Barbara & Earl
M'Lane

This book addresses fundamental questions in the philosophy of religion: Can religious experience provide evidence for religious belief? If so, how?

Keith Yandell argues against the notion that religious experience is ineffable, while advocating the view that strong numinous experience provides some evidence that God exists. He contends that social science and other nonreligious explanations of religious belief and experience do not cancel out the evidential force of religious experience. The core of Yandell's argument concerns the formulation and application of an appropriate principle of experimental evidence. A final chapter considers the relevance of non-experiential, conceptual issues.

An attractive feature of the book is that it does not confine its attention to any one religious cultural tradition but tracks the nature of religious experience across different traditions in both the East and the West.

The epistemology of religious experience

The epistemology of religious experience

KEITH E. YANDELL

UNIVERSITY OF WISCONSIN – MADISON

CAMBRIDGE
UNIVERSITY PRESS

Published by the Press Syndicate of the University of Cambridge
The Pitt Building, Trumpington Street, Cambridge CB2 1RP
40 West 20th Street, New York, NY 10011-4211, USA
10 Stamford Road, Oakleigh, Victoria 3166, Australia

First published 1993

Printed in the United States of America

Library of Congress Cataloging-in-Publication Data
Yandell, Keith E., 1938–
The epistemology of religious experience / Keith E. Yandell.
p. cm.
Includes bibliographical references and index.
ISBN 0-521-37426-X
1. Knowledge, Theory of (Religion)   2. Experience (Religion)
I. Title.
BL51.Y2715   1993
291.4'2'01 – dc20   92-3900
                                    CIP

A catalog record for this book is available from the British Library.

ISBN 0-521-37426-X hardback

For my wife:
  Sharon Dee Yandell
our children by birth:
  Karen Gail Yandell Buege
  Keith David Yandell
  Eric Thomas Yandell
  Merritt Katherine Yandell
and our children by marriage:
  Randy John Buege
  Julie Kay Yandell

Contents

Acknowledgments

An earlier version of the material in Chapters 6, "Nonepistemic explanation and belief," and Chapter 7, "Nonreligious explanation of religious belief," appeared as "The Nonepistemic Explanation of Religious Belief," in *International Journal for Philosophy of Religion* 27, No. 1, pp. 87–120 (1990); Associates for Philosophy of Religion, Inc., Box 828, Mocksville, N.C., U.S.A., *reprinted by permission of Kluwer Academic Publishers*. Part of Chapter 12, "The Argument Trimphant," appeared in an earlier form in "Sensory Experience and Numinous Experience," in *International Journal for Philosophy of Religion* 31, No. 1, pp. 1–29 (1991); Associates for Philosophy of Religion, Inc., Box 828, Mocksville, N.C., U.S.A., *reprinted by permission of Kluwer Academic Publishers*. Part of Chapter 8, "Self-Authentication and Verification," is a slightly altered version of "Self-authenticating Religious Experiences," in *Sophia*, Vol. XVI, No. 3, October, 1977, pp. 8–18; reprinted by the permission of the editor, Professor M. J. Charlesworth. Thanks are due to (Keith) David Yandell for lengthy discussions regarding the book, particularly the argument of Chapter 12, which greatly improved its content.

Introduction:
Is our task impossible or impolite?

There is a great deal of skepticism in our culture about any effort to argue that any religious belief is true or that any religious belief is false. Such attempts are often found offensive. Those whose beliefs are defended may feel that if the case for their beliefs is too strong, and this becomes known, then faith will be impossible. They worry that evidence may endanger faith. Those whose beliefs are criticized may feel that they are being subjected to personal attack. Regarding these matters, two things should be said. One is that there are accounts of religious faith wherein having faith and having strong evidence are perfectly compatible. At least philosophically, and arguably on religious grounds as well, these are more adequate conceptions of faith than those where the presence of evidence threatens faith. My faith in my good friends is not threatened because I have good evidence of their existence and integrity. Why should things be different concerning religious faith? The other thing that needs to be said is that the endeavor to tell if a religious doctrine is true, even if its outcome suggests that the doctrine is false, is not an attack on anyone who believes that doctrine. It is not even an attack on the doctrine. It is just an attempt to find out whether something (presumably something important) is true. Of course someone may still feel abused by an inquiry regarding the truth of some cherished belief. Then that person need not participate in the inquiry or read its results. But

1

for any interesting question there will be someone who has a stake in the answer's going one way rather than the other. If on those grounds we avoid raising any interesting question, we shall have made ourselves the intellectual prisoners of other people's fears.

Some people find it tempting to argue along some such lines as these:

(a) What we know is limited to things that lie within the reach of our senses and our limited cognitive powers.
(b) Discovering the truth or falsehood of religious claims is beyond the reach of our senses and our limited cognitive powers.

Hence:

(c) We cannot know whether religious claims are true or false.

Now (a) is intended to say more than simply that what we can know is limited to what we can know. It is intended to say what the limits of our knowledge are. But it is not clear what those limits are or what determines them. In trying to become clearer, we can make a useful simple distinction. To know the *truth-value* of something is to know that it is true (if it *is* true) or that it is false (if it *is* false). To know *whether* something has truth-value is to know whether it is true or false. You can know whether something has truth-value without knowing whether it is true as opposed to false. I know that *George Bush ate all of a hot dog yesterday* has truth-value – I know that it is either true or false – without knowing what its truth-value is. What the (a–c) argument suggests, then, is that while no doubt claims like *God exists* and *Nirvana can be attained* are either true or false, we cannot discover which they are (even though we want to know).

The argument has slight credentials. We seem to be able to discover that there are black holes, quarks, and neutrinos. If we discover that after all there are not these particular things, our doing so is likely to involve our discovering that they do not exist, because at least equally strange things exist with which black holes, quarks, or neutrinos cannot coexist. We can discover that, surprisingly, axiomatic systems of a certain power cannot be proved to be both consistent and complete. We can tell what the limits of our cognitive powers may be only by using them, and who knows what we may discover?

The argument does not need much by way of credentials in our current intellectual atmosphere. The assumption is that religious and moral matters are subjective. What this amounts to concretely came out nicely in two recent comments by students of mine. One asked in all innocence, "Why can't everybody just make up their own religion?" In contemporary America, the notion of do-it-yourself religion joins do-it-yourself home repair with no sense of disparity. My response was that I had no objection to this so long as no one claimed that his or her religion was true. Another student informed me, with great charm and earnestness, that truth in religion, like truth elsewhere, always was only *truth for me*. I pointed out that this amounts to saying that the objective truth for us all is that truth is subjective, which is self-contradictory. *A is true for me* just means *I believe that A*, which means *I believe that A is true*. One cannot sustain the notion of belief if one dissolves the notion of *truth* into that of *believed true*. In a world in which such basic points are news, an argument like (a-c) has nothing to fear. In fact, (a) is so vague about our limits that one cannot tell what follows from it. So (a) leaves us in the dark about why we should accept (b). The conclusion (c) follows from (b) alone; indeed, (c) just is (b) restated. So we are left with the vagueness of (a) and the sheer assertion of (b). Yet the (a-c) argument appears with regularity in student papers supporting the view that religion lies beyond reason's range.

The view the argument expresses is much like a view David Hume held, a view that goes like this:

(a') Anything that we cannot verify or falsify we cannot know to be true or false.

(b') The propositions that we can verify or falsify are lim-

ited to propositions that we can see to be contradictory (this will falsify them) and those that we can see
to have a contradictory denial (this will verify them)
and those that we can either verify or else falsify by
reference to sensory experience or introspection.

(c′) Characteristically, religious doctrines are not expressed by propositions that fall into any of the favored classes referred to in (b′).

Hence:

(d) We cannot verify or falsify religious doctrines.

Hence:

(e) We cannot know religious doctrines to be true or
false.

A problem arises regarding (a′): Given (b′), we cannot
verify (a′). No sensory or introspective evidence verifies or
falsifies that anything we cannot verify or falsify in the way
(b′) describes we also cannot know to be true or false, but
(a′) is not a necessary truth. So if we can tell whether (a′) is
true, we must be able to falsify (a′) (by seeing that it is
contradictory). If we can falsify (a′), then (a′) is false, and if
we cannot even in principle falsify (a′), then we cannot tell
whether (a′) is true or false. Then determining the truth-value
of (a′) is beyond our mortal knowledge. But if (a′) is either
false or such that its truth-value is not discernible by us, then
we cannot use it as a premise in an argument to show that we
cannot discern the truth-value of religious claims.

This nicely illustrates a deep problem with a priori attempts to show that we cannot discern the truth-value of
religious claims. The premises of the argument for this view
must be *strong* enough to yield the desired conclusion but
weak enough so that we still can know that the premises
themselves are true. I know of no set of premises that meets
these conditions. So far as I can see, any interesting or
plausible argument for the conclusion that we cannot discern
the truth-value of any religious doctrine rules itself out of

4

contention – it disqualifies itself because, on its own terms, we cannot know its premises to be true.

In spite of this, it is widely assumed that there is an argument that is valid, *plausible,* and has the conclusion *No human being can discern the truth-value of any religious claim.* A successful argument of this sort would have to meet certain conditions. The premises must have these features: (1) Their being true is compatible with their being known to be true; (2) their being true is compatible with their being verified; (3) they are not distributively or collectively contradictory; (4) what they assert to be generally true is compatible with their own truth. It is enormously hard, if not impossible, to deliver such an argument. I know of no successful argument to this effect for the intended conclusion, though I note that an argument could meet all of these conditions and have only false premises.

It also seems easy to think that it is somehow improper to suggest or even believe that someone else's beliefs – at least their religious beliefs – might be false. No doubt it is true that walking up to someone whose religious beliefs you know, and telling them their beliefs are unfounded, unreasonable, false, inaccurate, and really stupid, is not nice. But, besides this, what exactly is being forbidden? Consider these suggestions:

> (i) It is wrong to hold any belief such that, if that belief is true, then some religious belief is false.

On (i), it is wrong to hold any religious belief, for given pretty much any religious belief you like, if it is true, then *some* other religious belief is false. Given (i) it is wrong to be a materialist, for if materialism is true, then some religious beliefs are false. Indeed, it is wrong to think that you and I are distinct persons, since if that really is so (and not merely how things appear), then certain religious beliefs are false. Since it is not wrong to believe that there are distinct persons, (i) is false. In fact, some religious traditions hold (as part of their religious beliefs) that you should hold certain beliefs, and (i) is not among them; but holding (i) also is

5

incompatible with some religious beliefs, and thus if (i) is true, it is wrong to accept (i). There is no reason, then, to take (i) seriously. It is false and self-defeating.

> (ii) It is wrong to hold any belief such that, if you sincerely accept it and are consistent, then you also hold that some religious belief is false.

The descriptions *believing that the Koran is the Word of God* and *believing that those who think that the Koran is not the Word of God are mistaken* do not describe *two* beliefs; they describe but one belief. If you do not hold a belief accurately described by the second description, you do not hold the first belief either (or you are confused about this matter and it is hard for you even to tell what you believe). Since for almost any religious belief you like, if it is true, some other religious belief is false, then if (ii) is true and you sincerely hold any religious belief and are consistent, you are wrong to hold that belief. Again, various religious traditions hold beliefs that are (and that they would recognize are) incompatible with (ii). So if (ii) is true, it is wrong to believe that (ii). So (ii) fares no better than (i).

> (iii) It is wrong to try rationally to assess any religious belief – wrong to try to tell whether any religious belief (that anyone holds, anyway) is true or false.

This is an extraordinarily curious view. Why should we inquire into truth about everything else except religious matters? Because they are not important? On what standards, and how are those standards justified? Because we know that all religious claims are false anyway? If we know that, the assessment is already done – but where, and by whom, and what are the arguments? Because such assessment is another instance of cultural imperialism? First, many endeavors in rational assessment of religious belief occur *within* the same culture – arguments back and forth among Jains and Buddhists or Buddhists and Vedantins or between Jews and Christians or Protestants and Catholics, for example. They often occur *within* a single religious tradition – arguments back and forth among various schools of Vedanta or Islam, for example. Some of the things appealed to in these debates are shared perspectives, agreed on by the disputing traditions, *within* a culture; some of the things appealed to in these debates are not shared by the disputing traditions but nonetheless occur within a common cultural context. These *intracultural* assessments cannot be matters of cultural imperialism in which one culture tries to dominate another; so even given the present objection they are proper. A religious tradition often will transcend any one culture; that is, it will exist in various cultures. Are intratraditional debates that involve representatives from different cultures wrong just because they involve them? If so, why? If not, what then is wrong with debates between religious traditions, or between a tradition and its secular critics, even if they belong to both different cultures and traditions?

There is little rational basis for the suggestion that religious belief cannot be rationally assessed or that it is morally improper, or even impolite, to attempt such an assessment.

RELIGIOUS EXPERIENCE

Cross-culturally and over time, human beings report religious experiences. Judging from the reports, the contents of these experiences vary in interesting ways. There is not a division in which each culture contains its own brand of experience; various basic sorts of experience appear to occur at many times and in various places within diverse cultures. Our question is whether these experiences are evidence for anything besides social science generalizations about human beings and societies. Is religious experience evidence for religious belief?

This general question carries many other questions with it. For example, if some religious experiences are evidence for religious belief, must they all be evidence? What, if anything, are they evidence for? How could one tell?

7

Introduction

It is on these issues that the ensuing argument centers. What is offered here is a sustained argument with various steps. Most of the steps are controversial, and so require and receive defense. Critical consideration should be, and is, given to alternative views. By the time one has considered all of the relevant topics, a decent amount of the theory of knowledge, or epistemology, has been traversed.

PARALYSIS QUESTIONS

The question *Does religious experience provide evidence for religious belief?*, like the query *How can one know anything?*, is a paralysis question. Facing it, one is likely to experience intellectual paralysis, sunk into insensitivity by a Socratic sting. Behind the paralysis often produced by *How can one know anything?* is the pair of assumptions that there must be one way of knowing whatever one can know and that one must start from scratch, giving no heed to what one thought one knew but beginning all over again. Of course there is no one way of knowing what one comes to know, and no beginning from scratch. So, given the assumptions, one is finished before one can begin. So long as a skeptic can keep one from asking whether, and if so how, one knows that the assumptions are true, one remains paralyzed, at least until fatigue or the demands of one's environment break into one's reflections. Once it dawns on one that there is no single way by which one knows that one exists, that nothing can have incompatible properties, that elephants are larger than mice, and that torture for pleasure is morally wrong, and remembers that one does know them, one can escape the paralysis and break down the question into its various, more manageable parts.

Similarly, *Does religious experience provide evidence for religious belief?* invites paralysis. Whose religious experience? What sort of experience is it? Evidence to whom? Evidence for what? In fact, the class of subquestions is richer and more complex than this short list indicates.

8

Introduction

THE CHAPTERS

We possess a variety of descriptions of religious experiences, and a set of prospective claims that various religious traditions have related to these experiences, claims that these traditions characteristically, by way of description or evidence or inference, derive from these experiences. We thus, as it were, have a sampling of prospective legitimizers and prospective claimants. We do not possess much by way of general agreement, in precise terms, concerning the meaning of "religious" or "experience" or "religious experience." Thus our opening chapter, by way of definitions, examples, and a very modest typology, indicates what is meant here by "religious experience." Chapter 2 adds to the perspective begun by Chapter 1: It sketches in broad outline some of the central concepts of the theory of knowledge, or epistemology, as they relate to our overall enterprise. In Chapter 1 I discuss some of the salient characteristics of the structure and content of religious experiences, and in Chapter 2 I present some of the structure and content of epistemology of religious experience.

In Chapters 3–5 I discuss two sources of skepticism about the possibility of religious experience providing evidence. Both radically empiricist and positivist theories of meaning and zealous defenders of divine mystery proclaim the inaccessibility to language or concepts of what is religiously important. The claim is widely made that philosophical and religious considerations support the thesis that religious experience is ineffable. What is ineffable cannot be described. Since experience is evidence only under some description, ineffable experiences, on this view, cannot be evidence for anything. Unless these challenges can be defeated, the short answer to our overall question is negative; religious experience does not provide evidence for religious beliefs. Radically empiricist and positivist theories of meaning yield this result by denying that there *are* any religious beliefs, and hold that our question is misleading insofar as it suggests

9

otherwise. Some detailed arguments for such views are presented and assessed.

Chapters 6 and 7 deal with the question of whether social science and other nonreligious explanations of religious experience are not both obviously available and evidentially sufficient to cancel any evidential force that religious experience might be thought to have. Thus the notion and the consequences of nonepistemic explanation of religious belief require exploration.

Some have maintained that the subjects of religious experience enjoy a privileged status regarding not merely the content but also the cogency of religious experiences so that subjects are viewed as unchallengeable experts as to what their experiences are evidence for. Or, differently, some have held that religious experience, conceived as having evidential force, should be dealt with in the context of certain of the practices that define the religious tradition within which they occur (and which are constructed to favor those experiences). A sharply contrasting view contends that such experiences, imprisoned as they are in the conceptual cages of particular religious traditions, are thereby robbed of evidential significance. The first two sorts of views argue from the allegedly sheltered character of religious experience (its individual privacy or its occurrence within practices loaded in its favor) to its evidential power. The third sort of view argues from a differently conceived sheltered character of religious experience to its evidential impotence. In Chapters 8 and 9 I argue against all of these views.

Perhaps the philosophical core of the volume is formed by Chapters 10–12. The focus is on how best to formulate a defensible principle of experiential evidence – a clear and defensible answer to the question of what conditions must be met by an experience in order for it to constitute evidence for a proposition. Various candidates for the correct principle are considered, and while one version is defended in the context of the argument in Chapter 12, other versions could serve the same role in yielding the conclusion that the argument defends. Then, this question being answered, it is asked whether strong numinous experience provides evidence for the existence of God. Chapter 13 raises the same question regarding enlightenment experience, and the final chapter briefly considers the relevance of conceptual experience, or philosophical reflection and argument, to our topic.

Part I

The experiential data

1

Religious experience, "East" and "West"

The basic question this book tries to answer is, Does religious experience provide evidence for religious belief? In particular, my concern is with whether it provides evidence of the existence of God. While I have no particular brief for the terms "religious" and "religious experience" – the entire argument could be posed in other terms – and immediately grant that there are religions and religious experiences that are implausible, even evil, perhaps the most convenient way to indicate the rough range of what will be discussed is by the language used in the opening question. Hence a word about "religion" and "religious experience" is in order.

What I mean by a "religious experience" is simply an "experience doctrinally and soteriologically central to a religious tradition." What I mean by a "religion" or a "religious tradition" is "a conceptual system that provides an interpretation of the world and the place of human beings in it, that builds on that interpretation an account of how life should be lived in that world, and that expresses this interpretation and life-style in a set of rituals, institutions, and practices." Since our basic question is whether religious experience provides evidence for religious belief, we need some examples of descriptions of religious experiences.

At the conclusion of this chapter, there appear some descriptions of religious experiences, taken from various religious texts. Of course this is a very small sampling, but various sorts of religious experiences are represented. This

15

chapter presents, in an introductory way, some central considerations regarding the experiences of which this small sample is representative. The next chapter widens and deepens the discussion that this chapter begins.

The term "seems" has three senses. It may convey the notion "only seems, but is not" as in "She may seem unathletic, but she is the state's top player." It also has the sense of "weak opinion" as in "It seems to me that I locked the door before we left." Or it may express "how things appear, whether they are that way or not" as in "The wall seems beige to me, though given my sense of color it may or may not be that color." We will use the phrase "people seem to experience God" in the third sense – a sense that is neutral as to whether they do experience God or not. After all, that is what we want to try to decide, so we ought not to build an answer to our question into our use of the term "seems."

Since Rudolf Otto's *Idea of the Holy*, the term "numinous" has been applied to such experiences as that of Moses at the burning bush, Isaiah in the temple, or Arjuna on the battlefield. (Descriptions of these experiences are quoted at the end of this chapter.) Such experiences are matters of the subject at least seeming to be aware of a majestic, living, holy being of immense power. Strictly, Otto uses the term so that apparent experience of anything uncanny (for example, a ghost) is a numinous experience; our concern is with experiences of the sort just briefly characterized, and we shall refer to them as *strong* numinous experiences.

Descriptions using "seems" in the third sense typically are called phenomenological descriptions. A phenomenological description of a strong numinous experience gives us a way of describing that experience that skeptics, saints, and sideliners all can accept as accurate. Let a strong numinous experience, phenomenologically described, be an *apparent experience of God*. Such an experience will seem to its subject to be an experience of God; its accurate phenomenological description will require the use of the term "God" (or some referential equivalent). It may be a reliable or veridical experience (in which case it is really what it apparently is) or it may be *only* apparent. We can now put the view that religious experience provides evidence in favor of God exists along these lines: If one has an apparent experience of God under conditions in which there is no reason to think either that one would seem to experience God even were there no God or that one could not discover, if God does not exist, that this is so, then one has experiential evidence that God exists.

A phenomenological description of a religious experience is one that describes the experience "from within" or in terms of how things appear to the subject of the experience as she has the experience, without making any commitments to things being, or not being, the way they appear to the subject to be. If different experiences have different phenomenological descriptions, that is good, though not decisive, evidence that they are different sorts of experiences.

Every description of a religious experience can be transformed into a phenomenological description by the simple device of making a description of how things are into a description of how things seemed to be. The advantage of this is that typically there will be agreement that a person had an experience in which things seemed to them as they described; disagreement typically arises over whether things are as described. The nonphenomenological "I saw the Lord, holy and righteous" is phenomenologically recast as "I at least seemed to see the Lord, who appeared holy and righteous" (where this sentence is not read as entailing that there is, or is not, a Lord to be seen). The nonphenomenological report "I achieved Nirvana" is phenomenologically recast as "I at least seemed to achieve Nirvana" (where this sentence is not read as entailing that there is, or is not, a Nirvana to be achieved). Since the recasting into phenomenological form is easy, and it neutralizes much of the religious import of the description, I will leave the descriptions of religious experience contained in this chapter in their nonphenomenological originals.

The descriptions relevant to our concerns come from a variety of sources, some monotheistic and some not. Although we will focus on the question as to whether apparent experiences of God provide evidence for the existence of God, we will look as well at the question as to whether some other religious experiences provide evidence for the beliefs based on them.

SOME COMMENTS ABOUT RELIGIOUS EXPERIENCES

Various features of these experiences seem plain and should be uncontroversial. (Presumably they would be uncontroversial were it not an axiom in much academic study of religion that religion is essentially noncognitive.) First, there is a significant psychological component to these experiences; their descriptions quite naturally tell us something about how the people who have them feel and react. Second, that psychological component is not descriptive of the religiously most important aspect of these experiences; the religious point of having these experiences is not simply to feel a certain way. At any rate, this estimate of what is religiously important is the one we get if we listen to the formative figures of the relevant traditions rather than to some professors of religious studies. Third, and centrally, these experiences are *cognitive* in that, allegedly at least, the subject of the experience receives a reliable and accurate view of what, religiously considered, are the most important features of things. This, so far as their religious tradition is concerned, is what is most important about them. This is what makes them salvific or makes them powerful to save. Fourth, obviously the content of the experiences, as it is revealed in the phenomenological descriptions, is very different. For example, Isaiah sees himself as a sinner facing a holy God, desperately needing God's forgiveness; Isaiah is a creature facing his Creator. The experiences of Moses, John, and Arjuna echo this phenomenology. None of the nonmonotheistic experiences seems to share this feature, though it is a feature that makes Isaiah's experience what it is. Along similar lines, some religious experiences have a subject/consciousness/object structure whereas some have a subject/aspect structure. The former at least appear to the subject to be experiences of something quite clearly distinct from the subject; the latter do not. This structural difference makes dubious the claim that all religious experiences are really the same. Indeed, both phenomenological and structural considerations suggest that there are different sorts of religious experience. Since this point is often overlooked or explicitly denied, it is worth emphasizing.

SOME QUESTIONS REGARDING
RELIGIOUS EXPERIENCE

Religious experiences certainly do not all appear to be of the same thing. Not all of them are subject/consciousness/object in structure. Some of them do not even seem to be experiences of anything that exists independently of the experience's subject. Some of them seem to be experiences in which some aspect of the subject is discovered or discerned. Others of them plainly do seem to be experiences of something on which the subject himself or herself depends for existence. These differences in *structure* raise a deep problem for the idea that somehow these experiences are all experiences of the same thing. Further, if one considers *all* religious experiences that are subject/consciousness/object in structure – the experiences that seem to their subjects to amount to encounters with something not at all to be identified with the subjects themselves – their phenomenologies also differ significantly. Apparent experience of the Virgin Mary is quite different from apparent experience of Krishna. Their phenomenological content varies in important ways. There is no obvious reason to think that even all of the religious experiences that are of subject/consciousness/object structure, even assuming that they are reliable or veridical, are experiences of a single thing, or even a single *kind* of thing. The evidence suggests that there is no one thing that is the object of all religious experiences. Whether all or most apparent experiences of God are experiences of the same being, if they are experiences of any being at all, is an important question as well.

Still, many hold that all of these experiences do have a single focus, and are of one and only one thing (using "thing" in its broadest sense). Some do so almost obsessively. No doubt they do so from various motives and interests. I note but two of the most important, one religious and one philosophical. The religious motive is this: If all religious experience has a single object, that would provide one important link in a chain of considerations leading to the view that there is only one religion. The idea is that one would not have to choose between religions. The philosophical motive is that if all religious experience had a single object, that would provide one important link in a chain of considerations leading to the view that religious experience is not a source of evidence for conflicting religious beliefs.

Of course the same assumptions regarding there being but one object of religious experience can lead in the very opposite direction to the one just mentioned. Suppose, for example, that somehow all religious experience has the same object, and that object is Ultimate Reality. How, then, is Ultimate Reality to be conceived? Perhaps as the Hindu Brahman. But, then, how shall Brahman be conceived? One way in which Brahman is conceived is as the one worthy of worship, the one against whom sins are committed and who will forgive us if we repent our sins and ask for forgiveness. Another way in which Brahman is conceived is as a nonpersonal being altogether lacking in qualities. (I ignore here various difficulties in that notion.) The goal of religion, from the perspective that regards Brahman as a personal God, is forgiveness of one's sins by, and joyous service toward, a loving God – a service that continues after the death of one's body and that precludes any confusion between the worshiper and the God who is worshiped. The goal of religion, from the perspective that regards Brahman as an impersonal, qualityless Being, is something like absorption into Brahman. More carefully, it is an alleged recognition of the illusoriness of individuality and of an already existing identity of each apparent person with a nonpersonal qualityless being. Thus treating all religious experience as having a single object need not at all lead to there being one religion. For even if one thinks that all religious experience has a single object, the question remains, Which object is that? There are, of course, *more* than two answers to this question, but it is enough for my purposes here to have described only two.

Similarly, even if all religious experience has the same object, these experiences hardly appear to tell the same story about that supposed object. Since in one experience the supposed object seems to have properties incompatible with the properties it seems to have according to other experiences, the task of winnowing and sifting evidence remains even if one makes the assumption that all religious experience has one object. Even then, not all religious experience could be accepted uncritically. So even if all religious experiences were of one kind, this need not lead to the religious or philosophical motivations' being satisfied.

In any case, the structure, as well as the content of religious experiences, gives little encouragement to the view that all religious experiences are experiences of any one thing.

A MODEST TYPOLOGY

A rough and rapid survey of salient religious experience goes as follows. There are various sorts of enlightenment experience – Nirvana is central in the Buddhist traditions, *kevala* in the Jain tradition, *moksha* in Advaita Vedanta. Nirvanic experience is constituted by an awareness of the fleeting states of consciousness, or else of their cessation and the inner stillness that this constitutes. Kevalic experience is an awareness of the abiding self that underlies our fleeting conscious states and is presupposed by, though ignored in, nir-

21

vanic experiences. *Moksha* experience either is numinous or involves an awareness of the identity of oneself with quali-tyless Brahman. Numinous experience is awareness of God. Nature mysticism (another possibly distinct form of religious experience) involves a sense of empathy with nature directed at whatever part of nature is perceptually available to the subject of the experience while she has the experience. Given attention to experiential structure and phenomenology, each seems to belong to a different type of experience than the others.

Might it be the case that each sort of religious experience in fact is an experience of something quite different? If one simply considers the experiences, and leaves aside various external motives like the ones discussed in the previous para-graphs, the idea that religious experiences are of quite dif-ferent things is promising. There are various ways of developing this idea. Here is one way: *Moksha* experience is not awareness of anything; it is simply the mind resting. Or it is the same as quietistic/nirvanic experience. Nature mys-ticism is simply an awareness of nature plus an empathy with what one is aware of. Kevalic experience is awareness of a continuing self or mental substance plus an inflated sense of one's durability, powers, and importance. Numi-nous experience is awareness of God.

A monotheist may well be highly attracted to this reading. But it is not a religiously neutral reading of the experiences. Indeed, it is far from clear that there can be any religiously neutral reading of these experiences. One can simply offer phenomenological descriptions of such experiences. But there is no religiously neutral reading of their evidential value; why should, and how could, there be?

The interpretation just described, for example, will seem to a Theravada Buddhist to trivialize nirvanic experience. The Advaita Vedanta Hindu and the nature mystic will sus-pect the same regarding its readings of *moksha* and nature mysticism. The Jain will claim considerably more on behalf of the abiding self – for example, that it is dependent on noth-ing else for its existence, is implicitly omniscient and existentially secure. So long as the term "God" is used to mean "a holy, majestic, overwhelming, living person" a monotheist may well suppose that the interpretation is essentially sound. The interpretation we have described does not treat any of the experiences as nonveridical. It simply offers very thin, and largely merely psychological, descriptions of the experiences. Only reference to an enduring self, and of course to God, goes beyond this narrow scope. We can so thin out the relevant descriptions as to allow us to treat them all as reliable, though only by leaving out the religious significance of at least most of them. What we cannot do is retain that significance and have all of them reliable or veridical.

Religiously neutral descriptions of the evidential value of religious experience are not available, any more than mathematically neutral descriptions of the evidential value of a mathematical argument are available. Consider the argument: The set of all whole integers contains the set of all even whole integers as well as the set of all odd whole integers. Each of these sets is infinite, and the set of all whole integers is not contained in either of the other sets just mentioned. So sometimes one infinite set contains another one that does not contain it. This argument is sound and valid; it constitutes a proof. Neither *This argument is a proof* nor *This argument is not a proof* is a mathematically neutral description of the argument. We do not need for there to be a neutral description in order to tell which nonneutral description is correct. Similarly, we do not need a religiously neutral description of the evidential value of religious experience in order to tell which nonneutral descriptions are correct regarding that matter.

REVIEW

A brief look back at the ground we have covered may be helpful. The basic question regarding religious experience – at least, the basic question about how many *kinds* of such experiences there are – concerns whether there is *one* kind only, or *more* than one kind, not about whether there are (say) seven kinds as opposed to six or eight or fourteen. I have suggested that there are at least five kinds: numinous, nirvanic, kevalic, moksha, and nature mystical. Part of the basis for denying that there is just one sort of religious experience concerns the intrinsic structure of the relevant experiences – some are subject/consciousness/object and some are subject/aspect. The other part of the basis for recognizing different kinds of religious experience is their radical difference in phenomenological content. A phenomenological description of an experience says how things look, so to speak, from within the experience; an accurate phenomenological description of an experience expresses its content and reflects its structure. Subjects of religious experiences offer very different phenomenological descriptions of those experiences. It would be extremely high-handed to suppose that the descriptions offered by the subjects of religious experience are not phenomenologically accurate, whatever we may think of the evidential force of these experiences. Each sort of experience we have recognized has its own doctrinal setting, which we have briefly described. There is good reason, given their structure and content, to doubt that these kinds of experiences have any single object. Even if one thinks that they all have a single object, this by no means directly leads either to a justification of the claim that there is only one religion or to a confirmation of the view that we have no conflicting experiential evidence regarding matters religious.

There are, then, various nonphenomenological (but phenomenologizable) descriptions of religious experiences whose evidential significance we have yet to assess. While there are contemporary examples of these experiences, I will quote descriptions of them from religious texts that are regarded as authoritative by the traditions in which they are offered.

The traditions represented here should be briefly indicated. Monotheistic descriptions are taken from Jewish, Christian, and Vedantic sources. Then passages are taken from Buddhist sources, according to which one sees that the self is but a bundle of fleeting states; from Jain sources, according to which one sees that the self is an indestructible subject of experience; and from Hindu sources, according to which Brahman is experienced, either as a cosmic person or, quite differently, as qualityless. The descriptions follow.

MONOTHEISTIC EXPERIENCES

1. Moses, tending the flock of his father-in-law, Jethro, sees a bush that apparently is burning and not consumed by the fire. Then, the text of Exodus tells us, "And Moses said, 'I will turn aside and see this great sight, why the bush is not burnt.' When the Lord saw that he turned aside to see, God called to him out of the bush, 'Moses, Moses!' And he said, 'Here am I.' The he [God] said, 'Do not come near; put off your shoes from your feet, for the place on which you are standing is holy ground.' And he said, 'I am the God of your Father, the God of Abraham, the God of Isaac, the God of Jacob.' And Moses hid his face, for he was afraid to look at God" (Exodus 3:3–6).

2. "In the year that King Uzziah died I saw the Lord, high and holy and lifted up; and his train filled the temple. Above him stood the seraphim; each had six wings: with two he covered his face, and with two he covered his feet, and with two he flew. And one called to another and said: 'Holy, holy, holy, is the Lord of Hosts; the whole earth is full of His glory.' And the foundations of the thresholds shook at the voice of him who called, and the house was filled with smoke. And I said: 'Woe is me! For I am lost; for I am a man of unclean lips and I dwell in the midst of a people of unclean lips; for my eyes have seen the king, the Lord of hosts!' Then flew one of the seraphim to me, having in his hand a burning coal which he had taken with tongs from the altar. And he touched my mouth, and said: Behold, this has touched your lips; your guilt is taken away, and your sin forgiven.' And I heard the Lord saying, 'Whom shall I send, and who will go for us?' Then I said, 'Here I am! Send me.' And he said, 'Go' " (Isaiah 6:1–9).

3. "I [John] was in the Spirit on the Lord's day, and I heard behind me a loud voice like a trumpet saying, 'Write what you see in a book and send it to the seven churches.' . . . Then I turned to see the voice that was speaking to me, and on turning I saw seven golden lampstands, and in the midst of the lampstands one like a son of man, clothed with a long robe and with a golden girdle round his breast; his head and his hair were white as wool, white as snow; his eyes were like flame of fire, his feet were like burnished bronze, refined as in a furnace, and his voice was like the sound of many waters; in his right hand he held seven stars, from his mouth issued a sharp two-edged sword, and his face was like the sun shining in full strength. When I saw him, I fell at his feet as though dead. But he laid his right hand upon me, saying 'Fear not, I am the first and the last, and the living one; I died, and behold I am alive forevermore, and I have the keys of Death and Hades' " (Revelation 1:10–18).

4. "Father of all, Master supreme, Power supreme in all the worlds, Who is like thee? Who is beyond thee? I bow before thee. I prostrate before thee, and I beg thy grace, O glorious Lord. As a father to his son, as a friend to his friend, as a lover to his lover, be gracious unto me, O God. In a vision I have seen what no man has seen before; I rejoice in exultation, and yet my heart trembles with fear. Have mercy upon me, Lord of Gods, refuge of the whole universe: show me again thine own human form. I yearn to see thee again with thy crown and scepter and circle. Show thyself to me in thine own four-armed form, thou of arms infinite, Infinite Form" (Bhagavadgita [Song of the Blessed Lord], Chapter 11, paragraphs 43–6).

NIRVANIC EXPERIENCES

1. "This monk life leads to complete detachment, to freedom from desire, to peace, to superknowledge, to the highest insight, to nibbana [Nirvana]" (Digha Nikaya II, 251).

2. "This is peace, this is the highest, namely the calming of the activities, the rejection of all attachment, the destruction

of craving, the freedom from desire, nibbana" (Anguttara Nikaya V, 110).

3. ". . . freedom from pride, restraint of thirst, uprooting of attachment, cutting off of the cycle of existences, destruction of craving, freedom from desire, ceasing, nibbana" (ibid. I, 88).

4. "But when I comprehended, as it really is, the satisfaction of the world as satisfaction, the misery as misery, and the escape as escape, then I understood fully and accepted full Buddha status, and the knowledge and the vision arose in me: sure is the release of my mind: this is my last birth" (ibid. I, 259).

KEVALIC EXPERIENCES

1. "With the knees high and head low, in deep meditation, he [Mahavira, a founder of Jainism] reached Nirvana, the complete and full, the unobstructed, unimpeded, infinite and supreme, best knowledge and intuition, called Kevala . . . he was a Kevalin, omniscient and comprehending all objects, he knew all conditions of the world, of gods, men, and demons; whence they come, where they go, whether they are born as men or animals, or become gods or hell-beings; their food, drink, doings, desires, open and secret deeds, their conversation and gossip, and the thoughts of their minds; he saw and knew all conditions in the whole world of all living beings" (Jaina Sutras I, 201, 202).

2. "With supreme knowledge, with supreme intuition, with supreme conduct, . . . with supreme uprightness, with supreme mildness, with supreme dexterity, with supreme patience, with supreme freedom from passions, with supreme control, with supreme contentment, with supreme understanding, on the supreme path to final liberation, which is the fruit of veracity, control, penance, and good conduct, the Venerable One meditated on himself for twelve years. During the thirteenth year, in the second month of summer, in the fourth fortnight . . . on its tenth day, when the shadow had turned towards the east and the first wake

was over [the Venerable One] in a squatting position, with joined heels, exposing himself to the heat of the sun after fasting two and a half days without drinking water, being engaged in deep meditation, reached the highest knowledge and intuition called Kevala, which is infinite, supreme, unobstructed, unimpeded, complete, and full . . . he was a Kevalin, omniscient and comprehending all objects; he knew and saw all conditions of the world, of gods, men, and demons; whence they come, whither they go, whether they are born as men or as animals or become gods or hell-beings, the ideas, the thoughts of their minds, the food, doings, desires, the open and secret deeds of all the living beings in the whole world; he the Arhat, for whom there is no secret, knew and saw all conditions of all living beings in the world, what they thought, spoke, or did at any moment. [This is] final liberation" (ibid. I, 263, 271).

3. "Mahavira quitted the world, cut asunder the ties of birth, old age, and death; become a Siddha, a Buddha, a Mukta, a maker of the end (to all misery), finally liberated, freed from all pains" (ibid. I, 264, 265).

4. "Mahavira obtained the highest knowledge and intuition, called Kevala, which is infinite, supreme, . . . complete, and full" (ibid. I, 265, 266).

5. ". . . the highest knowledge and intuition, called Kevala, which is infinite, supreme, unobstructed, unimpeded, complete, and full . . . final liberation" (ibid. I, 265, 266).

6. "He reached Nirvana, the complete and full, the unobstructed, unimpeded, infinite and supreme, best knowledge and intuition, called Kevala" (ibid. I, 201).

7. "(The liberated) with their departing breath reach absolute perfection, wisdom, liberation, final Nirvana, the end of all misery" (ibid. I, 94).

8. "Having annihilated his Karman [= karma] both meritorious and sinful, being steadfast [self-controlled] [the enlightened one] crossed the ocean-like flood of worldly existence and obtained exemption from transmigration" (ibid. I, 111, 112).

9. ". . . what is called Nirvana, or freedom from pain, or perfection, which is in view of all; it is the safe, happy, and quiet place which all the great sages reach. This is the eternal place, in view of all, but difficult of approach. Those sages who reach it are free from sorrow, they have put an end to the stream of existence" (ibid. I, 128).

10. "[Kevalins] have obtained perfection, enlightenment, deliverance, final beatitude, and . . . an end to all misery" (ibid. II, 158).

11. "[A Kevalin] obtains perfection, enlightenment, deliverance, and final beatitude and puts an end to all misery" (ibid. II, 173).

MOKSHA EXPERIENCES

1. "When a seer sees the brilliant Maker, Lord, Person, the Brahman-source, then, being a knower, shaking off good and evil, stainless, he attains supreme identity with Him" (Mundaka Upanishad III, i, 3).

2. "Not by sight is it grasped, not even by speech, not by any other sense-organs, austerity, or work, by the peace of knowledge, one's nature purified – in that way, however, by meditating, one does behold him who is without parts" (ibid. III, i, 8).

3. "That which is the finest essence – the whole world has that as its self. That is Reality. That is Atman. That art thou" (Chandogya Upanishad VI, ix, 4).

4. "Now, when one is sound asleep, composed, serene, and knows no dreams – that is the self (Atman) . . . that is the immortal, the fearless. That is Brahman" (ibid. VIII, xi, 1).

5. "Then Usasta Cakkayan questioned him. 'Yajnavalkya,' said he, 'Explain to me who is Braham present and not beyond our ken, him who is the self in all things.' [Yajnavalkya replies:] 'Verily, he is the great, unborn self, who is this (person) consisting of knowledge among the senses. In the space within the heart lies the ruler, the lord of all, the king of all' " (Brhadaranyaka Upanishad III, iv, 1).

The experiential data

Besides numinous experience, *kevala*, Nirvana, and *moksha*, I am inclined to think there is another sort of experience that, perhaps in a borderline way, is (or is like) religious experience. For lack of another term, I propose to call it simply *nature mystical* experience. Here is an example from Richard Jefferies:

> I was alone upon the seashore as all these thoughts flowed over me, liberating and reconciling; and now again, as once before in distant days in the Alps of Dauphine, I was impelled to kneel down, this time before the illimitable ocean, symbol of the Infinite. I felt that I prayed as I had never prayed before, and knew now what prayer really is: to return from the solitude of individuation into the consciousness of unity with all that is, to kneel down as one that passes away, and to rise up as one imperishable. Earth, heaven, and sea resounded as in one vast world-encircling harmony. It was as if the chorus of all the great who had ever lived were about me. I felt myself one with them, and it was as if I heard their greeting: "Thou too belongest to the company of those who have overcome."

I do not, of course, pretend to have been exhaustive. Zen *sartori* may or may not fit into the modest framework set out here. But we have more than enough sorts of experiences to work with.

Obviously, some of these experiences are, and some of these experiences are not, described in subject/consciousness/object terms. In some cases, if the descriptions are at all apt, the subject seems to encounter something external to themselves – something they are in no danger of identifying with themselves or any aspect of themselves. In some cases, if the descriptions are at all apt, the experiences are subject/ aspect experiences. What the experiencer does is alleged to be this: She recognizes certain things about herself. There also are descriptions of an experience in which one, having achieved omniscience, is aware of just about anything you can name. There also are descriptions of experiences in which there is freedom from passion and misery and in which the subject has achieved complete insight, knowledge, and wisdom.

Both the Buddhist and the Jain experiences, seen in their native doctrinal context, allegedly involve freedom from illusion. The illusion one is said to be freed from differs. In Buddhist experiences, the illusion escaped is that of thinking that besides our momentary psychological and physical states, there is an enduring substantial entity – one that is numerically the same over time and through change of non-essential properties – that *has* these states. Our belief that we are such entities is a damning illusion if Buddhism is true. In Jain experiences, the illusion escaped is the belief that we depend on other things for our existence and that the limitations in knowledge and power that we commonly experience are essential to our lot rather than being an unfortunate feature of our reincarnated existence over which we can triumph by becoming enlightened. What one allegedly attains upon achieving enlightenment – indeed, what is constitutive of being enlightened – is the recognition that we inherently are independently existing beings that are numerically self-identical over time, through a lifetime and over lifetimes, capable of omniscience. Thus what the Buddhist sees as an illusion the overcoming of which is essential to enlightenment, the Jain sees as a recognition partially constitutive of enlightenment.

In these Advaita Vedanta texts, one finds descriptions of a different sort than one finds in the Old or New Testament. They differ as well from the description quoted from the Gita. But these descriptions differ also from those quoted from Buddhist texts and from Jain texts. These descriptions, while they say that the mind is purified, stainless, composed, and serene, and emphasize that the experience described is not sensory, emphasize awareness of a being with which the subject of the experience is alleged to be identical. "Thou are that": Brahman and the subject allegedly are one, not in purpose or intent or belief or action, but in very being; there allegedly is no distinction between them.

Our fundamental question concerns whether any of these

experiences provides any evidential basis for the religious beliefs typically associated with them. One might, of course, ask if they provide evidence for any other religious beliefs. In fact, it seems to me that (not surprisingly) the traditions in which they occur have gotten this much right at least: If they do provide evidence for anything, it is the beliefs typically associated with them.

2

Some basic epistemological concepts

In this chapter, the focus is on some basic concepts in theory of knowledge, or epistemology, that serve to define with some precision the issues raised by the question, Does religious experience provide evidence of the existence of God? An "apparent experience of God" is an experience that seems to its subject to be an experience of God. Suppose that Sharon has an apparent experience of God. Reflecting on her experience, she offers this little argument: (1) I had what seemed to be an experience of God. (2) If someone has what seems to be an experience of God, then there is evidence that God exists. Hence: (3) There is evidence that God exists.

Various questions arise about Sharon's experience. Is it evidence that God exists? Does it provide Sharon with evidence that God exists? Even if Sharon tells David about it, does it provide David with evidence that God exists? Can Sharon tell Eric about it in any way that would enable Eric to tell whether it gives Sharon evidence that God exists? Can it give Eric evidence that God exists even if Sharon does not take it to be evidence for any such claim? How can anyone tell whether it gives anyone evidence that God exists? And so on. It is such questions as these that will occupy us in this book.

TWO SIMPLE IDEAS

Two simple ideas are basic to the claim that we sometimes have experiential evidence of the existence of various sorts of things. One is that if someone seems to experience something, then that is reason to think that this thing exists. The other is that since sometimes things seem to exist that do not exist after all (since experience is not always reliable), a type of experience can be evidence for the existence of something only if there is some way to tell whether or not experiences of that sort are deceptive. We might call these "the basic positive idea" and "the basic negative idea." Although we will discuss various sorts of religious experiences, we will focus on one sort (those in which people seem to experience God). As we saw, often these are called (strong) "numinous" experiences; the subject at least seems to be aware of a majestic, awesome, worship-worthy being that she has no temptation to regard as a projection that she creates.

The idea that numinous experience provides evidence for the proposition *God exists* ultimately rests on simple grounds. An item A is an *object* relative to person S if and only if S *does not exist*, by itself or conjoined to a set of truths, does not entail A *does not exist*. Thus Susan herself, and Susan's thoughts, are objects relative to Sam, but not relative to Susan, whereas the moon is an object relative to both. An experience is *intentional regarding an object* A if and only if in order to give an accurate phenomenological description of the experience – to say how things at least appear to the experience's subject as she has the experience – one must use the concept of an A, where if A exists it is an object relative to the experience's subject. The simple ground behind the idea that numinous experience is evidence for the proposition *God exists* is that any experience that is intentional regarding an object provides evidence for the existence of that object, and that strong numinous experience is intentional regarding God, who is an object relative to the experience's subject.

The most profound challenge to this simple claim comes from another simple claim. It emphasizes that if an experience (or at least a kind of experience) can provide evidence for the existence of some item, then it must be possible that there be experiential evidence (perhaps from the same sort of experience) *against* the existence of that item – not that some experience of the same sort *must* or even *does* provide such negative evidence, but that it is *logically possible* that it do so. But (the claim is) numinous experience is not a possible source of evidence against God's existence. So it cannot be evidence for God's existence. Much of the epistemology of religious experience is based on attempts to clarify, defend, and apply various developments of the simple positive idea and the simple negative idea.

These two quite opposing simple ideas, as we shall see, lead to rather complex reformulations and refinements. The dispute as to which basic notion is fundamentally correct, or whether some plausible successors to these ideas are compatible, lies at the heart of the epistemology of religious experience, particularly as it deals with numinous experience. It lies at the heart of the notion of experiential evidence of *any* sort.

INTENTIONALITY

We can begin with an easy case. My present visual evidence is intentional regarding my office door. Were there no door where I now see one, I would notice this; not seeing a door on my outside office wall ordinarily would be sufficient evidence for the claim that it is not there. Here, experience that is intentional regarding an object is indeed evidence that the object is there. Doors, after all, are characteristically not invisible, or even hard to spot. We do not normally hallucinate doors that really are not there. If there is no door, typically we can tell.

If my door exists, it does so independently of my perceiving it. Anything that exists independent of me, let us say, is an *object* with respect to me. Concepts of objects, let us say, are *object concepts*. Sometimes, in order to say how things seem, I must use object concepts, even if I know that there are no objects in view, or even if I am unsure whether there are or not. If I ask, referring to the furry item that I just glimpsed in the next room, "Is that really a live bear?" I reflect the fact that it has just seemed to me that I saw a live bear in the next room and am unsure that my eyes are not deceiving me. Whatever is there, I seemed to see a bear. Experiences that seem to one to be of something that, if it exists, is an object with respect to oneself are *intentional* in their structure, and they are so in regard to the object (if any) in question. My seeing the bear in the zoo is intentional relative to that real animal; my seeming to see a bear in your dining room is intentional in structure, and is intentional regarding your real bear, if any.

One of our simple ideas tells us that having the property *being intentional regarding my office door* by itself is sufficient to give my current visual experience the further property *being evidence that my office door exists.* The other of our simple ideas denies this. It entails that my present visual experience must also have the property *being a member of a kind of experience that could provide evidence that my office door does not exist.* My current visual experience also has this property. The former of our simple ideas denies that my current visual experience *must* have this property in order for it to serve as evidence that my office door retains its slender hold on being.

THE KARMA PROBLEM

Philosophers seek arguments that are sound (have only true premises), valid (the premises entail the conclusion), interesting (the conclusion is significant), and are known to possess these features. Our basic problem is deciding whether Sharon's simple three-step argument (or some successor) is sound and valid (I will assume that it is interesting). Deciding this depends on solving what we might call "the karma problem." According to some varieties of Indian monotheism, the law of karma is really a description of God's providential activity. When a person dies without having achieved enlightenment, he must be reincarnated, and God's problem is to find the right body and environment into which to place this person, given the karma that he has built up. Of course, God being omnipotent and omniscient, the problem is easily solved. Having a little less to work with, we may find our karma problem harder to solve. There are various ways of embedding the simple positive idea and the simple negative idea into a single statement about when experience does provide evidence. Our karma problem is that of finding exactly the right embodiment – of discovering just the right way to blend the simple positive idea, and the simple negative idea, each appropriately qualified, into a unified *principle of experiential evidence*. Only getting that right will tell us whether or not religious experience provides evidence for religious belief.

KINDS OF RELIGIOUS CLAIMS

Religious claims come in many kinds. Some, for example, concern objects; some do not. More precisely, some are *object* claims and some are (what we will call) *aspect* claims. What this distinction amounts to bears examination.

In line with our earlier suggestion, let us say that item O, whatever it may be, is an *object* with respect to person S if and only if that S *exists* is false is neither logically nor causally sufficient for O *exists* being false. Thus my historian colleague who specializes in Indian history, friend though he be, in this sense is an object relative to myself, since God could obliterate me without also obliterating him.

Having defined "object," we need to define "object claim." Let C be an object claim with respect to person S if and only if it meets these conditions: (1) C is logically contingent (i.e., neither C nor C's denial is a contradiction); (2) C has the form "O is Q," where O refers to some item that is an object relative to S and Q refers to some property O is said to have (for simplicity's sake, let *existence* count as a property). Thus *My historian colleague is Scandinavian* is an object claim relative to me. A claim C is an object claim *by* person S if and only if C is an object claim with respect to S, and S asserts C.

Our concern is with whether religious experience provides evidence for religious beliefs. Let claim C be an *experiential object claim by person S* if and only if C is an object claim by S, and *S* asserts *C* (wholly or partially) on the basis of some experience *E* that *S* has had, and *E* meets the direct or indirect relevance conditions with respect to *C*. (I shall define the notion of a *relevance condition* later.)

One who feels fatigued or itches or wants to be warm though she is not also has an experience. These experiences lack items that are objects relative to their subject. John's fatigue depends for its existence on John's existence. Sam's itch, and Mary's wish to be warm when she is not, depend for their existence on the existence of their owners. Let us say that if an item *A* is so related to person *S* that *S does not exist*, by itself or together with some set of truths, entails *A does not exist*, then *A* is an *aspect* with respect to *S*. Each human person is an aspect with respect to herself. No human person is an aspect with respect to any other. John's hopes and fears, wishes and dreams, beliefs and attitudes, and pleasures and pains are aspects with respect to John but objects with respect to Mary.

RELEVANCE CONDITIONS

Not just any old experience can provide evidence for just any old claim. Seeing my golden retriever provides me with evidence that my dog is near but not that the stock market will take a plunge or that the president is about to announce his resignation.

If Sally hears the bell toll and pets her cat, she has evidence that the bell tolls and that her cat is present and accounted for. To generalize, if person *S* has an experience *E* that is a matter of its (phenomenologically) seeming to her that *O* has property *Q*, where *O* is an object relative to *S* if the experience is veridical, then the experience *E* meets the evidential *relevance conditions* relative to the claim *O has Q*. The experience *E* also meets the evidential relevance conditions for any claim that *O has Q* entails, such as *O exists* and *O has a prop-*

erty, though *E* may do so only by virtue of meeting the relevance conditions for *O has Q*.

Similarly, if William feels fatigued but euphoric after a long climb, he has evidence that he is tired but happy. To generalize, if person *S* has an experience *E* that is a matter of its (phenomenologically) seeming to him that he is aware of an item *A* that has property *Q*, where *A* is an aspect of *S* if *E* is veridical, then the experience *E* meets the evidential *relevance conditions* for the claim *A has Q*, as well as for any claims that *A has Q* entails. A *necessary* condition of some experience being evidence for some claim is that it meet the relevance conditions relevant to the claim.

One so favored as to observe little lines in a Wilson cloud chamber observes, we are told, the paths that electrons take. If we do not thereby observe electrons – if to observe their traces is not to observe their very selves – then at least there is a good theory that relates traces to electrons so that by observing the former I have evidence for the presence of the latter. If Susan knows that of her family only Tom likes date bars, and that only family has been home since she baked, then a very modest theory will explain the remarkable depletion in the local date bar population. In complex contexts, and in simple ones, an experience may meet evidential relevance conditions regarding a claim but do so only by mediation of a theory. To generalize, if *S* has an experience *E* that is a matter of its (phenomenologically) seeming to *S* that some item *X* has property *P*, and if there is a good theory that entails *If X has P then Y has Q*, then *E* meets the evidential relevance conditions regarding the claim *Y has Q*. Thus an experience may indirectly meet relevance conditions regarding a claim, or it may directly meet them.

Roughly, the content of my experience must match up with the content of the claim that I base on it. A more formal light touch on the notion of relevance conditions goes as follows: Janet's experience *E* meets the relevance conditions for the claim that *Item X has property Q* only if either (i) Janet's having *E* is a matter of its (phenomenologically) seeming to her that *X* has *Q* or (ii) Janet knows a good theory on which it is true that *If Y has P, then X has Q* and Janet's having *E* is a matter of its (phenomenologically) seeming to her that *Y* has *P*.

In sum, where *C* is the claim *O is Q, S*'s experience *E* meets the *direct relevance conditions* with respect to claim *C* if and only if *S*'s having *E* is a matter of there phenomenologically seeming to *S* to be an *O* that is *Q*, and *E* meets the *indirect relevance conditions* with respect to *C* only if *S*'s having *E* is a matter of there phenomenologically seeming to *S* to be an O^* that is Q^* and *S* reasonably accepts a theory that contains as an essential element the claim that *If O^* is Q^* then O is Q* and *S* infers *O is Q* from O^* *is* Q^* and *If O^* is Q^* then O is Q*.

DESCRIPTION/INTERPRETATION AND INFERENCE/DIRECT AWARENESS

If a person *S* has an experience *E* in which it seems to *S* that some object *O* or aspect *A* has some quality *Q*, then *S*, in saying how things seem, offers a description. If things are as they seem, what is being described is the object or the aspect. If, or insofar as, things are not as they seem, the description is false – false of the object or aspect if it is a matter of misidentifying the qualities of the object or aspect, false of the (physical or psychological or other) environment if there is no such object or aspect. No doubt there are cases of misdescription so errant in the qualities ascribed that it is dubious that there is any object or aspect that is being referred to. Neither exactly how to identify those cases nor whether description and interpretation are opposite ends of a spectrum or are different in kind is something we need to decide here. The claims that our argument needs can be made out on either account of the matter.

If a claim meets the direct relevance conditions relative to an experience, the person having the experience – or another who knows that she has had it – need make no inference in order to justify the claim; the claim merely reports the experience. If a claim indirectly meets the relevance conditions relative to an experience, then of course an inference is required from the description of the content of the experience to the claim evidentially based on that content.

THEORY AND REASONABLE ACCEPTANCE

Things may seem to have gotten out of hand. When *is* a person reasonable in accepting a theory? When is an element essential in or to a theory? Unless we know the answer to these questions, we seem likely to be unable to tell whether or not some particular experience meets indirect relevance conditions regarding some claim.

Perhaps, sometimes at least, we can tell whether a theory is reasonably accepted without being able to say what are the necessary and sufficient conditions of its being so. If we cannot, at least most people (including most philosophers) will not be able to say whether some particular person is reasonable in accepting some particular theory; there is no accepted account of when a person is reasonable in accepting a theory. Any account of such conditions presumably would be tested by reference to presumed paradigms. If such an account entailed that anyone would be unreasonable in thinking that prolonged stress can cause listlessness but reasonable in believing that eating six lemons will cause one to grow to over seven feet tall, then whatever the right conditions are for reasonable theory acceptance, *that* account of them is mistaken. This leaves the notion of a proposition being essential to a theory and the notion of a theory being reasonably accepted essentially untouched.

A theory, simple or complex, finds its epistemic rationale in its offering an explanation, answering a question, solving a problem, or the like. If we learn that Mary's beloved cat is ill, we may be able to explain why this usually gentle person snapped at us in the morning; concern leads to heightened irritability. If we learn that little Billy began school today, we may be able to answer our question as to why this normally hungry urchin left his breakfast untouched; new challenges can be threatening and produce anxiety that reduces appetite. We can solve the problem as to why the car will not start if we remember that Tom used it last night to run to the library and tends to leave the lights on. A proposition is essential to a theory if and only if it provides its intended explanation, answers its question, solves its problem, if that proposition is included in it, but not otherwise. It is reasonable to accept a theory that explains phenomena, answers questions, or solves problems otherwise left unexplained, unanswered, or unsolved, if it does so in a manner that requires us to believe nothing we have reason to think false and that links up the to-be-explained and the explanation thereof with conditionals that, if true, are explanatory. This not being a book on explanation, we shall have to leave these matters with this light touch.

HAVING AN EXPERIENCE

Suppose that at time t Kim (phenomenologically) seems to be aware of some item that is an *aspect* or an *object* with respect to Kim. Then, in the sense here relevant, Kim is having an experience at time t. I take *Kim seems to be aware of some item* to entail *Kim is conscious*.

Having an experience is an aspect of the experiences's subject. Experiences all have subjects, though not all have objects. That *having an experience* is an aspect relative to the one who has it of course does not entail that experiences cannot have objects. This account gives us sufficient conditions for *having an experience;* there may be other conditions also sufficient.

An experience is a conscious state in which a subject (phenomenologically) seems to be aware of an aspect or object.

John has a *perceptual* experience, one might say, if it (phenomenologically) seems to John that John is aware of an item that (if it exists) is an object with respect to John. If John (phenomenologically) seems to be aware of a lion, and there indeed is a lion that John is aware of, then (typically – we will consider exceptions later) John's experience is *veridical*. Given the notion of veridicality, we can rephrase the notion of a *perceptual* experience in this manner: John has a perceptual experience if and only if it (phenomenologically) seems to John that John is aware of an item that is an object relative to John if the experience is veridical.

Introspective experience, in contrast to perceptual, concerns aspects rather than objects. John has an introspective experience if John (phenomenologically) seems to be aware of something that (if it exists) is an aspect relative to John. Or, if one prefers, John has an introspective experience if John (phenomenologically) seems to be aware of something that is an aspect with respect to John if the experience is veridical.

While both perceptual and introspective experience receive a closer look further along in our discussion, it is perceptual religious experience that will receive the bulk of our attention.

DESCRIPTIONS

Experiences, among other things, are potential evidence for claims based on them. An experience is potential evidence under any description that is true of it, and is evidence only under some description or other. It matters, of course, what true description is offered. Suppose that Tim observes Ralph removing Mary's wallet from her purse, taking all the money the wallet contains, and returning the wallet to Mary's purse. Under the description *observing the movement in space of various physical objects*, Tim's observations will convict Ralph of nothing. Even if Tim knows that the purse is Mary's and that Ralph is known to be a thief, Tim's visual perceptual experiences are evidence for *Ralph stole Mary's money* only under the appropriate, if obvious, descriptions. A literally indescribable experience could be evidence for nothing.

TAKING AS EVIDENCE

Suppose that one has an experience that directly meets the relevance conditions for some claim. One nonetheless might not know that the experience met those conditions. One might know that it did and yet not *take* it to be evidence for the claim in question because one (rightly or wrongly) took the experience not to be veridical. There might be a true theory that related experience to claim indirectly without one knowing of the theory, or knowing that it was a true theory. Still, either an experience does, or it does not, directly or indirectly meet the relevance conditions regarding some particular claim. An experience might meet the relevance conditions regarding a claim without anyone, including the experience's subject, knowing that it did. That an experience meet the relevance conditions regarding a claim is a *necessary* condition of its being evidence for that claim. If *taking an experience to be evidence* also is a necessary condition, then an experience's meeting the relevance conditions regarding a claim is not sufficient for its being evidence for that claim.

Perhaps, then, we should distinguish between *de facto evidence* and *effective evidence*. Experience E is de facto evidence for claim C with regard to which it meets the relevance conditions; it is effective evidence if it both is de facto evidence for C and is taken as such. A person who had an experience that was de facto evidence might not take it as such; some other person might know that the first had had the experience and that it was de facto evidence. If the second person took it as evidence, it would be effective evidence for the second person (who did not have the experience) while it was not effective evidence for the first person mentioned (the one who had the experience).

As most persons reason from such facts as *The pot is empty* and *If the pot is empty then one cannot pour a drink from it* to *One cannot pour a drink from the pot* without having learned to formulate the explicit rule "If both P and If P then Q then Q," so most persons who have perceptual experiences in which it (phenomenologically) seems to them that a pot is empty take this as evidence that the pot is empty without having learned to formulate evidential criteria or to speak of relevance conditions. What relevance conditions an experience meets relative to what claims is not determined by who takes it to be evidence or by what anyone takes it to be evidence for. What evidence one actually has need not be what evidence one thinks one actually has, and the evidential potential of one's experiences need not be what one takes them to be. It can be more or less or just different.

While the evidential potential of one's experiences is not determined by what one takes it to be, and while one's taking an experience to be evidence for a claim does not entail that it is evidence for that claim, presumably people typically take their sensory experiences at least to be evidence for pretty much what they are evidence for. One's taking an experience as evidence for a claim can be altogether tacit. David now sees that his study door is open; he is not likely to reflect that his visual perceptual experience provides him with evidence for *My study door is open*, though it is likely that he is able to recognize that it does.

That one's experience provides one with evidence regarding the truth of some claim, and the fact that typically that evidence is defeasible – it is *always* overturnable regarding object claims and usually overturnable regarding aspect claims – does not entail that one should start doubting that claim. The state of the experiential evidence regarding a claim may rule out any practical doubt about the matter.

VARIETIES OF VERIDICALITY

Suppose that Jane has a perceptual experience that meets the relevance conditions regarding the claim *I see a green turtle*. Suppose, further, that a green turtle is what she sees. Suppose that every property the turtle seems to her to have, the turtle has. Then (again setting aside exceptions to be considered later) Jane's experience possesses *full veridicality*. Full veridicality can be viewed as having two components. Jane's experience E has *existential veridicality* regarding X if and only if E meets the relevance conditions concerning X *exists*, and X *exists* is true. Jane's experience E has *property veridicality* concerning X's having property Q if and only if E meets the relevance conditions for X *has* Q, and X *has* Q is true. A perceptual experience that altogether lacks existential veridicality regarding X will have nothing by way of property veridicality regarding X. An experience E will enjoy *full property veridicality* if and only if every proposition of the form *X has Q* that *E* meets the relevance conditions concerning is true.

It could happen, of course, that Jane sees a fake turtle – a highly realistic turtle sculpture, say – that she mistakes for a turtle. Then she is not simply hallucinating or having an illusion or dreaming or the like. She sees some object, but not the one she reasonably thinks she sees. Her experience then would have existential veridicality regarding a turtle sculpture and also have property veridicality regarding a green color and a turtle shape. But regarding turtles, it would have no veridicality at all.

It is also possible that Jane have an experience in which she is caused by an *X* that is not a *Y* and that has *P* but not *Q* to seem to see something that appears to be a *Y* and not an *X* and to have *Q* but not *P*. Then Jane's experience will have neither existential veridicality regarding *X* or *Y* nor property veridicality regarding either *P* or *Q*, unless there is a good theory that essentially includes *If one has an experience that meets the relevance conditions for "Y has Q" then one's experience is caused by an X that has P*. It might be necessary to refer to certain conditions that Jane must be in if this theory is to be relevant. Thus seeing little squiggles in the vapor of a Wilson cloud chamber can count as seeing electrons, or seeing the movement of electrons, given only that the theory that so explains the squiggles is a good one.

There are, of course, degrees of theoretical virtue. A theory might be good enough so that its explanation *Seeming to see an X that is P is caused by a Y that is Q* has *theoretical existential veridicality* in that *Y exists* is true but *Y has Q* is false, or that *Something that has Q causes one to see an X that is P* is true, but that *Y has Q* is false. *Full theoretical property veridicality* is present only if every property the theory ascribes to *Y* that *Y* must have in order to explain someone's seeming to see an *X* that is *P* is one that *Y* does have. *Full theoretical veridicality* is present only when *full theoretical existential veridicality* and *full theoretical property veridicality* join hands.

It might be held that Jane can experience something even

if that something has none of the properties that it appears to her to have – that Jane can have an experience that enjoys existential veridicality regarding X but has no property veridicality regarding X. This seems to me implausible, and I shall assume that sheer absence of property veridicality regarding X entails lack of existential veridicality regarding X. If this is mistaken, then I shall have made my case harder to prove than I needed, and this is no matter for concern. In any event, at the very least, typically an experience E that meets the relevance conditions for X *exists* is such that if it enjoys existential veridicality regarding X, there is some property Q of X regarding which E is veridical.

In brief, then, I shall operate within these claims regarding veridicality:

(V1) Any property veridicality regarding X presupposes existential veridicality regarding X.

(V2) Existential veridicality regarding X presupposes some property veridicality regarding X.

(V3) Full veridicality regarding X is composed of existential veridicality regarding X and full property veridicality regarding X.

(V4) Existential veridicality regarding X can be present with full property veridicality regarding X, and hence without full veridicality regarding X.

(V5) Theoretical property veridicality regarding X presupposes theoretical existential veridicality regarding X.

(V6) Theoretical existential veridicality regarding X presupposes some theoretical property veridicality regarding X.

(V7) Full theoretical veridicality regarding X is composed of theoretical existential veridicality regarding X and full theoretical property veridicality regarding X.

(V8) Theoretical existential veridicality regarding X can be present without full theoretical property veridicality regarding X, and hence without full theoretical veridicality regarding X.

COUNTERVAILING FACTORS

Various criteria for deciding when an experience provides evidence for some claim can be developed from these materials. One could maintain that any of the following serve as criteria for when a person's experience provides evidence. A *countervailing factor* is any consideration that would cancel out the evidence that S's experience that is intentional with respect to X otherwise would provide in favor of X *exists*. Consider the schema:

> (c) S's experience E in which there phenomenologically seems to S to be an X, where X (if it exists) is an object with respect to S, provides S with evidence that X *exists* if and only if . . .

Then consider these ways of completing the schema:

> (ca) S has no positive reason to suppose that some countervailing factor obtains.
> (cb) S has positive reason to suppose that no countervailing factor obtains.
> (cc) S has no positive reason to suppose that some countervailing factor obtains or S has positive reason to suppose that no countervailing factor obtains.
> (cd) S has no positive reason to suppose that some countervailing factor obtains and S has positive reason to suppose that no countervailing factor obtains.
> (ce) S has some positive reason to suppose that no countervailing factor obtains, and this reason must be stronger than any reason S may have for thinking that some countervailing factor obtains.
> (cf) S has some positive reason to think that no countervailing positive factor obtains, and this reason must be at least as strong as any positive reason S has for thinking that some countervailing factor obtains.

Among these possibilities, (ca) is correct even though it is the weakest condition. Suppose that I see my golden retriever begging for a dog biscuit. Unless I have some positive reason to think that my experience is not reliable – unless, for example, I know that my wife has taken our dog for a walk, or I am aware that the coffee I have been drinking is normal in all respects save that it produces golden retriever illusions – it provides me with evidence that my dog is begging for another dog biscuit. The mistake that something more is required rests in part on a mistaken epistemological thesis.

The thesis tells me that I do not know something is true if I can be mistaken about it. The following two theses are very different:

(T1) If I know that *P*, then *P* is true.
(T2) If I know that *P*, then I cannot be mistaken that *P*.

In the central sense of "know," (T1) is true, but (T2) (insofar as it is not an ambiguous way of stating what [T1] puts clearly) suggests that *knowing P* and *not being able to be mistaken about P* are coextensive.

If we ask what there is that we cannot be mistaken about, the answer is this: If I believe a proposition that is a logically necessary truth, then I cannot go wrong in believing that proposition. Or if the truth of a proposition follows from my believing it, then I cannot believe it and be mistaken. This will allow me to be secure in believing that 2 plus 2 equals 4 and *I exist*. But I cannot be similarly secure in believing *My golden retriever is begging for a dog biscuit*.

The mistaken thesis is this:

(T3) If *S* knows that *P* then *P* is a logically necessary truth, or *P is true* is entailed by *S believes that P*.

The point of (T3) is to restrict knowledge to propositions that meet this condition: *S believes that P and P is false* is self-contradictory. Such propositions, one might say, are *belief-secure*. To accept (T3) is to hold that one cannot know the truth of any logically contingent proposition whose truth does not follow from one's believing it, which of course is almost any logically contingent proposition you please. One must choose then between thinking that (T3) is true and thinking that one can know whether or not one has a head or a left hand or any children.

One who chooses to hold that (T3) and accepts the consequences might endeavor to keep the price of accepting (T3) low by rejecting:

> (T4) What one reasonably believes must be entailed by what one knows.

If (T4) is false, one could be reasonable in believing that one's golden retriever is begging for a dog biscuit even though one could not know this. Since *My golden retriever is begging for a dog biscuit* is neither a belief-secure proposition nor a proposition that is entailed by any belief-secure propositions, if (T4) is true, I cannot reasonably believe that my golden retriever is begging. It seems to me that I know that I have a head, two hands, and four children, so I reject (T3). But for anything I will argue for here, it would be enough that (T3) be true and (T4) be false. Thus if one insists that one might reasonably believe that God exists, but could not know this, no matter what the experiential evidence, because (T3) is true, this view will not be incompatible with anything I defend here. (I do not discuss the view that what I reasonably believe must be inductively derived from what I know, since it seems to me that this view fares at least as badly as does [T4].)

If one rejects either (T3) or (T4), it is possible that one know, or reasonably believe, a non–belief-secure logically contingent proposition and that one's knowledge of it be based on appeal to experiential evidence where the experience in question is not purely conceptual. Then, I suggest, it is the first way of completing the schema that yields a truth – that states (or comes closest to stating) a condition that one must satisfy relative to having an evidence-producing experience. I leave aside complications that would be introduced if we also considered the fact that one may have reasons that one is not aware of having; let our concern range only over reasons a person is *aware* of having under circumstances in which there are no negatively relevant reasons that she is culpably unaware of having. A consequence is that in knowing or reasonably believing that my golden retriever is begging for a dog biscuit, I do not have to rule out the possibility that there is an evil deceiver whose task it is to deceive me by providing me with misleading sensory experiences. That is a possibility that I need to worry about if and only if I have some reason to think that an evil deceiver exists.

It is a mistake to think that the logical possibility of there being an evil deceiver renders me unable to tell whether my dog is present. But if one makes that mistake, one by parity of reasoning ought to make the mistake of thinking that the logical possibility of there *not* being an evil deceiver is of equal evidential relevance. Then the two mistakes will balance each other out and one will be left where one should have been in the first place, namely, weighing the experiential evidence. In this rare case, two mistakes are better than one. Making neither mistake, of course, is better still.

PERCEIVING FACTS AND PERCEIVING THINGS

There is a distinction between *perceiving X* and *perceiving that it is X that one perceives*. If a package is a bomb, then if Ruth perceives the package, Ruth perceives the bomb, whether or not she perceives that it is a bomb that she perceives. In such circumstances, one might say that if Ruth has no reason to suppose that the package she perceives is a bomb (and, perhaps, if this is due to no fault on her part), then even though she sees a bomb, she has no perceptual evidence for any stronger claim than that she perceives a package. But if it ticks or if wiring is showing or a timer can be discerned through the wrapping, presumably Ruth should at least suspect that the package is a bomb. Her perceptual evidence then will be to the effect that it is a bomb she sees. Our main concern here will be with experiences that have this feature: If reliable or veridical, then they are experiences of the very sort of thing of which they seem to be experiences.

EXPERIENTIAL STRUCTURE

If one seems to experience an object, there nonetheless may be no object corresponding to one's experience. While subject/consciousness/object experiences, when veridical or reliable, typically inform one about items that populate one's mind-independent environment, they do not do so in a manner that is guaranteed free from error. Even if subject/aspect experiences typically inform one about some aspects of one's current consciousness in a way that is guaranteed from error, they do not inform one, in any way not subject to error, of one's being clinically depressed or physically hungry or physically diseased or the like. So whatever extra security attaches to subject/aspect experiences is purchased at a price concerning the scope of available information; whatever there is of such security concerns only the immediate momentary psychological states of the experience's subject. Even then, only a limited range of propositions about these aspects will be belief-secured. Such propositions concern only currently introspectibly observable properties of one's aspects.

An experience that is intentional need not be veridical. That S phenomenologically seems to experience an X is not decisive for whether or not X is there to be experienced. Were it, intentional experiences could never lack veridicality. Intentionality, in the sense defined here, is thus a feature of the structure of an experience, not a relationship between subject of experience and subject-independent object of experience.

COUNTERVAILING CONSIDERATIONS FINE-TUNED

The simple negative idea tells us that if Susan's at least seeming to experience an X is evidence that X exists, then it is at least logically possible or noncontradictory that Susan experientially tell that X does not exist, should that be the truth of the matter. The simple positive idea needs to be qualified so that it takes the negative idea into account. Suppose that Susan will seem to experience X, whether there is an X to be experienced or not. Experiences of X that occur under these conditions are not evidence that X *exists*. If Susan knows (or should know), as she seems to experience X, that she would seem to experience X whether there was an X to experience or not, she is justified in not taking her experience as evidence in favor of X *exists*. Further, she would not be justified in taking her experience to be evidence for X *exists*. So we have one qualification on the simple positive idea: If Susan has an experience that is intentional regarding X, and if X is an object with respect to Susan if it exists, then that experience provides evidence that X *exists* unless she would seem to experience X whether there was an X or not. This is *condition one* that any experience that is intentional regarding some X must satisfy if it is to provide evidence that X exists: It must not be the case that the subject of the experience would seem to experience X even were there no X to be experienced.

Suppose that Susan could never tell that X was not there to be experienced, even if it was not. This is *condition two* that any experience that is intentional regarding some X must satisfy if it is to provide evidence that X exists: It must not be the case that the subject of the experience could not tell that X was not there to be experienced, even were it not. Suppose that Susan always seems to see frogs; wherever she goes, and whatever she does, she seems to see at least one frog somewhere in her visual field. If her frog hallucinations blight all of her senses, then on her own she could not recognize a context in which frogs are absent, no matter how many contexts of this sort there might be. Thus if the proposition *A frog is present* is false, Susan cannot discover this fact – at any rate not by her own sensory experience. Then, according to our simple negative idea, Susan's seeming to experience frogs cannot be evidence that frogs are there to be experienced. Since she will seem to experience frogs whether any are there or not, she will not be able to tell by sensory experience that there are no frogs around, and so her sensory experience regarding frogs is worthless as evidence. So read, both the first and the second exception to our simple positive idea are illustrated by Susan's sad state. She could nonetheless learn that she was in this condition – someone that Susan trusted could discover it and tell her that the world contains fewer frogs than her experience has always suggested. Depending on how systematic her frog hallucinations were, Susan might discover this on her own. If she only visually hallucinated frogs, but was normal regarding hearing and feeling frogs – she hears frog sounds and feels frog surfaces only when there exist the appropriate croakings and damp smooth skins – she often could discover for herself whether her environment was frogless. She would always seem to experience frogs visually, and so her visual experience would be of no help to her in discovering whether she basks in the presence of frogs. But if her hearing and touch are normal, Susan's auditory and tactile experience can provide evidence regarding the frog population in her environment, even though her visual experience cannot. Hence her auditory and tactile experience of frogs is evidence of their presence. Susan's visual experience of frogs provides no evidence for their existence because it violates both condition one and condition two. Either violation is sufficient to render it void.

A jaundiced person's visual experience will present things as yellow, whether they are or not. Her unaided visual experience cannot be evidence that a thing is yellow, for if it is not yellow, she will not be able to discover this visually. Many instances that fit the *would experience X whether there was an X or not* description also fit the *cannot tell that no X is there, even if no X is* description. But any experience of X that fits either description fails thereby to be evidence in favor of *X exists*.

One might wonder whether there are *any* cases where the

second problem arises but the first does not. Are there cases in which (i) one appears to experience X, (ii) it is false that one would appear to experience X whether X was there or not, and (iii) it is true that one could not tell that X was not there even if it was not? In one respect, it does not matter much whether there are or not. If a particular perceptual experience (say, seeing a lake, having ingested a substance that produces what seem to be perceptions of a lake) is properly described as *appearing to perceive an X under conditions in which one will appear to perceive an X whether there is an X or not,* then let us say it has the feature of *being X-fixated.* If an experience has the feature of *appearing to perceive an X, where one could not experientially discern that there was no X, even were that the case,* then let us say that it has the feature of being *X-blind.* No experience that is either *X-fixated* or *X-blind* is evidence that there is an X. *Being X-blind* is a different property from being *X-fixated.* It does not matter deeply whether one can think of cases that are *X-blind* that are not also *X-fixated.*

Still, it is a point of some interest whether it is even logically possible that any experience be disqualified for failing to meet condition two that was not also disqualified for failing to meet condition one – whether it is at least logically possible that an experience be *X-blind* without its also being *X-fixated.* Obviously enough, this would be a matter of someone S's having an experience E that was intentional regarding an item X such that (i) S could not experientially discover that X did not exist even if it did not, while nonetheless (ii) S would not seem to experience X even if X were not there to be experienced.

If we leave fancy apparatus aside, perhaps this case will do. Suppose that Karen happens to perceive a dust mote. Although she will not seem to perceive nonexistent motes, her failure to see a dust mote does not tell her that none is present. Her experience is not dust mote–fixated, but it is dust mote–blind. According to the doctrine that experiences that provide evidence of objects with respect to which they are intentional must satisfy conditions one and two, Karen's seeing a dust mote cannot serve as evidence that there is one. Her experience does not satisfy condition two. It does satisfy condition one. Since it plainly is evidence that there is a mote, apparently we have an example of an X-blind but not X-fixated experience that also is a counterexample to the claim that evidence-bearing experiences must satisfy condition two. Plainly Karen's seeing a dust mote is evidence that it is there to be seen. So it seems false that satisfying condition two is a necessary condition of an experience providing evidence that something exists.

One can have evidence that a deer is in the thicket because one happened to see it move, whereas one's not seeing it there would not be evidence that the thicket was deerless; the deer knows how to hide well. But were one not able, under *any* circumstances, to discover the absence of deer in the thicket – if one's not seeing any deer even though one cut the thicket down an inch at a time until nothing remained would not enable one to tell that the thicket was deerless – *then* one's seeing the deer would not be evidence of its presence. Similar considerations apply with respect to dust motes. Upon reflection, then, condition two stands.

Karen's not seeing a dust mote, under the ordinary condition in which she sees one, is evidence that the mote exists even if, under similarly ordinary conditions, she might not be able to observe that no mote is present. But if there is not some circumstance in which motelessness is experientially detectable – not necessarily the same circumstance under which Karen observes her mote – some condition in which not observing a mote is evidence that no mote is there, then Karen's experience cannot confirm *There is a mote.* We need but state condition two with precision to achieve our desired results.

Hence we are able to allow Karen to see her mote, maintain that evidence-providing experiences must satisfy condition two, and have a logically possible example of an X-*blind* but *un–X-fixated* experience, all at once. We need only note that if in some condition one's seeming to experience an X is evidence that there is an X, then in *some* (the same one as before, or else another) condition one's not experiencing an X is evidence that there is no X. This provides us with an apparently unobjectionable way to state condition two. Whether or not this is exactly the way to put matters in the long run we will investigate later. This much will suffice for our introductory look at some basic salient epistemological concepts.

Part II

The challenge from ineffability

3

The outlines of ineffability

There is a brief argument for the claim that religious experience cannot be a source of evidence for religious belief. The argument goes like this: (1) If religious experiences are ineffable, then they cannot provide evidence for religious belief. (2) Religious experiences are ineffable. So: (3) Religious experiences cannot provide evidence for religious belief.

An item is literally ineffable only if it cannot be described. No concept applies to such a being. Any description of it is as good, or as bad, as any other. Such an item, if there is any, is equidistant from all possible descriptions.

It is a curious fact that people often expect God to be ineffable. Perhaps the idea is that since God, supposing there is a God, is so different from other things, yet another difference is not surprising. Nonetheless, the claim that God is literally ineffable is not obviously true. In fact, it is necessarily false.

Claims that something is ineffable often are not to be taken literally. A familiar hymn says that God is ineffably sublime. The same hymn, however, ascribes other properties to God, and perhaps even grounds the claim that God is ineffably sublime in the fact that God has these other properties. If God has these properties, then God is not ineffable. To be ineffably sublime presumably is to be as sublime as you can get, and thus to be omnipotent and omniscient, immutable and immortal, and the like. But then the concepts *being omnipotent, being omniscient, being immortal,* and *being immutable* apply to God, and God is not ineffable.

61

The term "ineffably sublime" is similar to such terms as "indescribably delicious" and "inexpressibly painful." A wound that is inexpressibly painful is painful, more painful than most, so painful that one would pass out if it were any worse. An indescribably delicious pie is delicious, more delicious than most, so delicious that no pie could surpass it. To say such things, of course, is to describe the wound and the pie, just as to say that God is ineffably sublime is to describe God. Metaphorical ineffability raises no philosophical problems. In that respect, literal ineffability contrasts with metaphorical ineffability.

The simplest and most basic problem with the claim that God is (literally) ineffable is that the claim is self-contradictory. *Being ineffable* is a concept. Nothing that falls under a concept – nothing to which a concept applies – is ineffable. So if God is ineffable, then God is not ineffable. Further, of course, if God is not ineffable, then God is not ineffable. So whether God is ineffable or not, God is not ineffable.

It is not unknown that someone embrace the view that God has contradictory properties. Divinity has its privileges, among which some count not merely freedom from the common cold but the option of both existing and not existing, or the state of being omnipotent and also not being omnipotent all at once.

The suggestion that God has this option, but (say) Moses does not, faces problems. Moses, being merely human, cannot both be saved and not be saved. *Being saved* is a property Moses either has or lacks. But if God can both save Moses and not save Moses, then it follows that Moses can both be saved and not be saved. Regarding saving Moses, then, either God can both do it and not do it (and not merely at different times or in different respects), or not. If God can save Moses and not save Moses, then Moses can both be saved and not be saved. Then Moses can have incompatible properties, and that alleged privilege does not belong to God alone.

A believer in God who thinks that God can have incompatible properties is not well placed for supposing that God will keep promises, or for taking any comfort even if God does keep promises. If God can have incompatible properties, then God's keeping a promise to bring those who believe safely to Heaven does not rule out God's putting them securely in Hell. The impact of such notions on the elements of the religious life (faith and hope, for example) is not cheering.

One attracted to the view that God can have incompatible properties may well wish to limit the range of such properties in order to avoid the sorts of problems the preceding paragraph illustrates. But it is not clear what rationale there is for supposing that while God can have contradictory properties, including of course having a property that God does not have, this can or does only occur when we like the results. At that point, a supposed divine privilege slips into being a function of human preferences.

The short way with such suggestions no doubt is the best. Contradictory claims are false by virtue of being contradictory, and claims about God do not differ in that respect from claims about frogs, trees, and doorknobs.

TWO SORTS OF ISSUES: CONSISTENCY AND JUSTIFICATION

The issues related to divine ineffability divide into two kinds. One concerns whether there is any consistent way of stating the claim that God is ineffable. The other has to do with whether anything like a rational justification has been offered for thinking that the claim is true. In this chapter we sample each issue; in Chapters 4 and 5 we deal with these issues, roughly respectively, in greater detail.

Consistency

If *God is ineffable* is contradictory, what will remove the contradiction? Perhaps we can move from the contradictory:

(1) God is ineffable,

which entails:

(1a) No concept applies to God, and the concept of ineffability applies to God,

which obviously is contradictory, to the apparently noncontradictory:

(2) Only the concept of ineffability applies to God.

The rationale for offering (2) is that is allows the concept of ineffability to apply to God.

Presumably (2) is intended to be true only if God exists; thus (2) entails:

(2a) God exists.

But if (2a) is true, the concept of existence applies to God, and if that is so, then (2) is false after all. Even if one reads (2) as identical to:

(2b) If God exists, then God is ineffable,

it still follows that if God exists, the concept of existence applies to God, so that (2b) is false. So (2b) will not do as a way of saving the notion of ineffability.

Basic concepts

Some concepts are basic in the sense that they apply to anything that so much as exists. *Being an existing item, having properties,* and *having only consistent properties* are examples of basic concepts. The problem with (2) is that it does not take basic concepts into account. This suggests that we take them into account by replacing (2) by:

(3) Only basic concepts apply to God.

The expression "concept C applies to item X" is ambiguous. It may mean that concept C is *true of* item X. In this sense, *being even* applies to the number two, and *being taller than average* applies to typical professional basketball centers. Or it may mean that a concept is *either true or false* of an item. In this sense, *being odd* applies to the number two and *being shorter than average* applies to a typical center. What is needed is a way of speaking that marks this difference.

A way as good as any is this:

> (i) Concept C *fits* item X if and only if C is *true of* X.
> (ii) Concept C *applies to* X if and only if C is true of X or C is false of X.

Thus *being even* fits the number two since *Two is even* is true, and *being odd* applies to the number two since *Two is odd* is false. Since whatever concept *fits* an item also *applies* to the item, the concept *being even* applies to the number two as well as fitting the number two.

On this understanding of a concept applying to an item, obviously there is a problem with (3). What (3) says is that only basic concepts apply to God. But *God is unable to move mountains* is false if there is a God. Hence *being unable to move mountains* applies to God, though it does not fit God. Obviously, the way to deal with this is to make a merely terminological adjustment:

> (3a) Only basic concepts fit (or are true of) God.

This raises the question as to whether it is possible that only basic concepts are true of God. Basic concepts fit all items, and so they characterize anything that they are true of only in a very abstract and general way. Nothing is characterized *only* by such concepts as *being an existing thing, having properties*, and *having only consistent properties*. These concepts are true of a carrot, of a groundhog, or of God only because other more concrete and determinate concepts are true of them. Whatever exists is determinate. Whatever exists is blue or not, round or not, immortal or not, omnipotent or not, and so on through an infinite list of properties. Necessarily, for any property P and item X, X has P or X lacks P. Everything that exists necessarily has properties, among which will be specific, determinate properties. Whatever has specific, determinate properties also is such as to fit specific, determinate possible concepts. So nothing can exist that only basic possible concepts fit.

The same point can be put briefly in another way. Some properties are maximally indeterminate; *being a property* is an example. Some properties are maximally determinate; *being exactly one centimeter long* is an example. Many properties fall between these extremes, being neither fully or maximally determinate nor fully or maximally indeterminate; *having length* is an example. Here is a necessary truth: Anything has a property that is not maximally determinate only by having a property that is maximally determinate. Here is another necessary truth: The properties that are not maximally determinate that a thing has are a function of – are completely determined by – the fully determinate properties that it has. It is logically impossible that anything have an indeterminate property without its having a corresponding fully determinate property as well. One might say that every fully determinate property *falls under* various indeterminate properties. *Being exactly a centimeter long* falls under *having length* and *being a property*, but not under *being conscious* or *having moral worth*. Then the way to put the relevant point is this: It is logically impossible that anything have an indeterminate property without having a fully determinate property that falls under it.

Basic concepts express indeterminate properties. Fully determinate properties are expressed by nonbasic concepts. Thus anything basic concepts fit will also be such that nonbasic concepts fit it too. Hence our most recent attempt to put the idea of divine ineffability in a logically consistent format fails.

There are, of course, deep and inescapable problems that are inherent in the claim that experiences are ineffable. For *being ineffable* is a property, and the concept of being ineffable is a concept. But to every property there corresponds a possible concept, and nothing to which the concept of ineffability applies is ineffable. Further, if the concept of ineffability is true of something, then of course at least one concept applies to that thing. But then note two things. One is that if a concept is true of something, then that thing must exist. In the sense relevant here, no concept is true of Santa Claus; there are just concepts that *would* be true of Santa Claus, were there any such fascinating person. So no concept is true (I suppose) of unicorns or trolls, there being none. What concepts are true of, there are some of – at least one. But whatever exists has properties; indeed, for any property you like, anything that exists either has it or lacks it, and nothing that exists can lack properties altogether. Whatever has properties, though, is describable, at least (as they say) in principle.

The other thing to be noted is that no concept is an island. A given concept gets its sense as a member of a community of concepts. Concepts, like human beings, are social by nature. The applicability of one concept brings with it the applicability of others. So the concept of ineffability cannot be the only concept that applies to something. The view, then, that religious experience is ineffable is multiply incoherent.

By the time the doctrine of the ineffability of religious experiences is revised in the direction of consistency so that it has any chance at all of being true, it is no longer a doctrine that precludes ever taking the subject's descriptions of their experiences as phenomenologically accurate – as saying how things at least phenomenologically seem to those who have such experiences, at least while they are having them.

SOME FURTHER CRITICISMS

We have considered the claim that the real significance of such experiences escapes language altogether. The claim is sometimes made that such experiences are ineffable, indescribable, inaccessible to concepts. This is a poor compliment to these experiences, as one can see if one simply notices its consequences. The suggestion that the experiences in question are ineffable is to be taken literally. It is not to be seen merely as an emphatic way of saying that we cannot *com-*

pletely describe them. We also cannot completely describe anything – anything you like has a plethora of properties that we are unaware of. Your ordinary orange or toenail or window pane has a history whose details escape us. It exists in a context of complex spatial and temporal relationships that we cannot rehearse. But it does not follow that an orange or a toenail or a window pane is ineffable. After all, what we can describe, even if not completely, is not ineffable. Partial describability rules out ineffability.

What is ineffable is equally distant from all concepts; all descriptions are equally bad (or equally good) regarding anything that is ineffable. So if religious experiences are ineffable, we need not in any way be bound by the descriptions those who had them happened to offer. We may, if we prefer, describe the experiences differently – perhaps as experiences of making cotton candy or being tortured by a real expert or eating a bran muffin or going to the dentist or singing the national anthem. *Any* description will do, as well or as badly, as any other. For anything that is really ineffable, we might as well study the menu on the wall of the local McDonald's as the descriptions offered by the experience's subjects. If that is absurd, then so is what it follows from, namely, the thesis that the experiences in question are ineffable.

To put the same sort of point in another way, an ineffable experience can have no religious significance. An experience can have religious experience only if it links up with some religious practices rather than others or none, with some religious institutions rather than others or none, with some religious doctrines rather than others or none, with some ways of living rather than others or none, and the like. An ineffable experience could have no content, nothing that could link up with anything.

SOME INEFFABILITY PASSAGES

Some sample passages relevant to alleged ineffability are the following:

1. Not inwardly cognitive, not outwardly cognitive, not both wise cognitive, not a cognition-mass (a state of potential knowing), not cognitive, not non-cognitive, unseen, with which there can be no dealing, having no distinctive mark, non-thinkable, that cannot be designated, the essence of the assurance of which is the state of being one with the Self, the cessation of development, tranquil, benign, without a second – (such) they think is the fourth. He is the Self. He should be discerned (Mundukya Upanishad, 7; said of Brahman).

2. (The liberated) is not long nor small nor round nor triangular nor quadrangular nor circular; he is not black nor blue nor red nor green nor white; neither of good nor bad smell; not bitter nor pungent nor astringent nor sweet; neither rough nor soft; neither heavy nor light; neither cold nor hot; neither harsh nor smooth; he is without body, without resurrection, without contact (of matter), he is not feminine nor masculine nor neuter; he perceives, he knows, but there is no analogy (whereby to know the nature of the liberated soul); its essence is without form; there is no condition of the unconditioned. There is no sound, no color, no smell, no taste, no touch – nothing of that kind (Jaina Sutras I, 52; said of an enlightened self).

3. The king said: "Venerable Nagasena, does he who does not receive nirvana know that it is blissful?" "Yes, he does." "But how can he know this without receiving it?" "Well, do those who have not had their hands and feet cut off know that it is a painful state to be in?" "Yes, they do . . . from hearing the sound of lamentation that they make (whose hands and feet are cut off)." "Similarly, Maharaja, it is from hearing the words of those who have seen nirvana that those who have not received it know that it is blissful" (ibid., III, iv, 8).

In the first passage, Brahman is said to be unknowable and beyond designation; Brahman is also said to be a tranquil, unique ("without a second") being that is to be discerned. In the second passage, the liberated one is said to be unknowable and indescribable, presumably because "there is no analogy" by which such knowledge or description can be converged. The third passage claims that Nirvana can be known to be blissful. Note how different (3) is in its emphasis from (1) and (2).

Justification

At least some things seem fairly clear about these passages. Sensory or observable properties, we are told, are not possessed by Brahman or a liberated being. It is added that Brahman is unique and the liberated one not analogous to anything in our experience. These contentions suggest two common premises in argument that conclude that something is ineffable.

One argument – the *uniqueness* argument – has this form:

(1) X is unique.
(2) If X is unique, then there is no property that X shares with anything else.
(3) If there is no property that X shares with anything else, then no property that anything other than X possesses can be truly ascribed to X.
(4) There is no property that X shares with anything else. (from [1] and [2])
(5) No property that anything other than X possesses can be truly ascribed to X. (from [3] and [4])
(6) If no property that anything other than X possesses can be truly ascribed to X, then X cannot be described.
(7) X cannot be described. (from [5] and [6])

Perhaps what lies behind (6) is the view that descriptions, at least in principle, are general; if a proposition of the from X *is A* is true, then at least Y *is A* (where X and Y are different) has got to be *possibly* true.

The other argument is the *analogy* argument. It has this form:

(1) There is no proper analogy between X and anything else.

(2) If there is no proper analogy between X and anything else, then X is ineffable.

(3) X is ineffable. (from [1] and [2])

Then appropriate values are suggested for the variable X – "Brahman" and "the liberated one" – for example.

The *uniqueness* argument relies on the claim that a unique item cannot be described. The argument envisions a *strongly* unique being – one having *no* property that anything else has. An item can be unique simply by having one property had by nothing else. An item can be unique simply by having a group of properties where nothing else has that particular group. An item can be unique just by virtue of having a unique spatiotemporal location. Having a property that nothing else has – being the most intelligent French speaker or being the oldest gorilla in captivity, for example – involves having properties that other things share. Being unique by having a uniqueness property grouping does not require having any property that something else lacks, save the complex property of having nonunique properties in an unshared combination. Being unique by virtue of having a unique spatiotemporal location involves an item's, like other things, having spatial and temporal location and again does not imply possession of only properties that nothing else has.

It is useful here to distinguish between a *property* and a *property instance*. If two shiny pennies (one 1991 and one 1992) both are copper colored, each has the property *being copper colored* though the instance of *being copper colored* that the 1991 penny has is different from the instance of *being copper colored* that the 1992 penny has. In this language, it is not properties, but proper instances, that things possess. Or they have properties only by virtue of their having property instances. If items A and B have instances of the same property, then A and B, to that extent at least, are describable in the same terms. If one wishes to make the maximal effort toward claiming that something is not describable, one is forced to deny that it has an instance of a property that anything else also has an instance of, by virtue of which the latter is describable. Hence these claims:

>(V1) X is strongly unique if and only if, for any property instance that X has, there is nothing else that has an instance of that property.
>
>(V2) Anything that does not have a property instance of any property of which anything else has a property instance is ineffable.

Then from *X is strongly unique,* with appeal to (V1) and (V2), one can infer to *X is ineffable.* This at least is one way of understanding the pattern of reasoning suggested in the first passage.

One is left, then, wondering what to make of the notion of something that is strongly unique. The notion fits nicely the idea that, for any property that we know anything to have, we must deny that anything strongly unique has it. But perhaps this does not leave us with any concept to which anything at all could correspond. We can formulate the concept of being strongly unique; that, of course, is not evidence that anything can satisfy or correspond to the concept. We also can formulate the concept of there not existing anything at all, to which nothing could correspond. (*There not being any state of affairs* is not another state of affairs.) The same goes for *something having logically incompatible essential properties.* Since we can recognize that there can be no such thing – that *Something exists that has logically incompatible essential properties* is necessarily false – we can form the relevant concepts requisite to this recognition.

Suppose that a strongly unique thing exists. What exactly will this amount to? Will it be enough, say, that a single red ruby exists in a world in which nothing else exists that is red, hard, material, spatially located, temporally placed, and so on, through all of the properties of which our supposed ruby has property instances? Presumably not, for such an item, if there could be one, would only be unique because of the contingent fact that no other such thing existed. God could destroy its strong uniqueness by (say) creating a pebble, which then would share with the ruby such features as *having shape* and *being material,* or by creating a second ruby, which would share *being red* and *being a ruby* with the original. Such happenstance and inessential uniqueness are of little interest.

If one turns to essential strong uniqueness, possessed only if every property an item has necessarily is not shared by another, perhaps the notion of strong uniqueness fares better. The Christian tradition, for example, speaks of the incommunicable attributes of God (independent existence and omnipotence, for example), these being viewed as properties that God cannot cause creatures to have or create creatures who achieve them. (Typically God also is viewed as having communicable attributes and so not as strongly unique.) But even incommunicable attributes do not support the notion of divine strong uniqueness. If God is omnipotent, then God can open an unlocked door, turn on the TV set, or pick up a copy of Kant's first *Critique,* sharing these properties with your typical human being and hence lacking strong uniqueness. It remains unclear, then, that there is any notion of a being that is essentially strongly unique – that has only properties that are essential and strongly unique.

Suppose that nonetheless some X is strongly unique. Then for any property Q that X has, X has a property instance of Q, and nothing else has a property instance of Q. Even were it possible that something be strongly unique, it is completely unclear why that thing should be indescribable. Why should it not be describable as the only thing that has (perhaps, that could have) Q?

At this point, we encounter familiar problems. Brahman is strongly unique. So Brahman is not intelligent. But Brahman is not stupid either. So Brahman is neither intelligent nor not intelligent. If this is not to entail that it is logically impossible that there be any such thing as Brahman, it must be the case that neither *being intelligent* nor *being not intelligent* applies to Brahman. Then Brahman is nonintelligent. So are rocks. So even if strongly unique items are ineffable, Brahman has a property instance of a property that rocks also have an instance of. So Brahman is not ineffable.

Presumably the reply is that both *bright* and *stupid*, and both *possessed of a mind* and *not possessed of a mind*, fail to apply to Brahman. The same will hold for any property we have any experience of. But of course our experience does not include encounters with *being omniscient* and *being omnipotent*, but we have concepts of these properties nonetheless. Experiencing an omnipotent being does not involve experience of the property *being omniscient* or *being omnipotent*. To experience a being who has a property Q is not always to experience Q. To experience X is to experience X's having some properties, but not therefore to experience X's having all the properties that X has. Unless there is something that only an omnipotent being can do, and we saw an omnipotent being do it, it is hard to see what *experiencing the property of being omnipotent* could amount to. I suspect that no one has ever had such an experience; certainly experiencing someone doing something that no human being can do would not be enough.

It is not easy to find instances of the notion *something that only an omnipotent being can do*, is opposed to the milder notion *something that no human can do*. Perhaps the best candidate is *creating something not made of anything that existed prior to its being made*. It would be hard to tell that one had observed this done, since it would be hard to eliminate the possibility that unobserved material had been used, but if one saw it done one might indeed have done what could be done by way of observing the property of being omnipotent. Even if one could not be sure that one had seen this done, if one saw it done, one would have observed omnipotence uniquely at work. But having such an experience is in no way a necessary condition of one's having the concept of omnipotence.

Similarly, unless there is something, X, that only an omniscient being can know, and we learned by experiencing some being that it knew X (presumably without our having to

74

know X), it is hard to see what *experiencing the property of being omniscient* would amount to. Of course we could not know this sort of thing without ourselves being omniscient. Perhaps, then, the relevant concept is *learning something from an omniscient being that only an omniscient being could know without having learned it from an omniscient being*. Again, simply learning something that no human being would know were she not to be told it by an omniscient being would not be enough; one would have to know that what one learned had this feature. The notion *something it is logically possible that no human know unless told by an omniscient being* also is hard to find instances for. It is stronger than the notion *something no human in fact could know without being told;* so an instance of the later notion need not also be an instance of the former. Thus even if there are things of that sort, one might learn some such thing, and have done what can be done by way of a nonomniscient being experiencing the property *being omniscient,* without one knowing that one had been so honored. I suspect that no one has had the experience of learning from an omniscient being something that only an omniscient being could know without having heard it from an omniscient being, and that this in no way prevents anyone from having the notion of omniscience.

In any case, whatever we have or have not experienced, the concepts *being omnipotent* and *being omniscient* are concepts we can have, and people do have them who have not done anything like experiencing the corresponding properties. It will not do to claim, for example, that an omnipotent being sustains us in existence so that we have moment-by-moment experiences of its effect; what that will give us moment-by-moment experience of is ourselves, and to experience an effect that X brings about by use of a power P is not thereby to experience X's *having P.*

The point, then, is this: Our having such concepts as a *being that can do anything it is logically possible that it do* and a *being that knows anything that it is logically possible that it know* is not likely to derive from our experience – not even if we encounter a being that has these features. The range of our concepts of properties is not limited to the range of properties that we have experienced things as having. Hence, a proposition of the form:

(1) *We have never experienced anything that has a property Q*

does not entail a corresponding proposition of the form:

(2) *We have no concept of property Q.*

And of course we could not know or believe that (1) was true without having the concept of the property in question. Similar remarks apply if we replace (1) with:

(1′) We have experienced something that has Q, but have never experienced its *having Q*.

What follows is that we can very well have the concept of properties that nothing in our experience has had an instance of, so even a strongly unique being can have properties of which we have concepts. It is not true, then, that if no property that anything other than X has can be truly ascribed to X, then X cannot be described.

There is the further fact that *X is strongly unique* entails *X is not ineffable,* and earlier we chased down the intricacies into which trying to elude this criticism leads.

The analogy argument rests on the notion of a proper analogy. A proper analogy has the form *X has Q and Y has Q*, which is like Q, so (in that respect at least) Y is like X.* Perhaps as good a way as any to put the idea is this: If there is a resemblance between one of X's properties and one of Y's properties, then there is a resemblance (and so a proper or genuine analogy) between X and Y. The claim, then, is that if X is liberated and Y is not, there is no pair of properties Q and Q^* such that X has Q and Y has Q^* and Q resembles Q^*. (The same will have to be true for any two liberated beings if either is to be strongly unique, but I leave that aside here.) The claim is that between a liberated one and anything else, there are no properties that can fill the role played by the properties that Q and Q^* would designate in a formulation of a proper analogy. (The notion of a "liberated one" is the concept of a person who has become religiously enlightened, and hence free from the alleged cycle of birth and rebirth. Enlightenment or liberation is variously conceived, and the argument here does not require that we investigate these variations.)

It is not a necessary truth that *If X exists, then X is spatial.* Neither *God exists, A mind exists* (on a Platonic, Vedantic, Leibnizian, Cartesian, Jain, or functionalist concept of mind), nor *Abstract objects exist* entails *Something has spatial properties.* I assume that if an item is eternal, then it exists with logical necessity (I do not assume the converse) and that God and abstract objects are the only serious candidates for logically necessary existence. Then whether it is a necessary truth that *If X exists, then X is temporal* perhaps is more problematic, but it is not if neither *God exists* nor *An abstract object exists* entails *Something exists now.* So perhaps *X is liberated* can entail *X exists* without entailing *X is in space* and *perhaps* without entailing *X is in time.* This much granted, our second passage perhaps suggests that no property (or no property but existence) that anything in our experience has is sufficiently like any property that a liberated one has to make a proper analogy possible.

This need not be encouraging. Unliberated people, possessing karmic debts and credits, are alive, conscious, self-conscious, aware of some of their past, and have fears but also hopes, pains but also joys. If being liberated blots out *all* of this, as it does if no property of a liberated being resembles any property of an unliberated being, then perhaps being liberated is not such an honor. Suppose what used to be the person Nagarjuna is now simply a nonconscious unchanging state – a state with no problems but also no joys. Or suppose what once was Nagarjuna – the one-time Nagarjuna stuff – now has combined with the stuff that used to be the person Dharmakirti and now is an apersonal hedonic tone and nothing else. Even if no proper analogy can be made to said states, it is not clear that such enlightenment is a goal worth pursuing. Further, one can conceive of such states without using analogies.

But the basic issue here concerns not the desirability of being liberated but the notion that a liberated being in no wise resembles an unliberated one. Consider two doctrines regarding properties:

(D1) For any item X and property P, exactly one of the following claims is true and one of them is false: (i) X *has* P; (ii) *X lacks* P.

(D2) For any item X and property P, exactly one of the following claims is true, and the other two are false: (i) *X has* P; (ii) *X lacks* P; (iii) *X neither has nor lacks* P.

I suggest that either (D1) or (D2) is the truth of the matter.

Suppose (D1) is true. Unliberated Saima is conscious and her favorite sari is not conscious. Liberated Sarvapalli is either conscious (and so resembles Saima) or not conscious (and so resembles the sari). The reply to this argument presumably is that *not being conscious* is not a property; to say X *is conscious* is to ascribe a property to X, but to say X *is not conscious* is simply to deny that X has that property.

There is something to this reply; how much depends on what exactly a property is. *Existing without consciousness* does seem to be a property that a sari possesses, and that a liberated being possesses unless it resembles Saima. A not implausible account of the notion of a property goes as follows: *There are no dodoes* does not ascribe any property to a dodo, so *expressing a truth* is one thing and *ascribing a property* is another, since our claim is true but ascribes no property to anything. *Dodoes are birds* is equivalent to *If anything is a dodo then it is a bird* and thus ascribes *being a bird* to each dodo there may be; it *conditionally* ascribes birdhood to dodoes. *There are dodoes, each of which is a bird*, categorically ascribes birdhood to dodoes, but it is false.

Consider, then, this suggestion: If proposition P is true of item X (categorically, not merely hypothetically, true of X), then P ascribes a property to X. If this is correct, then (given [D1]) either *The liberated being is conscious* or *The liberated being exists without consciousness* ascribes a property to this being, and one or the other property – whichever it actually has –

resembles properties had by other things. Hence there are proper analogies between the liberated being and those other things.

Suppose instead that (D2) is true. Then both *The liberated one is conscious* and *The liberated one is not conscious* can lack truth-value. Consider, however, that *being liberated* is intended to be incompatible with *being sad, being angry, being subject to rebirth*, and the like. Does this not entail that, for example, *X is liberated* entails *X is not sad*? Not necessarily; it may be that *X is liberated* is incompatible with *X is sad*'s being either true or false. Still, if a proposition of the form *X is liberated* is true, so is a proposition of the form *X exists*, and so are propositions of the form *X has property Q* – there will be one true proposition of the form *X has Q* for each property that falls within *X*'s property scope. How that scope is to be construed will depend on the particular doctrine of liberation being considered. But if there is no such scope, there correspondingly is no doctrine of liberation being offered.

One might object to the notion of *being a property* developed in the last paragraph. The proposition *My car is neither a prime number nor a county in Texas* is true of my car, but one might balk at the idea that it ascribes any property to my car. Perhaps the aforementioned proposition denies two properties to my car and (save for *being a car)* ascribes no properties to it. If we may take as reasonably clear the distinction between true propositions that ascribe a property to something (like *My car is red*) and true propositions that do not ascribe a property to something (like *My car is neither a prime number nor a county in Texas*) – allowing for mixed propositions (like *My car is red but not a prime number*) – it is proper to add to the definition of a property the requirement that the true proposition in question not be a non–property-ascribing proposition. Thus we have: *Q* is a property of *X* if and only if some proposition *P* is (i) not non–property-ascribing, (ii) true of *X*, and (iii) entails *X has property Q*. (Obviously, this is not a definition of "property" but an account of when something may properly be said to have a property.)

Some philosophers dislike such allegedly artificial properties as *neither a prime number nor a county in Texas* or *either a physical object or a forlorn hope*. I offer three replies, taking as my example the property-ascribing proposition *My car is either a physical object or a forlorn hope*. First, the distinction between artificial and nonartificial properties is both hard to make and not plainly not itself an artificial distinction. Second, *being a physical object* and *being a forlorn hope* seem perfectly ordinary properties. So do the properties referred to in our earlier argument, namely, *being conscious* and *existing without consciousness*. Third, while some would rule out (say) disjunctive properties (for example, *being red or blue*), doing so will not materially aid the ineffabilist's cause, and itself seems arbitrary if the disjunctive properties themselves are unproblematic.

The metaphysics of properties is, of course, too complex to try to develop here, nor need one do so to make the crucial point. For any liberated being X, *X is liberated* is true. The proposition *X is liberated* is understood in different ways by different traditions. Typically (perhaps always) it entails *X is not subject to further rebirth*. On various accounts, *X is liberated* will entail at least one of the following:

(1) *X is extinct.*
(2) *X is absorbed into a changeless state.*
(3) *X is part of a seamless being.*
(4) *X is in fellowship with God.*

A changeless state, an incomposite whole, and a soul in heaven are not ineffable. What does not exist can be neither effable nor ineffable. So there is nothing in (1–4) to comfort the ineffabilist.

4

Ineffability relative to particular languages

Since the claim (3a) *Only basic concepts fit (are true of) God* fails, perhaps we can do better by considering instead a more radical view. Some things, we might think, are ineffable relative to certain ranges of language but not relative to other ranges of language. Consider a modest language constructed of a limited number of elements. We begin with quantities: "all," "some," and "none." We then add connectives: "and," plus "or." We add negation: "not." We then add terms designating positive whole numbers ("one," "two," and so on). We also allow on board various operations that can be performed on numbers: "being multiplied by," "being subtracted from," "being divided by," and "being added to." We need "equals." Finally, we add terms expressing properties that a number necessarily has, like "being even," "being odd," and "being prime." Under such properties we shall count relations: "Being greater than" and "being the successor of" will express such relations. Then we quit. Call this language Mathese. In Mathese, we can say that two is even, three is the successor of two, and two divided by two is one. We cannot say that the Tower of Pisa leans or that the Eiffel Tower is not in Cleveland. The Tower of Pisa and the Eiffel Tower are ineffable, relative to Mathese. So is God. But of course Mathese is so limited in its descriptive range that being ineffable relative to it does not amount to much.

What would amount to considerably more would be the feature *being ineffable relative to any human language now available*. Perhaps what it is for God to be ineffable is this:

(4) God is ineffable relative to any human language available as of now.

This suggestion is limited in that it allows that there soon occur a linguistic breakthrough that allows us thereafter to describe God. One could supplement the suggestion with:

(4a) What has prevented God from being effable relative to any language we have developed thus far will prevent God from being effable relative to any language we shall ever develop.

What (4a) plainly raises, as does (4), is the question as to what explains divine ineffability relative to human discourse. Both (4) and (4a) leave us asking for a theory that will explain what they allege to be true. But for now our question is simply whether what (4) says is logically consistent and hence even *possibly* true. If it is not, then no theory that explains its truth is either necessary or possible.

Contrast (4) with:

(5) There is something that is ineffable relative to all human language.

Obviously, (4) seems much more specific, for it tells us that God is ineffable, and (5) tells us that something is, without specifying what. If "God" means "the Being worshiped by Jews" or "the Being called 'Father' by Jews and Christians" or "the One before whom the Hindu monotheists Ramanuja and Madhva bow," then, strictly, (4) is false. It is false because God is effable or describable at least to the extent that the descriptions just noted are true of God. On the other hand, while (5) does not suffer from this defect, it leaves us uninformed as to who or what it might be that is ineffable. One might try to give religious content to (5) by simply defining the term "God" as "that item or those items that is or are ineffable relative to all current human language." But since God, insofar as God is of deep relevance to monotheistic religion, is conceived of as existing, depending on nothing else for existence, omnipotent, omniscient, holy, morally perfect, and the like, God so conceived is not thought of as ineffable. The use of the term "God" in accordance with the definition just mentioned is related to the term "God" in typical monotheistic religious contexts rather as the term "bank" in the sentence "A bank is a place that provides financial services" is related to the term "bank" in the sentence "A bank is what keeps a river in place." You have one sound and one mark, but two very different meanings or uses, and hence two distinct concepts. Nor, of course, could you combine the two meanings or uses of "God" into a single, consistent meaning or use, for "God," used in typical religious fashion, is intended to refer to a holy and gracious, and hence effable, being.

INEFFABILITY AS RESTRICTED EFFABILITY

A careful look at even (5) raises more questions. What (5) at least says is that something exists that is ineffable relative to all current human language. But then (5) does entail that this item exists. Again, necessarily, if it exists, then it has properties, and has only consistent properties. If it has these highly indeterminate properties, it has fully determinate properties that fall under them. Further, at least (5) must be true of this rarefied item, which then is not ineffable after all.

One attached to (4) and (5) might wish to retain something as close as consistency allows to what they assert by replacing them by:

> (6) God is ineffable relative to any fully determinate concepts that we have any way of expressing.

One might distinguish between expressible indeterminate concepts and inexpressible (fully) determinate concepts, where expressibility is relative to the full range of current human languages. What (6) allows is that something be effable only relative to indeterminate concepts.

To be significantly in the spirit of a defense of ineffability, presumably (6) must be interpreted so as to make divine effability very limited. Thus *God exists, God has properties, God has only consistent properties,* and the like will be allowable, whereas *God is omnipotent, God is omniscient,* and *God knows that two and two are four* must be refused. If the latter sorts of claims are true or false, then God is not ineffable in the sense required by (6).

There is a point of dispute that should be mentioned here. On one view, for any item X and property P you like, it is true that X has P or true that X lacks P. On another view, this is not so. For some items, and some properties, it is alleged to be neither true nor false that those items have those properties. On the former account, such propositions as *God is bright yellow* is false, and *The number four, if it exists as an abstract object, is not red* is true. On the latter account, it is neither true nor false that God is bright yellow or that the number four is not red. I take the former account to be the correct one; the latter view may seem congenial to the suggestion that something or other, at least, is ineffable.

If one accepts the former view, then, as we have seen, a simple argument against ineffability can be mounted. For anything whatever, it is either true that it is red or else false that it is red. Hence the claim that it is red, being either true or else false, is meaningful. So is the claim that it is not red. Thus there is no escape from effability for anything. This seems to me exactly right.

There is no need to assume, however, that this is the truth of the matter. For the purpose of the present argument, I need not assume that such claims as *The equator can outrun any race horse* is false or such claims as *The square root of four is not blue* is true. Even if various kinds of items cannot be said, truly or falsely, to have certain ranges of properties, this forms no part of a case for ineffability. All that follows is that the general argument just offered must be restricted. The restriction goes as follows. For any item X, let the range of properties with regard to which it is either true that the item has it or else false that the item has it be an item's *property scope.* Then, necessarily, if it is possible that an item exist, then that item has a property scope. Whatever has a property scope is describable. No item that has a property scope is ineffable.

The defender of (6) will want here to press a legitimate distinction. It is true that for any item and any property, that item has or lacks that property (provided, if the second view is true, that the property falls within the item's property scope). That is a point about metaphysics; it speaks truly regarding what there is. But it may be that we have no words that express many of the properties that an item in fact has. What properties items have is one thing. What properties we can say that items have is another. What is inconsistent to hold is that anything exists without its having any properties, or that something has indeterminate properties without having fully determinate properties that fall under them. One need assert no such absurdities in order to embrace (6).

All that (6) favors is that there are certain limitations, not on what there can be, but on what we can say and what we can know. This sort of development of the idea behind (6) soon reaches a fork in the road. Consider the difference between:

(6a) God is ineffable relative to all of our fully determinate concepts

and

(6b) For no fully determinate concept can we tell whether it fits God or not.

What (6b) holds is a point about epistemology. It says that our knowledge about God has certain severe limitations. Nothing in (6b) by itself even suggests that *God knows when a sparrow falls* is neither true nor false. It is perfectly compatible with the view that, for any property you like, either it is true that God has it or it is false that God has it. Further, for any property you like, so far as (6b) is concerned, we can say

85

that God has or lacks it, although we shall not know if what we say is true. Thus (6b) is relevant to later portions of our argument, but it is no version of a claim that God is ineffable.

By contrast, (6a) says that God, relative to our fully determinate concepts, is ineffable. Correspondingly, however, (6a) allows that God *has* determinate properties that fall under indeterminate properties that we all have concepts of. We just lack, according to (6a), concepts of those determinate properties that apply to God and fall under the indeterminate concepts that we have. It is worth asking whether this view is logically consistent.

Is it possible that we have a concept of an indeterminate property and *no* concept of a more determinate property that falls under it? If I have the concept *being a property,* can it be true that I have no idea of such properties as *being a centimeter long, being chartreuse, being of a pound's weight,* or any other more determinate property? It is useful in approaching this question to remember that between the concept of a fully indeterminate property and the concept of a fully determinate property, there is a series of concepts of properties that (going toward full determinacy) are more and more determinate and also (going toward full indeterminacy) are more and more indeterminate. A short list of concepts going to full determinacy runs like this: *being a property, being a physical property, having weight, weighing exactly a pound.* A short list of concepts going to full indeterminacy runs as follows: *thinking that two is twice one, having a mathematical thought, having a thought, being in a mental state, being in some state or other, having a property.* Each concept that is not at one or another extreme of this continuum is both more determinate than a maximally determinate concept and more indeterminate than a maximally determinate concept. On our first list, each term but the last expresses a concept more indeterminate than that expressed by the term to its right. On our second list, each term but the last expresses a concept more determinate than that expressed by the term to its right. So many concepts are neither fully determinate nor fully indeterminate. If one is to have a concept at all, one must along with it – more carefully, as *part* of having it – grasp at least some portion of the conceptual continuum of indeterminacy/determinacy to which it belongs. If I do not know that *being tall, being tired,* and *being ill-tempered* are properties, and there are no other properties that serve me as recognized examples of *being a property,* then I lack the concept of being a property. I do not have the concept *being of some length* if I lack both the concept *being in space* and all concepts of specific length determinacy. I lack that concept if I lack *either* the concept *being in space* or all concepts of specific length determinacy. The answer to our question, then, is negative. One cannot have an indeterminate concept without also having some more determinate concept that falls under it. Of course (6a) does not require that one can do this. It requires only that one have an indeterminate concept that applies to God without our having any determinate concept that both falls under it *and* applies to God.

On the face of things, at any rate, this sort of ineffability seems not very deep. The idea behind it is that an indeterminate concept C has (say) determinate concepts C_1, C_2, and C_3 that fall under it. If C_3 fits God, and we have C, then we can have only C_1 and C_2. Since C_3 is a determinate concept that falls under a concept that we have, one wonders if the block to having C_3 can be very deep or hard to overcome.

What a supporter of (6a) requires is that whenever we have an indeterminate concept C that applies to God, none of the determinate concepts that we have that fall under C applies to God. One need not, of course, have *all* of the fully determinate concepts that fall under an indeterminate concept in order to have that concept. No doubt, interior decorators have many color concepts that I lack; while I have the concept *being colored* and know that *being orange, being green,* and *being purple* fall under it, various fully determinate concepts that fall under it are concepts that I lack, not necessarily but in fact. So, (6a) tells us, while there are determinate concepts that apply to God, and that fit God, none we have does so. We are lucky to have any indeterminate concepts that apply to, and fit, God. Then one must have some set of more determinate concepts that fall under them and lack divine fit. This allows that there be other more determinate concepts that fall under these indeterminate concepts that we do have, but do not fit God.

What this line regarding divine ineffability, on inspection, amounts to is something like:

> (7) Whereas we have highly indeterminate concepts that fit or accurately describe God, and various fully determinate concepts that fall under these highly indeterminate concepts, no fully determinate concepts that we have fit or accurately describe God.

While (7) does not entail that God is ineffable regarding indeterminate concepts, it asserts that God is ineffable regarding fully determinate concepts relative to those fully determinate concepts that we have. Thus it may seem to capture an appreciable part of what unrestrained advocates of ineffability favor. This appearance vanishes once one asks why in the world anything that fits only such concepts that we have as *exists* and *satisfies only indeterminate concepts among those we have* and *satisfies no determinate concept that we possess* should be called "God"? Why give it honorific titles? So far as we know, it is merely a vague something or other of no known interest or value or relevance to anything we care about. At best, so far as our knowledge of it extends, it is something of a curiosity.

In other ways, too, (7) is dubious. The concept *knowing that two plus two is four* is a fully determinate concept. Given (7), it is not true – it is either false or neither true nor false – that God knows that two and two are four. That God not have managed this modest feat is surprising, but (7) entails that it is true. The same holds for such claims as *God exists independently of anything else, God loves Mother Theresa,* and *God can cause the sun to explode.* All of these apply fully determinate concepts that we have to God. Hence, given (7), none of them is true. The same goes for such concepts as *calling Abraham, giving the law to Moses,* and *forgiving one of Saint Paul's sins.*

While (7), then, is intended to express a claim about the limits of human language, it entails a surprising amount of theology. For any specific person you please, and for any of that person's sins, (7) entails that God has not forgiven that person that sin. It follows from this that God has forgiven no sins at all, or at any rate none of which any human being has any fully determinate concept. According to (7), the claims *God made David king,* and *God revealed the Koran to Mohammed,* since they invoke the application of fully determinate concepts that we have to God, are meaningless. Hence, embracing (7), far from being a *defense* of Judaic, Christian, or Islamic monotheism, is incompatible with accepting typical versions of these types of monotheism.

This last comment is a *criticism* as opposed simply to a *consequence* of (7) only insofar as we have reason to think that (for example) *Either God made David king or God did not make David king* is true, or (7) is taken as an exposition or defense of some typical version of monotheism. But it is clear that there are deep barriers to there being a monotheistic religious rationale for (7). Similar considerations hold relative to nonmonotheistic religious traditions.

What (7) tells us is that something exists to which none of our current batch of fully determinate concepts applies but to which some of our indeterminate concepts apply. Suppose that (7) is true. Then something exists (allegedly, God) that currently is ineffable relative to our fully determinate concepts. Why suppose that this has any religious relevance? One might suppose that if the being in question is God, then (7) has religious relevance. Indeed, (7)'s religious relevance, as was noted earlier, would be significant and highly negative. It just lacks *positive significance for most religious traditions.*

TWO SORTS OF JUSTIFICATION OF INEFFABILITY

At this point, then, we turn to our second question – namely, what reasons have been offered for accepting some version of the claim that God is ineffable? Essentially, the reasons have come in one of two kinds: that God is ineffable because

God is too big to be effable, or because we are too small to have an accurate concept of God. The former alleges that God's nature precludes divine effability. The latter focuses on allegedly limiting features of human language, human cognitive capacities, or human experience.

At least for those who claim that God exists necessarily, the concept *being in existence* is indeterminate. Indeed, this is so for those who hold that the notion of logically necessary existence is meaningful, whether or not they hold that God enjoys logically necessary existence. The fully determinate concepts that fall under it are those of *existing necessarily* and *existing contingently*. An item X exists necessarily if and only if X *does not exist* is necessarily false or contradictory; equivalently, X exists necessarily if and only if X *exists* is a necessary truth. An item Y exists contingently if and only if Y *exists* is true but Y *does not exist* is not necessarily false or contradictory. The concept of necessary existence, then, is a fully determinate concept, and hence a being that enjoys logically necessary existence is not ineffable in the sense specified by (7). The concept of logically contingent existence is also fully determinate. So if one holds that *God exists* is logically contingent, one thinks that a fully determinate concept fits God. Since *God is ineffable* entails *God exists,* one who holds that God is ineffable holds a view that entails that some determinate concept fits God. Thus (7) must at least be revised so as to allow a fully determinate concept of existence to fit God and any determinate concepts that fit God by virtue of a fully determinate concept of existence doing so. For example, *God is either eternal or everlasting* follows from *Necessarily, God exists,* and *God is either eternal, everlasting, or temporally finite* follows from *"God exists" is logically contingent.* Even if one held that we only know *Either God exists necessarily or it is contingently true that God exists,* we would know that some fully determinate concept that we have applies to God; either *exists with logical necessity* or else *exists logically contingently* fits.

Assuming that these concepts are consistent, the concepts of omnipotence and omniscience are fully determinate. Thus one who holds that God has one or both of these properties must forgo the claim that God is ineffable in the sense that (7) specifies, and one who holds that God is ineffable must forgo these claims.

One characterization of God asserts that God exists necessarily and links necessary existence with simplicity or complete lack of complexity. On this account, God has no one property that is distinct from any other of God's properties, nor is God distinct from the property that God has or is. Thus it is impossible that God lose any property that God has.

It is not obvious that this doctrine is logically consistent. An omnipotent being presumably lacks no knowledge that it is logically possible that it possess. But a being that was omniscient might know how to do things that it nonetheless lacked the power to do. If these things are so, then it is logically impossible that an omnipotent being lack omniscience but it is logically possible that an omniscient being lack omnipotence. If that, in turn, is the case, then *being omnipotent* is one property and *being omniscient* is another property. Further, *being morally perfect* presumably includes both *having acted rightly* and *never having acted wrongly*. It would appear that a being could be both omnipotent and omniscient and yet lack either or both of the properties included in being morally perfect. *Being necessarily existent,* which simplicity supporters ascribe to God, seems plainly a distinct property from any of the others mentioned. In sum, if *God's being omniscient* is entailed by, but does not entail, *God's being omnipotent,* then they are different properties. Similarly, if *God's being omnipotent and omniscient* neither entails nor is entailed by *God's being morally perfect,* then these are different properties.

There are two general strategies for avoiding the result that various divine properties are distinct. One endeavors to show that for any two properties you pick from the list of properties that God has, necessarily God has the one if and only if God has the other. Then if A and B are two divine properties, *God has A* entails, and is entailed by, *God has B.*

Then, the argument continues, *God has A* means the same thing as *God has B; A* and *B* have identical connotations. But if that is so, then *A* and *B*, the claim is, are the same property. The other strategy allows that if *A* names a divine property and *B* names a divine property, then *A* may connote or mean one thing and *B* connote or mean something else. But the claim is that *A* and *B* will still refer to or denote the same property.

The former strategy argues something as follows. Suppose, to begin with, that God is omnipotent. It follows that God is omniscient. Even being able to do wrong, let alone doing wrong, is a weakness. An omnipotent being will not have any weakness. So an omnipotent being will also be morally perfect, and not even capable of not being so. To be omnipresent simply is to be capable of acting anywhere at any time. Thus, being omnipotent entails being omnipresent. And thus, there is at least one divine property – namely, being omnipotent – such that God's having it entails God's having such other divine properties as being omniscient, morally perfect, and omnipresent. One might call this the *omnipotence derivation* strategy, as it infers the presence of the other divine attributes from the presence of omnipotence. A more general version of this strategy relies on the notion of a perfection, arguing that God is a perfect being, a perfect being has all perfections, and having *any* one perfection entails having all of the others. This more general strategy obviously relies heavily on the notion of a perfection, and I know of no criterion for being a perfection that both is plainly correct and adequately serves the purpose of one who follows the strategy.

What the identical connotation strategy requires is that this be true: If *P* entails *Q* and *Q* entails *P*, then *P* has the same meaning as *Q*. Every necessary proposition entails every other. Thus *Two is even* entails, and is entailed by, *If George is embodied, then George is embodied* and *Every unicorn is single-horned* and *Either George Washington exists or he does not exist*. One would suppose it obvious that these propositions are not the same, and the sentences that naturally express them in English are not identical in meaning. Nor will this change if one expresses them instead in Telugu, Hebrew, or Ugaritic. Hence this strategy presupposes a mistaken theory of meaning.

Typically, on the simplicity strategy, God necessarily has (perhaps necessarily *is*) the one property that God has. So for any predicates *A* and *B*, *God has A* and *God has B*, if they are true at all, are necessarily true. So *God's having A* and *God's having B* are necessarily coinstantiated, both because *A* and *B* (on the view under discussion) have the same meaning and because every necessary truth entails every other, so that *God has A* entails, and is entailed by, *God has B*. Reference, then, to predicates rather than propositions will not save the view.

Besides requiring a false principle of meaning, the first strategy has other defects. On one influential and plausible conception of moral perfection, one is a moral agent only if one is free or autonomous regarding morally significant actions. A morally significant action is one that it is morally right or morally wrong for the agent to perform. An agent has autonomy regarding an action only if she both can perform it and can refrain from performing it. A moral agent, then, can perform wrong actions and refrain from performing right actions. A perfect moral agent, of course, is a moral agent. So even a perfect moral agent could have trod a path other than that of moral perfection. On this view, *being able to do evil* is not a weakness, and *doing good though one is able to do evil* is a significant strength. Thus, if this influential and plausible account of morality is correct, the alleged link of entailment between omnipotence and moral perfection cannot be forged. Omnipotence will include the power to do evil.

Another example raises the same sort of problem. As was noted earlier, a being exists necessarily if and only if it is logically impossible that it not exist. The claim that God exists necessarily is the claim that *God does not exist* is contradictory. This, of course, is not merely a claim about language or thought. If God exists necessarily, then on a concept of God that is adequate regarding representing God's existence,

God's necessary existence will be reflected in the necessary truth of *God exists* and the necessary falsehood of *God does not exist*. It will not be identical to, or dependent on, its being so reflected. It is possible that something exist necessarily but not be omnipotent. Some have held, for example, that true mathematical propositions are true by virtue of the qualities and relations of numbers conceived as abstract entities. So conceived, the number two is distinct from the concept *two*, which exists only if people have it, and of course from uses of the word "two," which occur only if people use it. The number two is viewed as a nonspatial, perhaps atemporal, and certainly necessarily existing abstract object. But the number two has no power at all, and so falls considerably short of being omnipotent. On the other hand, an omnipotent being might be a logically contingent being. A logically contingent omnipotent being could prevent anything from putting it out of existence. *Being logically contingent* does not entail *being in some way dependent for existence on something else*. While an omnipotent being can enjoy secure existence, the security need not be that of logically necessary existence. It can be that of a being that nothing else can endanger without its own permission. Neither *being omnipotent* nor *being logically necessary* is such that anything having the one property must therefore have the other. Here, too, the relevant properties are not connected as simplicity theory requires. *God's being omnipotent* and *God's enjoying logically necessary existence* are distinct properties, since neither entails the other.

One might object to these arguments by suggesting that while they are correct so far as they go, they do not refute simplicity doctrine. That doctrine requires, not *Necessarily, being omnipotent mutually entails being morally perfect*, but *Necessarily, God's being omnipotent mutually entails God's being morally perfect*. Our examples have been *being omnipotent, being morally perfect*, and the like, not *God's omnipotence, God's moral perfection*, and the like. The problem with this reply is simply that the entailment relations between *being omnipotent* and *being omniscient*, and between *God's being omnipotent* and *God's enjoying logically necessary existence,* mirror one another, and we have cast part of our argument in the latter terms.

There is, however, the other strategy mentioned earlier. Consider any convex surface. Its opposite surface is concave. Necessarily, if X has a concave surface, its opposite surface (the surface seen from the other side, as it were) is convex. The meaning or connotation of "being concave" is distinct from the meaning or connotation of "being convex." The defender of divine simplicity presumably will view the connotatively distinct terms as having identity of denotation or reference. *Being concave* and *being convex,* in the same item, will be the same property. The simplicist, then, embraces the general doctrine that:

> (8) If it is a necessary truth that something has a property P if and only if it has a property Q, then property P is identical to property Q, though the meaning of the term P need not be identical to the meaning of the term Q.

Thus regarding Euclidean triangles, a triangle's *being three-sided and closed* is the same property as its *being three-angled.* Regarding Fridays, a given Friday's property *occurring after a Thursday* and its property *occurring before a Saturday* are the same property. The number two's property of *being divisible by two* and its property of *being the successor of an odd number* are one property. In each case, the proposition that says that the item in question has one of the properties mentioned and the proposition that says it has the other property mentioned are necessary truths. Every necessary truth entails every other. So the propositions regarding the same item enjoy mutual entailment, and the item has the one property if and only if it has the other.

Suppose, for the sake of the argument, that (8) is true. What its use requires, if the strategy we are concerned with is followed, is that it be logically impossible that (say) God be omnipotent but not logically necessarily existent, or that God be omniscient but not omnipotent, or that God be omnipotent but not morally perfect. We argued that these things are not impossible. Those arguments rested on such propositions as *God has logically necessary existence* and *God is omnipotent* not entailing one another. They do not rest on the view (which is false) that mutual entailment requires connotational identity. In the absence of mutual entailment, one lacks necessary coextension between "having logically necessary existence" and "being omnipotent." Claim (8) was appealed to as a way of suggesting that there might be necessary identity of reference or denotation even in the absence of identity of meaning or connotation. But if necessary coextension is lacking, (8) is of no help.

Such terms as "greatest defensive basketball center ever" and "first African-American coach in the National Basketball Association" are different in connotation but not in denotation, as are "Morning Star" and "Evening Star." Such cases need raise no particular philosophical puzzles. It is more problematic whether such terms as "closed, three-sided plane figure" and "three-angled figure," applied to one item, refer to one property of that item or to two. Suppose, for the sake of the argument, that they refer to one. What we lack is any reason for supposing that such claims as *God is omnipotent if and only if God is morally perfect* or *God has logically necessary existence if and only if God is omnipotent*, and similar claims regarding all other properties properly ascribed to God, turn out to be true. Without that, appeal to (8) is of no avail.

5

Reasons in ineffability's favor

We turn next to arguments that suppose that we are too small to have any concept of God. Such arguments walk on a razor's edge. They must rely on enough of a notion of God to serve as a basis for the argument's strong conclusion, but not enough of a notion of God to subvert that conclusion. It is as if one were commissioned to produce a zero balance on a complex account from which unpredictably large expenditures were continually being made, so that one had to make sure that there was just enough deposited to prevent going into the red – only harder.

The simplest version of the argument runs: God is infinite, and the infinite surpasses our comprehension. But of course one is owed an explanation of some sort as to what "God is infinite" means and why its proper meaning excludes our knowing anything about God. Read in anything like a typical monotheistic way, "God is infinite" does not entail that God is everything there is. My pen is not God or part of God – not at least on any typical version of monotheism. (If the question arises as to why this matters, it should be remembered that our overall topic concerns whether or not religious experience provides any evidence for religious belief, and in particular for the belief that God exists, as that belief is understood in those traditions.) If A is not identical to B, neither is B identical to A. Since my pen is not God, God is not my pen. Even if God is infinite, God's being so need not get in the way of that being true, and known to be true. It cannot

97

be simply that God is construed as having an infinite number of properties, for quite modest items have that distinction. The smallest armadillo in Texas has the infinitely complex property of being nonidentical with any of the natural numbers. If one does not like this example, consider all the spatial properties and temporal properties that our armadillo possesses. (If two or more Texan armadillos tie for smallness, consider any one.)

One might consider only nonrelational properties; perhaps God alone has an infinite number of nonrelational properties. If knowing that something is true is a relation between the knower and what is known, being omniscient involves being in a great many relations. Being omnipotent perhaps involves something like this. Consider the power, relative to some action *A*, to be able to do *A* and to be able to refrain from doing *A*: One might describe this as having a *dual capacity* regarding doing *A*. Perhaps *being omnipotent* is a matter of a being's having a dual capacity regarding any action that it is logically possible that being perform. A capacity is perhaps best construed as a nonrelational property, so perhaps an omnipotent being does have an infinite number of nonrelational properties. But such a being would be able to make a rosebush bloom, make it rain in Toledo, or turn on the lights on the White House Christmas tree. Any being that could so act would not be ineffable. Indeed, a being with an infinite number of nonrelational properties would seem a splendid candidate for being infinitely far from ineffability.

Quite a lot is known about infinite sets. The set of all whole, positive, even integers (two, four, six, and so on) is infinite. So is the set of all whole, positive, odd integers (one, three, five, and so on). So, too, is the set of all whole integers, whether even or odd. Call these, respectively, the *even* set, the *odd* set, and the *big* set. The big set contains the odd set and the even set. The odd set contains neither the even set nor the big set. The even set contains neither the big set nor the odd set. But the big set does not contain more members than the even set or more members than the odd set, even though in each case it contains an infinite number of members that the contained set does not. That much information about mathematical infinity need not paralyze the human mind, and of course it does not exhaust our information on the subject. So "infinity" need not be an inherently mystifying term.

When God is said to be infinite, the idea is not that God is composed of an infinite number of members. The core notion is that God is not limited in various ways. Even the world's strongest human is unable to do lots of things that it is logically possible that he or she do. Even the world's most intelligent human does not know even close to everything that it is logically possible that he or she know. Even the oldest human depends for her existence on something other than herself. To say that God is infinite is to say that God is able to do anything that it is logically possible that God do, that God knows everything that it is logically possible that God know, and that God depends on nothing else for existence. It is to say that God lacks moral fault. None of these descriptions is beyond human ken, and they are part and parcel of what *God is infinite* means. Hence divine infinity provides no cheer to the defender of divine ineffability.

ANALOGICAL PREDICATION

Sometimes God is said to be a rock. This claim does not lie on the border of theology and geology. It says in nonliteral terms what *God is reliable* puts literally. Sometimes God is said to be a father. This claim does not fall between theology and biology or sociology. It puts nonliterally what *God is our loving and providential cause* says literally.

Claims of this sort are analogical; they compare familiar things with God, doing so on the basis of an alleged similarity. If you rely on a rock to support your weight, typically it will not fall apart; if you trust in God, God will not forsake you. Our understanding analogical claims about God rests entirely on our understanding the property that God and rocks (or father or whatever) share. Without such understanding, our use of analogies will not involve our making any intelligible claim. Without such an understanding, not even revelation cast in terms of analogy will yield any knowledge of God. One *might* be in a position to claim something like this: *God is like a rock in some way or other, but I cannot specify in what way.* How one could know this is unclear, as is what religious significance it might have. *God is a rock* entails *God is reliable.* What of religious interest is entailed by *God is like a rock, but in some unspecified way* is more puzzling.

Some have claimed that, God being a member of no genus or sharing no genus membership with anything else, claims about God are *purely* analogical. A claim is purely analogical if and only if it has two features: (i) it has the form *God is like X;* (ii) one cannot state in nonanalogical terms the relevant respect in which God is like X. The consequence of such a view is simple. On it, claims about God are not thicker or more interesting than the nearly contentless *God is like a rock in some unspecified way* mentioned earlier. So, presumably, are the number seventeen, the oldest golden retriever in Wisconsin, and every goldfish like God in some unspecified way. Such claims are utterly trivial and of no religious or other interest.

On the other hand, if we can specify the property or properties on which an analogy trades, there strictly is no *need* for the analogy, however useful it may be for purposes of pedagogy or worship. One can simply assert that God has the relevant property, leaving aside noting that something else has it as well.

PROPORTIONAL PREDICATION AND "AS IF" PREDICATION

Sometimes it is suggested that God has a property characterizable in these terms: As strength is to a rock, so is this property to God. The property cannot be *being reliable,* since *God is reliable* (on this view) is not allowable. But somehow God has a property that is proportional in God to strength or solidity or durability in a rock. A similar suggestion is that God acts *as if* God were trustworthy or reliable; God has the relational property *treating human beings trustworthily*, but lacks the intrinsic property *being trustworthy*. On the former account, as on the latter, nonrelational properties cannot be ascribed to God. On the latter account, relational properties can be so ascribed, but they lack their ordinary basis. *God acts lovingly toward human beings* is so construed as not to entail *God loves human beings*, but also so understood as not to entail *God acts hypocritically*.

Here too one faces familiar difficulties. A sentence of the form *X loves Y* entails *X is conscious*. Both dogs and humans typically are conscious, and since God (it is said) cannot share nonrelational properties with anything else, *God loves human beings* does not entail *God is conscious*. Further, *God acts as if God were trustworthy* entails *God acts*, which entails (on the view being discussed) that *God acts as if God were trustworthy* must be rejected, for if one accepts that claim one must grant that God acts and this view rejects that notion. Or, it will be said, the claims *God loves human beings* and *God acts as if God were trustworthy* must be interpreted so as not to entail *God is conscious* or *God acts*. Short of ascribing unconscious action to God, which would also be rejected, it is hard to see what this new, restricted interpretation could amount to. If God does not act at all, then God cannot act as if God were trustworthy.

Put one way, the problem is this: To know what (say) *Some apples are tart* means is to know what else is true if it is. It is to know what *Some apples are tart* entails. The views in question require that one follow this strategy: For any proposition of the form *God does A*, delete every proposition that such a proposition would entail were it to have some subject other than "God" and do not replace them by adding any proposition that says that God has some nonrelational property. By the time one tries to follow this strategy, one loses one's grasp of what is supposed to be asserted.

Put another way, any proposition of the form *X acted* that supposedly fails to entail *X is conscious* is either self-contradictory or contentless. It is of the form *X did A, doing A entails having property P, and X lacks P* or "*X did A*" is true but *no (nonrelational) proposition entailed by the proposition "X did A" is true.* The former is contradictory. The latter leaves us not knowing what proposition X *did* A is supposed to express. No successful defense of divine ineffability comes from such notions as these.

CONCEPTS

A somewhat more interesting line of reasoning than that which appeals to infinity begins with an account of human concepts. There are various accounts that can serve the purpose, and we will take our example as representative of others. The account contains two distinct and separable elements: an account of the *nature* of concepts and an account of the *source* of concepts. Strictly, the suggestion goes, what needs analysis is *what it is to have a concept.* That account goes as follows. John has the concept *cow* to the degree that John knows what is true if and only if there are cows. John has the concept of being red to the degree that John knows what is true if and only if something is red. Put generally and abstractly, John has the concept *being (an) X* to the degree that John knows what is true if and only if *something is (an) X.* Thus, to have a concept is to possess a piece of conditional knowledge.

The source of our concepts, the suggestion goes, is sensory and introspective experience. It is taste, smell, sight, touch, and hearing, as well as being in pain, feeling tired, being aware of tasting chocolate, feeling cold or dizzy or elated or nauseated or happy or depressed, and the like. To each sensory sense, there corresponds a particular sort of property: colors, sounds, tastes, odors, and tactile features such as roughness and smoothness. Then there are various objects of various inner senses, namely, a variety of inner sensations and emotions, including pulse and heartbeat, dizziness and fatigue, and joy and anger.

Our descriptive concepts, the story goes, derive from inner and outer sensations. Our indefinable descriptive words name, denote, or otherwise correspond to, the objects of

102

outer and inner sense, and thereby get their meaning or connotation. Definable descriptive words are made up from their indefinable descriptive siblings.

Not all of language is descriptive or semantic. Some of it is structural or syntactic. Thus we have quantifiers, connectives, inference terms, and negation. These provide the glue with which to put indefinable or simple words together to make definable or complex ones, and to attach words together to yield sentences. Obviously "all," "or," "therefore," and "not" name, correspond to, or refer to no objects of observation. Any theory of the source of our concepts will have to give attention to the origin of these important concepts, but for the sake of the argument let us suppose that such an account that is adequate can be given that fits nicely alongside the account of descriptive terms already sketched.

Trying to define "God" by reference to such terms as "red," "sour," "smooth," and "joyful" is not encouraging. So the theory of concepts that we have been sketching may offer promise for a theory of divine ineffability. Of course, it also offers promise for the view that all talk about divine existence and properties is sheer nonsense.

RANGES OF EXPERIENCE

Whether this has any chance of being so depends on what sorts of objects of sensation and introspection are allowed. Suppose that we are held to be acquainted with ourselves as minds in the sense of enduring agents that have cognitive and moral capacity. It is not extravagant to suppose that we know ourselves not to be omnipotent, omniscient, or morally perfect. But then we can conceive of God as an agent that is omniscient, omnipotent, and morally perfect. If the concept of something being atemporal is in order, then we can both know that we are not atemporal and (if such is our view) claim that God is. If the notion of atemporality or eternity is inconsistent, then nonetheless, we know that we are not everlasting and can claim that God is. In sum, if introspection or sensation gives us acquaintance with self-conscious agents and their powers, then, given that the concept of an agent who, in sharp contrast to us, possesses these admirable properties will be God, it will turn out that God is effable.

Alternatively, if the objects of outer and inner sense are short-lived states, such as momentary flashes of redness, smoothness, sourness, dizziness, or elation, and physical objects and minds are conceived as nothing more than sets of these transitory states, things may be different regarding divine ineffability. If even the concept of an apple is nothing more than the concept of *red now, round now, smooth now,* and the like, how shall we construct the concept of God? This question sometimes has seemed unanswerable, save by saying that we cannot construct the concept of God from such materials or others like them. If these materials, and others like them, are all the materials we have, we shall not be able to construct the concept of God.

There is cause for hesitation before one accepts this conclusion. How are we to understand the claim that the concept of God cannot be derived in any way available to us? Don't we need to *have* the concept of God in order to make such a claim? The argument that one does not needs the following sorts of premises: (1) Any concept that counts as a concept of God must meet condition *A*, and (2) no concept that we have can meet condition *A*. The idea, then, is to find some content for *A* on which (1) and (2) are true. Were one to argue that (1) any concept of God must be the concept of an infinite being, and (2) we cannot have the concept of an infinite being, one would offer a second premise whose truth would be incompatible with one's understanding either (1) or (2), and hence incompatible with knowing or believing that (1) or (2) was true. If (2) is true, then all there is to (1) that we can grasp is *any concept of God must be the concept of,* which of course is no premise at all. So one has to be careful how one formulates an argument of this sort; one can easily slip inadvertently into offering premises that presuppose their own falsehood as well as the falsehood of the conclusion one is trying to establish (namely, that one has no concept of God).

The two-stage strategy recently outlined tells us that all concepts, and hence the concept of God if we have it, must meet a certain condition. If it is an indefinable, descriptive concept, it must name or correspond to or refer to some object of inner and outer sense. If it is a definable, descriptive term, then it must be definable (immediately or through steps) in terms of indefinable descriptive terms (plus syntactical terms). Objects of inner and outer sense all are momentary states. So if "God" is a meaningful term – if we have the concept of God – then "God" is definable by reference to words referring to momentary inner or outer states.

In order to assess this sort of argument, it is useful to leave the concept of God aside for the moment. Consider, instead, such terms as "onion," "apple," and "leaf." On a very familiar perspective that is ordinary if anything is, an onion is a thing that has certain properties and endures for a certain while. It exists whether anyone senses it or has any momentary experiences, and it is not a collection or bundle or concrete set of momentary states.

One central issue in metaphysics concerns what things are *individuals* – items that are not made up of other simpler items that could exist on their own. On one account, both *bodies* and *minds* are individuals. But on the account of the two-stage strategy that we are considering, it is momentary *states* that are individual.

If a body is an individual, then it is a physical substance – a thing that has properties, is not itself a property, is not a collection of properties, has states, is not itself a state, is not a collection of states, and endures over time and through change. If minds are individuals, then a mind is a thing that has properties and states, is not itself a property, and so on. If momentary states are the only individuals, then bodies and minds are not individuals, but are instead collections or bundles of states.

The objects of inner and outer perception – of sensation

and introspection – the suggestion is, are these momentary states that are the only individuals. So an indefinable descriptive term refers to an individual momentary state. The claim, then, is that "God" does not refer to some momentary state and does not mean "collection of individual momentary states" and thus the concept of God cannot be constructed out of the concepts of individual momentary states.

This theory of language obviously contains a significant amount of metaphysics. What there is determines what actual items there are for words to refer to; descriptive language, on this view, should contain an inventory of what things there are. A list of indefinable terms should provide an account, if not of all the individuals that there are, at least of a significant number of them. Concepts of nonexistent things, on this view, must be concepts of *complex* things, things composed of individuals rather than being individuals themselves. As we have seen, the view is polemically more promising if its metaphysical element includes the view that the only individuals are momentary states.

This view, however, faces deep problems. One is epistemological; the other is metaphysical. Simply put, the epistemological problem is that such terms as "theory," "meaning," "language," "concept," and "condition" are as dubious as candidates for being defined in the approved manner as is "God." The same goes for "term" (taken as a bearer of meaning), "refers to," and "is constructed of." Plainly meaningful terms cannot be defined in the approved manner and clearly are not indefinable on this view's criteria. It is certainly more clearly true that these terms are meaningful than that the theory is true. Further, the theory itself cannot be stated if they are meaningless. Thus, religious concepts aside, there are strong reasons to reject the theory.

This view also faces a metaphysical difficulty. That a person has a mind entails his having a variety of mental capacities: being able to remember having had breakfast yesterday, perform numerical calculations, make inferences, develop character, and the like. If bundles of momentary states can perform the sorts of cognitive tasks, and possess the sorts of dispositions and tendencies, that minds construed as mental substances can possess, then perhaps persons can be bundles of momentary states (although it does not follow that they are). But then there seems no reason to think that it is logically impossible, on the view in question, that a bundle of momentary dispositions be omnipotent, omniscient, and morally perfect. If bundles of states can be parts of persons, doing so in such a way as to provide a solid basis for personal identity, self-consciousness, memory, responsibility, and the like, then perhaps persons are bundles of momentary states after all. But it is not clear why having the concept of a person will provide any problem. Then a divine person will be one whose possession of knowledge, power, and goodness, unlike those of our friends, is full and complete.

On the other hand, if bundles of states cannot perform these sorts of tasks, and possess these sorts of properties, the persons who do possess them are not bundles of states. But then the concept of a person, insofar as it is accurate, is not the concept of a bundle of momentary states, and cannot be constructed only out of concepts of such states plus syntactical concepts.

SYNTACTIC CONCEPTS

The sort of theory of concepts that we have been discussing, like classical accounts in Locke and Hume, says little about "logical tissue" or syntactic concepts. What criticisms of it strike the mark partly depends on exactly what syntactical concepts include. Correspondingly, of course, so does what follows from such a theory and what sort of promise it may hold for ineffabilists.

The term "is" has at least three senses. In *Mark Twain is Samuel Clemens*, "is" means "is the same as." In *Larry Bird is a great player*, it means "has the property of being." In "17 is a prime number" it (on one reading, anyway; one can give a predicative reading to the sentence instead) means "is a member of." There is the "is" of identity, the "is" of predication or property ascription, and the "is" of class membership.

Temporal notions, such as *being successive, being simultaneous, being momentary, enduring over time,* and the like, are not part of an austerely defined list of logical terms. Neither is *being a substance.* Yet the "is" of predication is logically tied to the notion of something that has properties, and it is easy to smuggle the notion of a substance into discourse by hiding it beneath the cloak of the predicative "is."

The notion of a thing that has properties can be constructed out of the quantifier *there is an* X and a supply of property variables or property constants. The notion of a bundle that is composed of states can be constructed out of a supply of variables or constants construed as ranging over states and the notion of *being a member of a class.* The former results in the concept *an* X *that is* P *and* Q, where the "is" is that of predication. The latter results in the concept *a set that comprises* A *and* B, which obviously uses the "is" of class membership. Temporal notions can be added in various ways.

Strictly, neither *enduring substance* nor *momentary state* is a syntactical term. If one allows temporal terms plus the "is" of predication and the "is" of identity, then one can construct the notions *enduring substance* and *momentary state* from syntactical plus temporal concepts. In that respect, there is no reason to give one concept pride of place over the other. Indeed, they go together; since momentariness rules out enduring, if I have the concept of a momentary state, I have the concept of a state that does not endure, and hence have the concept *something that endures.* Possession of the concepts requisite for understanding the claim *Everything is momentary* includes possessing the concept *enduring thing* – that is, *substance.*

The two-stage strategy combines a metaphysical thesis (*only momentary states are individuals*) with an epistemological claim (*our indefinable descriptive concepts correspond to individuals*). If the metaphysical thesis is true, then persons are composed of individual states and are enduring composites possessed of a variety of complex cognitive properties. If this is so, then our concept of God can be the concept of an everlasting (or else eternal) composite that possesses complex cognitive capacities of the highest order, and whose composing states never fall apart or fail to be replicated (or else are eternal). If the complex properties that persons possess cannot be exhibited by composites of momentary states, then the account of our concept of being a person that the two-stage strategy offers fails to be adequate for persons. (It might, for analogous reasons, be inadequate even as an account of our concept of a physical object.) Either way, as a defense of divine ineffability, the strategy fails.

VERIFICATIONISM AS A ROUTE TO INEFFABILITY

A different strategy claims that there is nothing that could provide evidence either for or against the claim *God exists* and hence that the claim is not genuine – that in fact nothing is asserted when one apparently alleges that God exists. *God exists*, the suggestion is, is but a pseudo claim. Like *Zambala egretulates*, it has form and sound without benefit of sense. This sort of argument sometimes has been launched from a premise that asserts *An alleged claim is not genuine unless there is some in-principle-available observation that would provide evidence for or against it.* There being no observation that satisfies this characterization relative to the premise itself, the premise expresses no claim if it is true and hence is self-defeating. That sort of appeal, then, does not lend any credence to the general verificationist strategy.

On one notion of God, *God exists* is a necessary truth and *God does not exist* is a contradiction; call this *Anselmian* theism after Saint Anselm. On another notion, *God exists* will be true though logically contingent, and *God does not exist* is false though not a contradiction. Call this view *plain* theism (*Biblical* theism perhaps would be presumptuous). Either sort of monotheism embraces *Necessarily, God does not depend for existence on anything distinct from God.* It is consistent with either sort of monotheism that God's existence be proved, though a proof of God's existence if *God exists* is necessary can contain only necessarily true premises, and a proof of God's existence if *God exists* is logically contingent must contain at least one logically contingent claim.

Even if *Necessarily, God exists* is true, there might be evidence that God does not exist. There might be an argument, for example, that was plausible and concluded that while if God exists, both *God is omniscient* and *God is morally perfect* are true, no being can be both omniscient and morally perfect, so there can be no God. Whatever reason one had to think that argument correct would be a reason to think that *God exists* is a false claim. Of course if there is a sound and valid proof of God's existence, there is something wrong with the plausible argument to the contrary. But then there is no contradiction between *We have plausible and apparently unanswerable evidence in favor of proposition P* and *In fact, P is false,* or between *We have plausible and apparently overwhelming evidence against P* and *In fact, P is true.* It is not obvious that no version of the ontological, teleological, or moral argument provides some evidence for the existence of God, or that no version of the argument from evil provides some evidence against God's existence. Nor is it obvious that all experiential evidence is irrelevant to the question of God's existence. So it may well be that, even were it the case that *If there could be no evidence pro or con regarding God's existence, then "God exists" would only seem to express a claim to those unaware of its lack of content,* the fact is that there is relevant evidence and so *God exists* is either true or false. Accepting verificationism would be a mistake, but one who made that mistake need not in all consistency make the further mistake of supposing *God exists* to lack truth-value.

The thesis that an apparent claim is only a pseudo claim unless there *can* be evidence pro or con concerning it is compatible with no human being now having, or ever coming to have, any such evidence. So even were one to show that currently the evidence regarding *God exists* is nil, either in favor or against, this would do nothing to show that *God exists* is neither true nor false.

All of this, in a way, circles the issue without meeting it directly. The fact is that it is not true that, if an apparent proposition is true or false, then there must be some possible state of affairs the obtaining of which would make it false. At best that is so only for contingent propositions, true or false. It is not true for *Everything that exists has only logically compatible properties*, which is necessarily true, and hence true, precisely because there is no possible state of affairs the obtaining of which would make it false. It would be mistaken to suppose that therefore it asserts nothing at all. On the contrary, it says something that is true of absolutely everything that exists. In that regard, its information content is quite high, exceeding that, say, of the Chicago telephone directory.

Assume, however, that *God exists* is a logically contingent claim. The current attempt to show that God is ineffable, then, requires that there be no logically possible evidence against *God exists*. It is mistaken if it is even logically possible that anyone (perhaps quite mistakenly, but nonetheless with at least a smidgen of plausibility) believes that he or she has been given reason to think that the concept of God is contradictory, for a person who so believes has evidence that *God exists* is false. Since it plainly is possible for someone to be so situated, the attempt fails. If all that is required for *God exists* to be a genuine claim is that it be logically possible that someone has some evidence that it is false, then the claim indeed is genuine. There is, then, little reason to think verificationism true, or to think that, were it true, it would render *God exists* truth-valueless. There is no more reason to think that, were *God exists* truth-valueless, this would establish ineffability; if *God exists* cannot be true, then God cannot exist (and so cannot be ineffable).

MODALITY

There are some interesting, and perhaps surprising, connected issues, as a brief excursion into modal logic can reveal. A proposition is anything that is either true or false. Where *having truth-value* is a matter of *being either true or false*, what has truth-value is a proposition. Belief *in*, or trust, presupposes belief *that*, which is propositional belief.

Now for the modal logic. A proposition is either *necessary* or *contingent*. A necessary proposition is either necessarily true or necessarily false. A proposition is *necessarily true* if and only if its denial is self-contradictory. A proposition is *contingent* if and only if it is not necessary, neither it nor its denial being self-contradictory. A contingent proposition is either true or false. Necessarily true propositions, and contingent propositions, are *possible* or *possibly true*; necessarily false propositions are not possible or possibly true. *Being necessarily true, being necessarily false, being contingent,* and *being possible* are *modalities* of propositions. A necessary truth is true and so, of course, is possibly true; it has no chance of being false. A necessary falsehood is false, and not possibly true. A contingent truth is true, and both possibly true and possibly false; it *could* have been false. A contingent falsehood is false, and both possibly false and possibly true; it *could* have been true. This distinction between necessary propositions and contingent propositions is deep and basic; it is relevant to a great many issues in philosophy.

Monotheism, we noted, comes in two varieties. For one variety, *God exists* is a necessary truth, and *God does not exist* is contradictory. For the other variety, *God exists* is logically contingent; it is true, and both possibly true and possibly false. Both traditions hold that it is a necessary truth that *If God exists, then there is nothing distinct from God on which God is dependent for existence;* neither perspective supposes God's existence to be shaky or endangered.

As we noted, it is widely and plausibly held that a proposition possesses its modality with necessity. A necessarily true proposition is *necessarily* necessarily true; *being necessarily true* is not a hat that can be put on or taken off. The same goes for *being necessarily false, being contingent,* and *being possible;* these features are necessarily possessed by what has them. If follows that *Necessarily, God exists* is itself either a necessary truth *or a contradiction.* Similarly, *"God exists" is a logically contingent proposition* is either a necessary truth *or a contradiction.*

The variety of monotheism that embraces the claim *Necessarily, God exists* can be called *necessitarian monotheism.* Its corresponding atheistic view is *necessitarian atheism,* which holds that *Necessarily, God does not exist* is true. Necessitarian atheism is true only if the concept of God is contradictory – only if it ascribes to God logically incompatible properties. The variety of monotheism that contends that *God exists* is a true, logically contingent claim can be called *nonnecessitarian monotheism*. The corresponding version of atheism is *nonnecessitarian atheism*, which holds that *God does not exist* is a false, logically contingent claim. Both nonnecessitarian theism and nonnecessitarian atheism assume that the concept of God is not contradictory; they share this view with necessitarian monotheism.

Suppose that necessitarian monotheism is true. Then necessitarian atheism (but also nonnecessitarian theism) and nonnecessitarian atheism are not merely false but necessarily false or contradictory. Suppose that nonnecessitarian monotheism is true. Then necessitarian monotheism is necessarily false, as is necessitarian atheism, and then nonnecessitarian atheism is contingently false, not necessarily false.

It is perhaps surprising that either necessitarian monotheism or nonnecessitarian monotheism is necessarily false or contradictory. But this is not more surprising than the fact that either necessitarian atheism or nonnecessitarian atheism is necessarily false. The logic of the situation, then, is interestingly complex. But I know of no reason to think that this complexity makes more plausible than otherwise the view that religious experience does not provide evidence that God exists, or for that matter the opposite view more plausible than otherwise. Further, exactly one of these views must be true. If that is so, of course God is not ineffable, no matter which view is true.

TWO THEORIES REGARDING EVIDENCE

Broadly speaking, there are two kinds of theories of evidence. One is called *confirmationism,* and its basic idea is that if one proposition entails another, then the truth of the second proposition to some degree confirms the first. On this view, *P entails Q* and *Q is true* entail *Q to some degree confirms*

P, with the proviso that *P* not be a contradiction. What confirms a proposition to some extent provides at least a bit of evidence for that statement.

The other theory of evidence is called *falsificationism*. It builds on the sound idea that if one proposition entails a second, and the second proposition is false, it follows that the first proposition also is false. Thus if *P* entails *Q*, and we have evidence that *Q* is false, we also have evidence that *P* is false. For a proposition of the form *X has P*, where *X* is some observable object and *P* some observable property, of course if one observes *X* and observes that *X* has *P*, one thereby confirms *X has P*. The theories in question agree on this much. But their focus is not on propositions that say that some observable object has an observable property. Falsificationism, like confirmationism, is most interested in theories. Confirmationism requires that a good theory be confirmed in the sense noted. Falsificationism sees no reason to suppose that a theory should be to any degree confirmed by the mere fact that it entails some truth. But if a theory explains the truth of a proposition whose truth is not easy to explain and also, on strenuous effort, as yet has not been shown to entail anything false, then that theory has significant information value and is unfalsified, and perhaps that is as close to enjoying confirmation as a theory can come.

Consider, then, the claims (1) *God is an omnipotent, omniscient, morally perfect agent*, and (2) *An omnipotent, omniscient, morally perfect agent, if she creates, will create nondivine agents*. It is the case that (4) *There are nondivine agents*. Plainly, (4) is the sort of proposition that might have been false. Plainly, (1) and (2), plus the claim (3) *God created* entail (4). So for a confirmationist, (4) confirms the conjunct of (1), (2), and (3). If that conjunct is true, *God exists* is true. So (4), on a confirmationist perspective, somewhat confirms, and so provides some evidence for, *God exists*. Along falsificationist lines, the conjunct of (1–3) explains the truth of (4), which surely needs explanation. If we have no evidence against that conjunct, it forms a theory that has significant informational content and is not falsified.

The idea here, then, is not to argue in favor of the existence of God, but to point out that on standard theories of evidence, it is neither impossible nor false that there is some evidence that God exists. At the very least, it is neither impossible nor false that there are some evidential considerations relevant, pro or con, to the proposition *God exists.* (This way of putting things assumes, for simplicity, that for the falsificationist, to put things roughly, *P explains things otherwise hard to explain and has not been falsified* entails *There is some reason to think P true;* if it confers some other epistemic honor on *P* that too should suffice for the present argument.) So *God exists* is not meaningless, and no basis is found along confirmationist or falsificationist lines for the claim that God is ineffable.

CONCLUSION

We have considered various versions of the claim that God is ineffable. Taken literally and at full strength, it is a logically contradictory doctrine, sharing with all contradictions the inelegance of being false. Taken in more restricted terms, it has some surprisingly negative consequences for the monotheistic traditions of which it is supposed to be an interpretation and possibly a defense. Its weaker versions suffer deep conceptual disabilities. There seems to be no good reason to accept the ineffability theme in any of its versions, and good reason to reject each of its versions that we have discussed. Of course, one could dream up others, but there is no reason to think that they would fare any better.

The witches in Shakespeare's *Macbeth* "make themselves into the air, and vanish into it." So, apparently, does the claim that God is ineffable. Nothing is lost with its departure.

Part III

The social science challenge

6

Nonepistemic explanation of belief

It is quiet on Elm Street at 3:00 A.M. No traffic disturbs the street. No wind troubles the trees. All is silent, save in little Johnny Wise's room at 411 Elm, where, tonight as always, a tape deck plays the sound of Mrs. Wise's gentle voice. Sometimes the tones she uses are those with which she comforts Johnny in his distress, calms his fears, and restores his peace. Sometimes the tones she uses are those with which she praises his triumphs, offers his favorite foods, and expresses her love. But the message of the tape is always the same: "God exists, God rules, God loves you" – over and over again while Johnny sleeps. Because of the tape, and for no other reason, Johnny comes to believe that God exists, God rules, and God loves him.

Some distinguish between reasons and causes. If Randy believes that he will get a horse for Christmas because he has seen the papers with his name listed as owner and heard his rich uncle tell his father that Randy has an equine surprise coming on Christmas morning, whereas Ruth believes she will get a horse for Christmas because the clouds overhead seem to her to have a horsey shape, Randy believes for reasons and Ruth believes from causes. On this view, Johnny believes from causes, and hence not for reasons. Some distinguish between causes that are reasons and causes that are not. On this view, the cause of Randy's belief is the reason he has for thinking it true, and the beliefs of Ruth and Johnny have causes that are not reasons.

A nonepistemic explanation E of person S's belief that P perhaps will meet at least this condition: E will explain S's belief that P by reference only to causes that are not reasons. On either account, Johnny's belief that God exists will receive a nonepistemic explanation.

BELIEF AND RELIGIOUS BELIEF

Our concern is with the nonepistemic explanation of belief in general and religious belief in particular. I will not say much about the notion of *belief*. For Ralph to believe that proposition P is for Ralph to take it that P is true. So (in the sense relevant here) *Ralph believes that P* is not incompatible with *Ralph knows that P*. "Belief" is ambiguous between what Ralph believes and Ralph's believing it; the former I will refer to as *propositional belief* and the latter as *psychological belief*.

Nor will I say much about the notion of *being a religious belief*. Perhaps, strictly speaking, only persons, not beliefs, can be religious or irreligious; perhaps the same goes for *being philosophical, being political,* and *being scientific*. For all that, talk of religious, philosophical, political, or scientific beliefs is perfectly in order. I will take a belief to be religious if it is essential to a religious conceptual system, and take a conceptual system to be religious if it contains answers (including negative ones) to such questions as: Does God exist? What is God's nature? What purpose does human life have? What is the goal of history? What constitutes human nature? Does a person survive the death of his or her body? What constitutes salvation? With these light strokes over *being a belief* and *being a religious belief*, I turn to the topic of the nonepistemic explanation of religious beliefs.

SOME DEFECTIVE CHARACTERIZATIONS OF "NONEPISTEMIC EXPLANATION"

We have not yet been told what, exactly, a nonepistemic explanation of someone's belief may or must include. The tentative suggestion made earlier was that if E is a non-epistemic explanation of S's belief that P, then E will explain S's belief that P by reference only to causes that are not reasons. In fact, this is too stringent.

Suppose that S reads William Rowe's *Cosmological Argument*, follows carefully the argument – call it (R) – that Professor Rowe says makes belief that God exists rational for one who reasonably accepts its premises (as, perhaps, one may do). Suppose that S agrees that if one accepts (R), then one is rational in believing that God exists, and that S is correct about this matter. S, that is, rightly accepts (R1) *There is an argument – namely, (R) – that renders belief that God exists rational for those who accept it, and S accepts (R).* But this by itself, we shall suppose, is not sufficient to bring S to believe that God exists, through S does believe this. S also believes that (P1) *Satan exists if and only if there is an argument that renders belief that God exists rational* and (P2) *God exists if and only if Satan exists.*

Suppose that S reasons: (R) and (P1) are true. Together, they entail *Satan exists.* That proposition, plus (P2), entails *God exists.* Only because he accepts this argument, S accepts the conclusion *God exists.* Let E be the explanation that S accepts *God exists* because S accepts the indicated argument. Given its somewhat less than stunning epistemic quality, the explanation E is nonepistemic. Perhaps (R) is evidentially or epistemically sufficient in the sense that *S believes that God exists because S accepts (R)* and *If one accepts theism because one accepts (R), then one's acceptance of theism is rational*, which entail *S's belief that God exists is rational*, are true. On our assumptions, however, (R) is not – and S's acceptance of (R) is not – sufficient to explain S's theism. If proposition P is essential to explanation E of phenomenon A if and only if (i) E includes P, and (ii) were E not to include P then E would not explain A, and (iii) P is not merely descriptive of one of A's background conditions, it seems that (on our assumptions) S's belief that (P1) and S's belief that (P2) are essential to E. But so is S's belief that (R). So an explanation of S's belief that *P* can be nonepistemic, which nonetheless makes essential reference to evidence that is *P*-preferring, or even evidentially or epistemically sufficient for belief that *P*.

Indeed, it seems that a nonepistemic explanation *E* of *S*'s belief that *P* may have the (in the context) somewhat curious feature of essentially referring to true propositions that entail that *P* is true without thereby compromising its nonepistemic character. Suppose it is true, and *S* (without any evidence) believes that, *God created S with a disposition to believe in God – a disposition that is elicited by experiences S was bound to have.* Having had such experiences, *S* believes in God and, being less confused than various contemporary theologians and philosophers, thus also believes that God exists. But suppose also that *S* believes (a) *There is evil* and, having read Hume, Flew, and Mackie, but not Pike, Mavrodes, or Plantinga, mistakenly supposes (b) *If there is evil, then God does not exist*, and suppose that *S* is reasonable in accepting (a) and (b). Then it is true that *S* believes that God exists, and also true that *S* (so far, anyway, as *S* is aware) believes this against his evidence. Presumably, then, the explanation of *S*'s belief is nonepistemic.

In fact, that *S* believes that God exists because he believes (without any evidence) that he was created by God to have a disposition to do so – a belief *ex hypothesi* (so far as *S* knows) against *S*'s evidence – plus the fact that *S* believes that this disposition has been activated, *constitutes* (under the conditions stated) a nonepistemic explanation of *S*'s belief, even though if the propositions essentially referred to in the explanation as objects of *S*'s beliefs are true, then the belief that is being explained is also true.

Indeed, one could accept *Some beliefs are nonepistemically explicable* in such a manner that a nonepistemic explanation was true of one's acceptance and hence sufficed to confirm the belief's content. So a characterization of "nonepistemic explanation" that forbids such an explanation's making essential reference to sufficient evidence for, or the truth of, the belief being explained will not be adequate. It is not as easy as it might seem, then, to explicate the notion of a nonepistemic explanation, and when I return to this topic later, my argument will not rest on strict criteria for what will count as a nonepistemic explanation.

NONEPISTEMIC EXPLANATION AND DISCREDITATION

If S's belief that P has a nonepistemic explanation, this is often taken to discredit something – perhaps S, or perhaps, in some circumstances at least, S's belief. Let one who offers such an explanation of someone's belief be a *discreditor* – of a person or a belief, as the case may be. It is not obvious on what sort of perspective the fact that a belief is nonepistemically explicable will serve as fuel for the discreditor's fire.

NONEPISTEMIC EXPLANATION AND
SOME ONTOLOGIES

Presumably, if some variety of materialism is true, then every mental state M is identical to one or another physical state N. As a physical state, N presumably is explicable in physical (and so nonepistemic) terms. If I have explained the existence of N, and N is identical to M, then I have explained the existence of M. So if materialism is true, every mental state (and so every belief, if beliefs are mental states) has a nonepistemic explanation. And if that fact discredits either belief or believer, or both, then if materialism is true, either every belief or believer, or both, is discredited. Given the high implausibility of the varieties of behaviorism, I will assume here that having a belief does involve being in a mental state, at least in the case of "occurrent beliefs"; that is, I will assume that if person S is entertaining (thinking about) P at t, and believes that P at t, then S is in a mental state at t. This assumption at least simplifies exposition of the argument.

The obvious objection to this argument is the claim that it is false that if $N = M$, then an explanation of the existence of N is an explanation of the existence of M. One might distinguish between (i) the existence of the item designated by both M and N, (ii) the fact that "N" designates that item, and

(iii) the fact that "*M*" designates that item. Ordinarily, to explain (i) is not to explain either (ii) or (iii). So it is one thing to explain the existence of *X*, and another to explain *X*'s being describable in one way and its also being describable in another. This way of putting the objection, though, perhaps is defective. It suggests – given that *M* is *ex hypothesi* a "mentalese" term (a term such that it properly applies to an item only if that item is mental) and *N* is a "physicalese" term (a term such that it properly applies to an item only if that item is physical) – that *being mental* and *being physical* are both, as it were, *relative to description;* so construed, it assumes that nothing is, in itself, mental or physical, beyond our saying so.

Suppose, rather, that items are, if physical, then intrinsically so, irrespective of description, and similarly for items that are mental. Then the explanation of the fact that *S* is in a physical state at *t* of a particular sort need not by itself also be an explanation of the fact that *S* is in a (corresponding or identical) mental state at *t* (though we will have such an explanation if we add *To every physical state of the sort in question, there corresponds a mental state*) and the explanation of the fact that *S* is in a physical state of a certain sort at *t* need not by itself also be an explanation that *S* is in a mental state of a particular kind at *t* (though we will have such an explanation if we add *To every physical state of that sort there corresponds a mental state of M's particular kind*).

In sum, we might put things as follows. If materialism is true, then if we explain the fact that *S* is in physical state *N*, and there is a mental state *M* such that *N* and *M* are identical, then we have also explained that the state exists with which *M* is identical, but we have not explained the fact that *M* is identical with it. Still, the materialist supposes both that every state (whatever else it is) is a physical state and (whatever else it has) has a purely physical explanation. Purely physical explanations, I take it, are nonepistemic. They include reference only to causes that are not also reasons. So every state (allegedly) has a purely nonepistemic explanation.

Nonepistemic explanation of belief

Suppose that S's state X at t is a mental state of kind K. *Ex hypothesi*, X is identical to a physical state Y of some kind K_1. *Ex hypothesi*, Y has a purely physical (and so a purely non-epistemic) explanation. *Ex hypothesi*, the propositions (i) *Every mental state is identical to a physical state* and (ii) *Every mental state of kind K is identical to a physical state of kind K_1*, or some similar propositions, are true. Neither (i) nor (ii) is an epistemic explanation, and neither is such that its introduction into a nonepistemic explanation need render that explanation epistemic. Suppose E is a nonepistemic explanation of S's being in Y at t, and let E include the claim that X is identical to Y, or let this claim be part of E's background conditions. Introducing (i) and (ii) into E will give us an explanation of S's being in X at t; if E explains (indeed, entails) *S is in state Y of kind K_1 at t*, then E plus (i) plus (ii) explains (indeed, entails) *S is in state X of kind K at t*. So if materialism is true, then for any mental state anyone is in at any time, there is *ex hypothesi* a nonepistemic explanation of their being in that state at that time.

Of course there may also be epistemic explanations of persons being in mental states at particular times if materialism is true. Presumably the materialist will admit that persons sometimes have excellent reasons for thinking that certain propositions – for example, those essential to some favored version of materialism – are true, and sometimes accept those propositions in the light of their having those reasons. So presumably the materialist will hold that sometimes a person's beliefs are causally or at least explanatorily overdetermined, for unless they are overdetermined no one's beliefs are both purely physically explicable and also epistemically explicable – held *both* "from causes" and "for reasons" (or both from causes that are not reasons and from causes that are). Thus the materialist must allow for – indeed, must insist on – the sacrifice of a certain somewhat attractive form of explanatory simplicity; she must think it not inelegant that rationality (the occurrence of beliefs for reasons) itself requires, in a materialist world, the overdetermination or overexplicability of beliefs. A materialist who allows for belief that materialism is true being a reasonable alternative apparently must reject what might be called *the principle of explanatory simplicity* – the claim that for any item X (beliefs included), if we have one (correct) explanation sufficient to account for X's existence, then we need a special reason to suppose that there is also another (correct) explanation sufficient to explain X's existence, and also reject the claim that it would be unreasonable to make exceptions to this principle on the magnitude of one exception for each reasonably held belief. The only escape from this conclusion would seem to be to deny that an epistemic explanation of a belief is ever sufficient to explain anyone's having any belief whatever.

Of course one need not be a materialist in order to insist on this. One might be a dualist and yet maintain that mental states have a basically physicalistic sufficient explanation. Consider, for example, a *state dualism* that holds that mental states and physical states are of irreducibly different kinds, or a *substance dualism* that holds that mental substances and physical substances are of irreducibly distinct kinds, where in both cases it is added that for every mental state M of any kind K that S is in at t, S's being in M is causally determined by, or is otherwise entirely a function of, the physical states S is in at t. Then it will be held that (iii) *Every mental state is correlated to some physical state on which it, in some fashion, completely depends,* and (iv) *If S is in mental state M of kind K at t, S's being in M is entirely due to S's being in some physical state N of kind K1 at t.* And given a purely physicalistic explanation E of S's being in physical state N of kind K1 at t, plus (iii), plus (iv), one will have a nonepistemic explanation of S's being in M at t. For such varieties of dualism as these, there will also be overdetermination or overexplicability of beliefs if any beliefs are rationally or reasonably held.

The general sorts of dualism briefly described here, given their adherents' views concerning the tight dependence of mental states on physical states, might be called *physicalistic dualism*. If materialism, or physicalistic dualism, is true, and if any beliefs are rationally or reasonably held, then some mental states (beliefs) are overdetermined or overexplicable.

I do not offer this as a *criticism*, much less a *refutation*, of materialism or physicalistic dualism, though materialism – at least in the respect specified – is less parsimonious than might have been thought, and some of its proponents have leaned heavily on its alleged allegiance to explanatory simplicity as one of its particular virtues.

In any case, one alternative to holding that beliefs (at least, reasonably held beliefs) are overdetermined or overexplicable is to hold that every explanation of a belief – even if it has a physicalistic component – must also have an epistemic component. If S is in mental state M, and M is a belief that S is reasonable in having, then while S's being in some physical state N may be a necessary condition of S's being in M, S's having some ground or reason (and so S's being, or at least having been, in some mental state M_1) is also a necessary condition of S's being in M. One might allow that reference to both N and M_1 appear in the same seamless explanation. Or one might require that reference to N occur in one explanation and reference to M_1 in another, and view these explanations as belonging to different kinds such that no single explanation could participate in both kinds, but hold that a *full* explanation of M will conjoin both explanations into an account of S's being in M whose component parts cannot commingle. Whichever alternative is chosen, on this view a physicalistic explanation of a mental state of S at t is not a sufficient explanation of that state in the sense that crucial features of the state – features that render the state *mental* rather than physical, or features that render it the *sort* of mental state it is – are not determined by the physical states S is in at t (or *was* in before t). Such a view seems properly referred to as *idealistic*, or at least *nonphysicalistic, dualism*.

The other alternative would be to hold that all explanation is epistemic, and none physicalistic – that apparently physicalistic explanations are all translatable into, or that all physicalistic explanations are replaceable by, epistemic explanations, and that there is good enough reason in each case to make the translation or replacement. Presumably this view is most at home in, and perhaps it is required by (and requires), mind-body idealism (the view that all there is is minds, mental states, and qualities and relations of minds and mental states). What idealism and idealistic or nonphysicalistic dualism relevantly share is the view that the mental states of S at t are not completely causally determined by, or otherwise purely functions of, the physical states of S at, or before, t. Thus a mental state can be epistemically explicable without its being overdetermined.

NONEPISTEMIC EXPLANATIONS: COMPONENT, COMPANION, GENERIC, POSITIVE, NEGATIVE

Suppose that S is irrational or unreasonable in believing that P. There may still be (in one sense) an epistemic explanation of S's belief – one that, roughly speaking, traces S's belief to bad reasons or bad reasoning or lack of grounds for belief or lack of evidence or presence of contrary grounds or evidence relatively near the surface of S's belief system or the like. The notion of an epistemic explanation can be generic or inclusive – roughly, an explanation is generically epistemic if it essentially contains reference to mental states. This makes all psychological explanations epistemic. One could restrict epistemic explanations to those mentalese explanations that made essential reference to *cognitive* states (states of believing, knowing, inferring, etc.) rather than *affective* states (hoping, fearing, etc.) or *conative* states (choices). And one could refine things further in various ways; how this is done, and whether it is done, is irrelevant here. The class of generic epistemic explanations will include cases in which S's belief that P is so explained that S is not reasonable in believing that P, and cases in which S's belief that P is so explained that S is reasonable in believing that P. Also needed, then, are the notions of a *positive* epistemic explanation (explanation E of S's belief that P is positive if and only if E is *the correct explanation of S's belief that P entails, by itself or with other truths, S is reasonable in believing that P*) and of a *negative* epistemic explanation (E is a negative epistemic explanation of *S*'s belief that *P* if and only if *E is the correct explanation of S's belief that P* entails, by itself or with other truths, *S is not reasonable in believing that P*). If any *positive* epistemic explanations are correct, and if materialism or physicalistic dualism is true, then at least some beliefs are overdetermined or overexplicable. And if every belief is such that its holder is either reasonable or not in holding it, and either materialism or physicalistic dualism is true, then every belief is overexplicable.

Another complication, thus far ignored, is relevant. Being reasonable or not with regard to one's belief may be analogous to being moral with regard to one's actions at least to this extent: just as an action may be right, wrong, or neutral, so may a belief be reasonable, unreasonable, or neither. Suppose *S*'s belief that *P* is caused by hypnotic suggestion (and *S* had no role in *S*'s being under hypnosis save that of being an utterly passive patient – to be redundant for the sake of emphasis). Then *S*'s belief is not one that *S* can be held responsible for having. It is not one *S* can be *blamed* for having, and so perhaps it is not one *S* is unreasonable in having. The same goes for a belief *S* has because *S* has an overpowering innate disposition to believe that *P* (a disposition activated by experiences *S* was bound to have, and so has had). But *S* also is not reasonable in having these beliefs.

Yet one could also argue that if, say, belief that *P* is almost surely false – perhaps it runs against the grain of loads of evidence to which everyone has long had easy access, or flies in the face of new, solid, and widely published data – then, in believing that *P*, *S* (who has access to the evidence) is somehow unreasonable even if not culpable. Obviously, the notion of *being reasonable* is partly normative, partly descriptive. Let us say that *P* is *conceptually confirmed* to *S* if and only if *S* sees that *not-P* is a contradiction; *P* is *reflexively confirmed* to *S* if and only if *S* sees that *S believes that P* entails *P is true*. The locutions "inferring Q from *if Q then P* and *P*" and "believing that *P* when *not-P* is conceptually or reflexively confirmed to one" are descriptive. Yet insofar as they apply to *S*, *S* is epistemically defective.

One issue, at least, in the debate concerning the ethics of belief is over which of these propositions is true:

(E1) For any person S and proposition P, if S has neither evidence nor grounds for P, and believes that P, it follows that S's believing that P is wrong.

(E2) For any person S and proposition P, if S has neither evidence nor grounds for P, and believes that P, it does not follow that S's believing that P is wrong.

One begins with epistemic descriptivity, progresses to the epistemically defective, and comes to the morally objectionable or morally permissible; though perhaps the last step requires appeal to moral or quasi-moral principles such as (E1) and (E2). One has *the epistemically descriptive, the epistemically normative,* and *the morally normative.*

It seems possible that what is epistemically normative conflicts with what is morally normative. Suppose (so far at least as S, on careful examination, can see) S's total relevant evidence supports proposition P, where P is of the form *S ought to do A at t* and where doing A is flagrantly wrong – torturing for sport or killing for pleasure, or the like. Perhaps, in order to be in such a position, one must already have done something significantly wrong, morally or epistemically. Whether or not this is so, suppose S is in such a situation – a situation, so to say, in which S's epistemic duty (if such there be) is to believe that P – at least S's overall evidence favors P – and so to believe that A ought to be done (where A is an action of, say, torturing for sport or killing for pleasure) – and yet within S's system of belief is the proposition *Torturing for sport or killing for pleasure is wrong.* It is at least not obvious that this type of thing cannot happen, and so at least not obvious that there cannot be a conflict between one's epistemic duty and one's moral duty (or between one's duty regarding believing in accord with the evidence and one's duty to regard persons with respect, or between believing what one's evidence points to and doing what one's moral principles – or perhaps those moral principles that are not directly epistemic [those that do not specify epistemic duties] – require). Even to say exactly what sort of conflict there might be is not easy and would require careful analysis. But it is not at all clear that there cannot be some such conflict or tension as has been hinted at here.

If there can be this sort of conflict, it is not clearly the case that any moral impropriety involved in having one or another belief in one or another circumstance necessarily is a consequence of (or supervenes on) some prior epistemic impropriety. Nonetheless, our concern here is with epistemic impropriety, whether or not such impropriety carries with it, by itself or in conjunction with some moral principle, a moral inelegance as well.

Two explanatory pictures for beliefs have been broadly sketched. On one picture, some beliefs, at least, are overdetermined or overexplicable; for any belief *B,* there is a physicalistic explanation, and for at least many beliefs there are at least generic or inclusive epistemic explanations. If any beliefs are held in such a manner as to render their owners reasonable in their possession, some beliefs have positive epistemic explanations. On the other picture, (at any rate, nonepistemic) explanations provide at most partial explanations, or descriptions of necessary conditions, of at least many beliefs, and physicalistic explanations of these beliefs are completed by epistemic explanations, positive or negative. In the former picture, a belief for which there is a generic epistemic explanation will have a *companion* physicalistic, nonepistemic explanation; in the latter picture, a belief that has a generic epistemic explanation will also be such that its generic epistemic explanation is part of a larger explanation in which there is a physicalistic *component.* The presence of a physicalistic *companion* or *component* is not viewed as incompatible with the presence of a generic (and so a negative or a positive) epistemic explanation. The price of this denial would be either the denial that any beliefs are reasonable or unreasonable, or the denial that beliefs, either in *companion* or *component* fashion, have physicalistic explanations.

For strongly idealistic dualism and idealism, then, beliefs have no physicalistic explanations. For physicalistic dualism and materialism, beliefs have physicalistic explanations, in whole; but this fact is not incompatible with their having generic (and so positive, or else negative) epistemic explanations. And for interactionistic dualism, beliefs have physicalistic explanations, in part; but this fact is not incompatible with their having generic epistemic explanations, in part.

Relative to physicalistic explanations and beliefs, idealism and strongly idealistic dualism form one cluster (the *idealistic*), physicalistic dualism and materialism form a second cluster (the *physicalistic*), and the varieties of interactionistic dualism form a third cluster (the *dualistic*). These clusters agree that:

> (P1) The presence of physicalistic explanation of a belief does not prevent that belief from being generically epistemically explicable, and so being reasonably or unreasonably held.

Of course the idealistic cluster holds this because it thinks that no beliefs have any physicalistic explanations; (P1), as it were, is but vacuously true for the idealistic cluster, for it is at least open to one who identifies with that cluster to hold:

> (P1a) Were there any actual physicalistic explanations of any beliefs, the presence of those explanations would render those beliefs inaccessible to even generic epistemic explanations.

It is just as open to one who identifies with the dualistic cluster to hold:

> (P1b) If there is a physicalistic explanation of belief *B* that is not merely a component of a statement of the sufficient conditions of *B*, but a full statement of those conditions, then there is no even generic epistemic explanation of *B*.

But for each cluster, it is the presence of generic epistemic explanation that is a condition of belief possession being reasonable or not. Further, for each cluster a necessary (and sufficient) condition of *S*'s belief that *P* being reasonable is that belief's having a positive epistemic explanation. Each cluster, thus, holds that de facto no belief or believer is ever discredited by its being the case that some (or perhaps all) of his or her beliefs are physicalistically (and so nonepistemically) explicable.

For each cluster, persons identified with it do not suppose that all beliefs are rationally held and that all holders of beliefs are paragons of rationality. One thing that discredits S, by virtue of S's believing that P, presumably from the perspective of any cluster, is that S's belief that P has a negative epistemic explanation: *not-P* is conceptually or reflexively confirmed to S and S knows this; S inferred P from Q and *if Q then not P;* or the like. Perhaps S has simply made a mistake in reasoning. Perhaps S has believed against overwhelming evidence only because S is proud of having "thought up" the content of P. Very broadly put, S is irrational only if (or to the degree that) something is epistemically awry in, or with, S's system of belief. S is not irrational only if (or to the degree that) things are epistemically not awry in, or with, S's system of belief. And perhaps S is rational only if (or to the degree that) S's system of belief lacks epistemic inelegancies altogether – that is, if S is not irrational. (I will not worry here about whether *rationality* in this sense is in fact identical with presence of beliefs and absence of irrationality.) Perhaps (if one wishes to distinguish between *rationality* and *reasonability*) S is reasonable only to the degree that S makes changes in S's belief system only in ways that S knows, or has good reason to believe, will epistemically improve that system in content or structure.

The truth of *All or part of S's system of belief is physicalistically* (and hence nonepistemically) *explicable* will be any reason to be suspicious about S's rationality only given views on which at least not all beliefs are physicalistically explicable – on which S's beliefs are, by their very physicalistic explicability, set apart from other beliefs that are not so explicable. The reason for this is not that *rational believer* or *reasonable possessor of belief* is a contrastive term to *irrational believer* or *unreasonable possessor of belief,* and so must apply to something, and hence there are rational believers or reasonable possessors of beliefs; *striped giraffe* and *pink elephant* are contrastive concepts too (what concept is not?). Rather, the reason is that any view that can be non-self-defeatingly held must allow for at least its own epistemic respectability. It is somewhat curious that members of the physicalist cluster should sometimes attempt to discredit religious beliefs or believers by appeal to the alleged fact that all religious beliefs are physicalistically (and so nonepistemically) explicable, since the success of this sort of discrediting procedure would devour its own flesh in its gnashing at others.

7

Nonreligious explanation of religious belief

If P's truth is more likely given Q than it is given not-Q, let us say that Q is P-preferring; if S knows that Q is P-preferring, believes that P, and bases belief that P on belief that Q, let us say that S has some P-preferring reason for accepting P.

One argument a discreditor might use begins as follows:

(1) If S's belief that P can be explained without reference to any P-preferring reasons that S has, then S is unreasonable in believing that P.

It will continue by asserting of some person-belief pair that the former accepts the latter in the absence of any belief-preferring reason, and concludes that the person is not reasonable in having the belief in question. If the discussion in the preceding chapter is roughly correct, one who grants that many beliefs are reasonably held can either reject the physicalistic culture or the principle of explanatory simplicity – even in the relatively mild version that says only that special reason is always required if it is alleged that the principle is violated (and denies that special reason is always present in a case of reasonable belief). Thus one can either reject the principle or embrace a member of the dualistic or idealistic clusters (assuming, as I do here for convenience, that the three clusters exhaust the alternatives). In order not to have to worry about which choice to make, it is possible to revise (1) as follows:

(1a) If *S*'s belief that *P* can be explained without reference to any *P*-preferring reasons that *S* has, and *S*'s belief that *P* is not overdetermined, then *S* is not reasonable in believing that *P*.

Or one might replace (1) with the milder

(1b) If *S* has no *P*-preferring reason, and *S* believes that *P*, then *S* is not reasonable in believing that *P*.

Presumably, however, if *S* has beliefs, not all of them are epistemically based on other beliefs that *S* has; presumably some will be basic. At any rate, presumably the discreditor will wish her strategy to apply to those persons some of whose beliefs are basic. The locution "a *P*-preferring reason" is such that appropriate values of *P* are bearers of truth-values – are propositions, if you like. Presumably one's having a basic belief is a matter of one's taking a proposition to be true without basing that acceptance on the acceptance of another proposition.

Given this plausible account of basic belief, plus (1b), it follows that no one is reasonable in having any basic belief whatever, for a basic belief that *P*, being based on no propositional acceptance whatever beyond acceptance of *P*, is not based on the acceptance of any *P*-preferring proposition. Hence, given (1b), one could not be reasonable in accepting any value of *P* as basic.

Claim (1a) fares no better. For suppose that *S* sees that the proposition (N) *Nothing can have logically incompatible properties* is true, accepts (N), has no (N)-preferring reason, and that *S*'s belief that (N) is not overdetermined. Then, according to (1a), *S* is not reasonable in believing that (N), and this seems obviously false. Of course *S* might accept (N) on the basis that (N1) *For any value of "X," "X has logically incompatible properties" is contradictory* and (N2) *Contradictions are always false.* But *S need* not rest reasonable belief that (N) on acceptance of (N1) and (N2), and if *S* did, similar considerations would arise concerning *S*'s acceptance of (N1) and (N2). It would seem, then, that (1a) and (1b) should be rejected and that the successors

136

of (1a) and (1b) will have to include some consideration of basic belief – some consideration of the conditions for holding basic beliefs that are reasonable.

On current accounts of epistemic basicality, *being basic* is an extrinsic property of a belief that has it. S's belief that P is basic if and only if there is no proposition Q such that S bases her belief that P on her belief that Q. Of course, this sort of characterization is not lucid. For example, *S bases his belief that P on his belief that Q* is not lucid. It might mean *S's evidence that P includes Q;* and if this is so we might say that for S, Q has *evidential association* with P. It might mean *S psychologically associates P with Q in such a manner that were S to cease to accept Q, S would also cease to accept P.* If we describe this sort of psychological association as *associative dependence,* and describe the whole of S's beliefs as S's *epistemic constellation,* then for P to be basic for S at t will be for P to be in S's epistemic constellation, and (on the epistemic account) for there to be no proposition Q in S's epistemic constellation such that Q is included in S's epistemic constellation and Q is in evidential association with P; or (on the psychological account) that there is no proposition Q in that constellation on which P is associatively dependent. It would seem that a proposition might be basic on one of these criteria but not on the other. S might hold P in such a manner that P was in associative dependence on Q, although Q was not evidence for P and S did not regard it as such, and there was no other proposition S took to be evidence for P. Then P would be basic on the epistemic, but not on the psychological, criterion. S might hold that Q was evidence for P, but nonetheless might so hold P that there was no proposition (including Q) in S's epistemic constellation on which P was in associative dependence. Then P would be basic on the psychological, but not on the epistemic, criterion. It would *not* do to say: P is basic to S only if there is no Q in S's epistemic constellation such that were S to reject Q, S would reject *P*, for a belief may both be basic and subject to *modus tollens* dislodgement.

Perhaps if *P* is associatively dependent on *Q* in *S*'s epistemic constellation, then *S* should take *Q* to be evidence for *P*; assume this is so, and describe an epistemic constellation in which *P* is psychologically basic if and only if *P* is epistemically basic as *properly coordinated*. Suppose *S*'s epistemic constellation is properly coordinated. Then what beliefs may *S* properly include among her basic beliefs?

A strong sort of relativism regarding proper basicality goes as follows: for any proposition *P* and person *S*, if *S* believes that *P* and *P* is basic to *S*, then *P* is properly basic to *S*. A person who thinks that some beliefs are properly basic need not think that all are; she need not embrace relativism regarding proper basicality. But what conditions of proper basicality are appropriate?

Some seem obvious. Let us say:

(i) If *P* is contradictory, and *S* sees this, then *P* is *conceptually falsified* for *S*.

(ii) If *S believes that P* entails *P is false,* and *S* sees this, then *P* is *reflexively falsified* for *S*.

(iii) If *S* knowingly observes (i.e., visually sees, hears, tastes, smells, or tactilely discerns) that some object has some property or that some process is occurring, then the proposition that says that that object lacks that property or does not exist at all or the proposition that says that that process is not occurring is *observationally falsified* for *S*.

It seems clear that if there are criteria for proper basicality, one of them is:

(C) If *P* is conceptually, reflexively, or observationally falsified for *S*, then *P* is not properly basic to *S*, and *not-P* is properly basic to *S*.

So we have a trio of sufficient conditions for proper basicality. It seems clear that (C) will not do as *the* criterion for proper basicality – as stating all the conditions under which a believed proposition is (or is not) basic to its believer.

One reason why this seems clear is that one can think of cases that (C) does not cover. For example, if I claim to know the proposition expressed by *No one knows any proposition that is expressed by use of an English sentence of more than twelve words*, what I claim cannot be so; my claim to know is inconsistent with what I allege knowledge of. But the falsehood of the proposition in question does not follow from my believing it, nor (I suppose) is it a contradiction. Of course, one might add:

> (iv) If *P* is such that *S knows that P* is logically incompatible with *P is true*, and *S* knows this, then *P* is not properly basic to *S* (and, *perhaps*, one might add: *not-P* is properly basic to *S*).

And no doubt one could continue to add conditions to (C). But even if we add something quite general like:

> (v) If *S* knows *P* to be false, then belief that *P* is not properly basic to *S*,

it will be the case that (C), in an important sense, is incomplete. It obviously leaves out propositions that do not satisfy (i – v). For example, the proposition (C') *S's belief that P is properly basic if and only if it is not disqualified by* (C) is not such that it satisfies (C). Claim (C'), for example, is not such that its denial is conceptually or reflexively falsified, or observationally disconfirmed, to *S*, or that its denial is false if *S* believes it true. Nor is it clear that such propositions as *It is wrong to torture for pleasure, Anyone capable of correctly translating Kant's works into English knows German well*, and *Nothing that begins to exist lacks a cause of its existence* satisfy (C). Perhaps none of these propositions ought to be properly basic to anyone. But even if this is so, that it is so does not follow merely from the fact that they do not satisfy (C). Nor is it clear, to me at least, how to complete (C) so as to make it informative and exhaustive of legitimate conditions of proper basicality.

At this point, then, perhaps the thing to do is to make a virtue of one's modest epistemic possessions. The following seems right:

(C1) if P is such that it is conceptually, reflexively, or observationally falsified to S, or that its falsehood follows from S's believing it true, then belief that P is not properly basic to S.

Perhaps we can add:

(C2) For any time t, proposition P, and person S, either P is properly basic to S at t or P is not properly basic to S at t.

(C3) If P is not not properly basic (is not improperly basic) to S at t, then if S believes that P at t, and P is basic to S at t, then P is properly basic to S at t.

Perhaps there are beliefs that, sometimes anyway, *ought* to be basic to some or all persons, and beliefs that, sometimes anyway, merely may be basic to persons, but (according to [C3]) if P is basic to S at t, whether it ought to be or merely may be, it is properly basic to S at t if it is not improperly basic to S at t.

On this conception of properly basic belief, the following seem to be correct:

(1) A basic belief need not be important, in the sense either of *having many ramifications* or of *concerning significant epistemic, moral, scientific, metaphysical, or religious matters* or of *being presupposed by beliefs that are important in any of these senses*. (E.g., *I now feel a tickle in my left heel* may be properly basic.)

(2) While *P and not-P* is not properly basic to anyone, *P* may be properly basic to S at t and *not-P* may be properly basic to S at t_1, and, at t, *P* may be properly basic to $S1$ and *not-P* to $S2$.

(3) Where P is properly basic to S, and Q is not basic to S, S may come to see that Q (directly or together with

other basic or nonbasic beliefs of *S*) entails *not-P* and
so come to reject *P*, without epistemic impropriety.
(4) If *P* is basic to *S*, then while *S* may have propositional
evidence *e* for *P*, it cannot be the case that were *S* to
reject *e*, or to reject *e is propositional evidence for P*, then
S would reject *P*. One need not hold as nonbasic that
for which one has evidence.

A proponent of the view that beliefs that do not satisfy the
positive portions of criteria like (i – iv) may nonetheless be
properly basic can allow that properly basic beliefs may be
justified by (and accepted on the basis of) *grounds*, though
they may not be accepted on the basis of evidence. Thus if,
at *t*, *S* sees a tree (in Chisholmese, *is treely appeared to*), converses with a friend, or remembers having breakfast, then *S*
may properly believe that *S* sees a tree at *t*, *S*'s friend exists
at *t*, or that *S*, earlier than *t*, had breakfast. The suggestion is
that these perceptual, conversational, or memory experiences provide *S* with grounds, though not evidence, for *S*.
Although the matter is not lucid, it looks to be the case that
if the relation between *Q* and *P* is that *Q* is *S*'s evidence for
P, then *Q* and *P* are propositions and *S* infers from *Q* to *P*,
whereas if the relation between *g* and *P* is that *g* is *S*'s
grounds for *P* then *g* is nonpropositional and (hence) *S* does
not infer from *g* to *P*. Since (on the account in question) *S*
bases P on x entails *S infers from x to P*, *g is S's ground for P*
entails *S does not base belief that P on g*. For all that, *S's having
g* may constitute superb epistemic credentials on behalf of *S*'s
believing that P, and perhaps *S* may even accept *P* because of
its being favored by *g*. Apparently, though, on this account,
while a properly basic belief may be such that its owner has
grounds for it, *S's belief that P is properly basic* does not entail
S has grounds for belief that P, and *S has grounds for belief that P*
entails neither *P is true* nor *S is reasonable in believing that P*
(since while *S* may have grounds for believing that *P*, and
know this, *S* may also have better grounds, or evidence, on
behalf of believing that *not-P*, and know this too).

The social science challenge

BRIEF REMARKS ON "THE ETHICS OF BELIEF"

Much of the concern about properly or improperly basic beliefs comes from concern with "the ethics of belief," particularly with W. K. Clifford's account of this ethic. If there is an ethic of belief, presumably some such principles as these are true:

(A1) One ought to have a properly coordinated epistemic constellation.
(A2) Belief that *P* is improperly basic to *S* if *S* knows that *P* satisfies the negative portions of any of (i – v) in (C).
(A3) If *P* is improperly basic to *S*, then *S* ought not to accept *P* as basic.

And (perhaps more debatably):

(A4) If *P* is not improperly basic to *S*, then it is permissible that *S* accept *P* as basic.

Presumably the idea will be that insofar as a person's epistemic constellation contains improperly basic beliefs, he is irrational or unreasonable.

DISCREDITATION AGAIN

It is time to return to the task of our discreditor. Perhaps the proper revision of (1a) or (1b) relevant to basic beliefs will go as follows:

(1a1) If *S*'s belief that *P* is basic but not improperly so, and can be explained without reference to any *P*-preferring grounds that *S* has, and *S*'s belief that *P* is not overdetermined, then *S* is not reasonable in believing that *P*.

And:

(1b1) If *S*'s belief that *P* is basic but not improperly so, and *S* has no *P*-preferring grounds, then *S* is not reasonable in believing that *P*.

Basic beliefs that satisfy (1a1) and (1b1) presumably will be *unreasonable basic beliefs*, and the reformulations of (1a) and (1b) regarding nonbasic beliefs wil go as follows:

> (1b) If *S*'s belief that *P* is nonbasic, and *S*'s belief that *P* can be explained without reference to any *P*-preferring proposition *S* believes that is not itself an unreasonable basic belief, and *S*'s belief that *P* is not overdetermined, then *S* is not reasonable in believing that *P*.

And:

> (1b2) If *S*'s belief that *P* is nonbasic, and *S* has no *P*-preferring evidence, then *S* is not reasonable in believing that *P*.

The gist of (1a1) and (1b1) is this: A belief that is not improperly basic is still such that one is irrational in having it unless one has grounds that epistemically favor it. A belief that *P* can be such that it is unreasonable of *S* to have it even though belief that *P* is properly basic to *S*. This arises from the facts (or alleged facts) that *S*'s lacking grounds that epistemically favor *P* does not appear among the conditions of improper basicality, that a belief that is basic to *S* but not improperly basic to *S* is properly basic to *S*, and that a basic belief for which *S* has no grounds is one that *S* is irrational in having. The gist of (1a2) and (1b2) is this: A nonbasic belief for which *S* has no evidence is a belief *S* is irrational in having. If it is assumed that for any person *S*, proposition *P*, and time *t*, if *S* believes that *P* at *t*, then *S*'s belief that *P* at *t* has an explanation, and that it is irrational or unreasonable on *S*'s part to have a belief if the explanation of *S*'s having that belief is nonepistemic, the relevance of (1a), (1b1), (1a2) and (1b2) to the topic of nonepistemic explanation becomes clear; roughly, belief that is (by these criteria) unreasonable has a nonepistemic explanation. (It may also have a negative, but may not have a positive, epistemic explanation.) According to (1a1), if *S* has a basic belief that *P*, but lacks *P-preferring* grounds, then even if the criteria for proper basicality are not violated – even if *S*'s belief that *P*, on these criteria, is not improper – nonetheless *S* is unreasonable in believing that *P*. Reference to lack of overdetermination will be requisite only if one embraces some member of the physicalistic cluster, and I set that issue aside here. Plainly put, on this view beliefs that have nothing epistemic going for them are avoided by reasonable persons.

Consider proposition (B): *For any item X, if X has a beginning of existence then X has a cause of its existence.* As Hume notoriously noted, propositions like (B) do not have contradictory denials and cannot be properly inferred from particular cases of items that are known to possess both a beginning and a cause. Observational confirmation of (B) – or of not-(B) – is unavailable. It very much appears to be the case that none of the properties along the lines of reflexive confirmation or disconfirmation is available for (B). It is hard to find reasons in favor of (B) that are more clearly justified than is (B) itself. Perhaps, then, neither (B) nor its denial can properly appear in anyone's epistemic constellation, either as basic or as nonbasic. And (B) seems representative of many other propositions – propositions that are *structural* in the sense that their presence and relations within a conceptual system determine – and at least in large part comprise – the form of that system. But it is typical of wide-ranging theories to include structural propositions, so (1a1) will ban our accepting such theories on pain of irrationality.

Structural propositions, of course, are found in the social science theories that provide the sources of nonepistemic explanations (or negative epistemic explanations) of religious beliefs. Consider such remarks as these: "Human beings, in the course of their externalization, project their meaning into the universe around them. These projections are objectivated in the common worlds of human societies" (Peter Berger, *The Sacred Canopy*, p. 88). "The concept of humanity as distinct from animality . . . is always latent in men's customary attitudes and behaviors even when it is not explicitly formulated in words" (Edmund Leach, *Lévi-Strauss*, p. 36; Leach is here expounding Lévi-Strauss). Such propositions express theories and define an interpretative context for understanding data. It is often unclear what conditions would have to hold for any conceivable data to refute them. If they are treated as nonbasic, they are hard to derive, in any unproblematic way, from any data; if they are treated as basic, the questions arise as to whether they are somehow more correct than various competitors and what could possibly ground them. Insofar as structural propositions appear in social science explanations of religious belief, these explanations, as much as any religious beliefs, are unreasonably accepted if (1a1) or (1b1) is true.

Notoriously, (1a1) does not satisfy the conditions it sets for other propositions; more carefully, *S's belief that* (1a1), if it is basic and not improper, will still be groundless and *S* will be irrational insofar as *S* has allowed (1a1) basic membership in *S's* epistemic constellation. The attraction of (1a1) is that it is itself a structural proposition. It has an important role in those epistemic perspectives in which it is basic. Many find these perspectives highly plausible; this seems often psychologically to outweigh the considerable inelegance of embracing a proposition that cannot pass its own standards. Such, apparently, is the rational need for structural propositions that even structural propositions that are self-condemning find acceptance. In any case, (1a1) cannot, on its own terms, be rationally accepted as basic.

It is clear that (1b1) shares the epistemic defect of (1a1); if *S* accepts (1b1) as a not improper basic belief, that acceptance seems plainly groundless (what experience would ground it?) and so its acceptance marks *S* as irrational in *S's* acceptance of (1b1) as basic. The interesting question, then – beyond our scope of inquiry here – is how to choose between the various structural propositions whose presence in anyone's epistemic constellation (1a1) and (1b1) apparently veto. The point relevant here is that (1a1) and (1b1) cannot appear as basic in *S's* epistemic constellation without *S's* being rendered irrational on the basis of their acceptance.

In one respect, at least, things are different with regard to (1a2) and (1b2) than they were regarding (1a1) and (1b1), for the former may be properly accorded the status of not improperly basic beliefs without their believer falling under the condemnation of the content of her belief. According to (1a2), if S's belief that P is nonbasic and unfavored by evidence, then S's belief that P is not a reasonable belief – S, that is, is irrational in having it. The rough idea behind (1a2) and (1b2) is that a proposition that appears in an epistemic superstructure without visible means of epistemic support is a kind of cognitive anomaly; such an epistemic building is architecturally unsound, such an epistemic constellation is improperly ordered, and such a belief would reside in midair – resting on, and hanging from, nothing at all. So to say, it would be a *levitated* belief.

With this perspective, I will not pick a quarrel. What is interesting, in the present context, about (1a2) and (1b2) is that in order to tell whether S is irrational in their light, one must tell whether a belief is supported by evidence, at least in S's epistemic constellation. And of course, since it may lack support in S's constellation but be blessed by an abundance of support in $S1$'s constellation, or lack it in S's constellation at t but possess it in S's constellation at t_1, in order to be sure that it is not due to S's idiosyncrasy or ignorance or the like, one who condemns the belief and not merely the believer must gain what confidence one may that *no* evidence for it is available. In any case, examination of the belief's evidential environment in S's epistemic constellation (if it is psychological belief, relative to S, that is under review) or of the belief's evidential environment overall (if it is the reasonability in general of the belief in question that one is investigating) is required. Hence the presence or absence of nonepistemic explanation is here not the central focus of the inquiry regarding the rationality of belief or believer. I will return to the relevance of this in concluding this chapter.

NONEPISTEMIC EXPLANATION AND THE DISCREDITATION OF PROPOSITIONAL BELIEF

Sometimes S's *belief that P's being nonepistemically explicable* is alleged to be grounds, in some manner, for *P's being false*. Of course one can see easily enough how, under certain conditions, the two might be connected. If *P* is conceptually, reflexively, or observationally falsified to *S*, then of course *P* is false, and further perhaps *S* can believe that *P* only if *S* is conceptually confused or not very penetrating or perceptually inattentive, or the like, and perhaps such conditions on *S*'s part are physicalistically, and so nonepistemically, explicable.

Under such circumstances as these, it will be true that if *S* believes that *P*, then the relevant epistemic explanation, if such there be, is negative or that perhaps a nonepistemic explanation may be sufficient. But in such cases the chain is forged in a certain direction – *P*'s probable or certain falsehood (and *S*'s easy access to this falsehood or to what reveals it) provides reason for thinking that *S*'s believing that *P* deserves no positive epistemic explanation. If we call propositions whose falsehood seems something the average adult should be able to figure out without undue hardship *accessibly false propositions*, then perhaps *P is accessibly false* and *S (an average adult) believes that P* provides reason for thinking it the case that *S's belief that P has no positive epistemic explanation.* Such arguments from *P*'s discerned and easily accessible falsehood to its being unreasonable to believe that *P* are easy and characteristically uninteresting, and they do not apply to many theological beliefs. Nor is the chain forged by such considerations one that leads in the intended direction. It goes from falsehood to unreasonability, not (as was desired) the other way around. But if one's strategy is to argue from *P has property A* to *P is* (or: *P is probably*) *false*, where *A* of course is not *is* (*probably*) *false*, one's effort is needlessly cumbersome if one has first to establish *P*'s falsehood or *P*'s probable falsehood. Arguing in this fashion would be like driving home in order to get one's bike so one can ride home; one is at one's desired destination before one uses one's favored means to the end of arriving there. Arguments to falsehood from nonepistemic explicability are aimed at circumventing the task of assessing *P*'s truth-value in any direct manner, and hence are pointless if they presuppose direct assessment.

Say one wishes to develop some argument of the form:

(1) *S's belief that P has A;*
(2) *Beliefs that have A are (probably) such that they have no positive epistemic explanation (or: if they have any epistemic explanation, it is negative);*
(3) *Beliefs that have no positive epistemic explanation (or: if they have any epistemic explanation, it is negative) are (probably) false;*
(4) *S's belief that P is (probably) false.*

One has the task, by virtue of propounding (2) and (3), of relating *being A* and *being false*. And (3), of course, will have to be restricted, in a manner that is also reflected in (2). For example, if $S1$ knows that P is true, or has good reason to think that P is true, $S1$'s learning that S's belief that P has no positive epistemic explanation will not generally be any reason for $S1$ to start doubting that P is really true, or to think that probably P is false. Perhaps a restriction should be included that deals with *accessible falsehood* (with some account of just what this amounts to). It is some varieties of (2) and (3) on which this discussion will focus.

For some values of A, of course, the connection between *being A* and *being false* will be that P is A entails P is false. This will be so for *is contradictory, is false if believed and is believed, is false if entertained and is entertained,* and the like. But it seems highly implausible that religious doctrines, in general, and across the board, actually have such properties as are expressed by these values of A. If they have some property A that relates in some interesting way with *being false*, I shall assume that the connection between *being A* in that sense, and *being false*, is logically contingent.

A fairly popular candidate for being a value of A that many believe would make (2) true is (i) *not being arrived at through a reliable method* or perhaps *being arrived at through an unreliable method.* Another is (ii) *being associated with a prescientific world-view.* Still another – though here *not known to be true* replaces *false* – is (iii) *is not empirically testable.* Unless *seeing that P is necessarily true* is a reliable method (though it seems not to be a *method* at all), the proposition (PC) *Nothing can have incompatible qualities* seems to be associated with falsehood on the first suggestion – that is, on (i). If Aristotle's worldview is prescientific, (PC) does no better on (ii), and it fares worse on (iii). So much the worse, of course, for those criteria. But perhaps it is only logically contingent propositions that are in question.

The strategy of discreditation involved here, in one way, is clear. One endeavors to find some (simple or complex) property A such that (a) A defines a class K of propositions such that more (preferably many more) than half the members of K are known to be false, and (b) in some relevant and plausible sense of "religious," religious propositions comprise K or some substantial subset K_1 of K such that more (preferably many more) than half of K_1's members are known to be false. But plainly some propositions that belong to K – and if religious propositions comprise some subset K_1 of K, perhaps some propositions that belong to K_1 – must be directly discovered to be true or false; member P of K or K_1 must, that is, be discovered to be true or false (or probably true, or probably false, or the like) on the basis of P-relevant grounds or evidence and without its being requisite that P be a member of K or K_1. And presumably anyone who cared greatly about the truth-value of some particular member of this class would do what he could to follow a direct procedure in the case of that member, especially if the indirect test seemed negative. Nor would this appeal to direct test – to inquiry concerning the grounds or evidence relevant to the proposition whose truth-value one cared about – be in any way irrational or unreasonable, since if I have grounds or evidence that P, this may well overcome whatever negative epistemic prejudice membership in K or K_1 may involve.

In order to develop this discrediting strategy one may wish to reject the principle that (KM) *If proposition P belongs to area of discourse K, then not-P also belongs to K,* for this (allowing the looseness of "area of discourse") entails *If P is a religious proposition, then not-P is a religious proposition,* and exactly half the religious propositions will be true, no matter how anyone came to believe or disbelieve them. Of course it will not follow that half of the *believed* religious propositions are true, and one may wish to restrict the strategy to *believed* religious propositions and accept principle (KM), with the result, so to say, that if the strategy is correct, then people have been unfortunate in the religious propositions they have come to believe – their epistemic success has fallen short of what sheer chance would provide.

Still, if S accepts a system of religious claims – say, C_1 through C_{10} – then even if all C_1 through C_{10} are false, accepting C_1 through C_{10} has prevented S – insofar as S's religious beliefs remain stable and S is consistent – from believing any other false religious propositions. Moreoever, consider the set R of all religious propositions. (What makes a set of propositions "religious" can be determined by whatever standard the discreditor has in mind so long as satisfying that criterion does not by itself entail being false – for otherwise the discreditor's strategy becomes otiose.) Set R presumably will contain a very large number of propositions, even if it is so conceived as to contain only all the propositions people who are usually thought to have been religious held true as part of their religious belief. Suppose, for the sake of convenience, that R contains a thousand and twenty such propositions. *Ex hypothesi*, if we subtract from R both S's favored religious beliefs and their contradictories, R contains a thousand other members. S's epistemic score is *zero true, ten false,* and on a *one belief pair/one act* principle it is *zero correct epistemic acts, ten incorrect epistemic acts.* But among the thousand remaining propositions, there are five hundred deficiencies on S's part (five hundred truths that S has failed to believe) but also five hundred errors S has not made (five hundred falsehoods S has failed to believe). Whatever reasons one has for thinking S's epistemic record is *zero correct, ten incorrect* regarding his own system of religious claims may – if they are given to S, and assuming that their introduction into S's epistemic constellation gives S reason to agree to this assessment – reverse S's record. But S's poor record does not by itself give grounds for pessimism regarding S's religious epistemic future – not objective grounds in the propositions themselves (here his chance in each case is .5), and not subjective grounds concerning S himself, for twenty in a thousand and twenty is not much, and in any case, if S has accepted the reasons in question, S's record has become *ten true, zero false* or *ten corrected errors, zero errors remaining* or the like, which augurs well as far as it goes.

The discreditor, however, probably has in mind some such view as this. There are *affirmative* religious beliefs – beliefs that this or that god exists and has this or that property, that this or that state is such that attainment of it is the key to life and time and happiness, and so on – and *negative* religious beliefs – beliefs that this or that god does not exist and that this or that god (therefore – to be Russellian) lacks this or that property, that this or that state is such that the attainment of it does not even provide the key to Santa Monica. If one wishes to maintain principle (KM), and to hold the view that to be religious is (no doubt among other things) to accept religious beliefs (*whether positive or negative*), then the discreditor is all for being religious. She just recommends that we achieve our religiosity by way of accepting only *negative* religious beliefs. Then the argument will focus on *positive* religious beliefs and go: (1') *S's positive religious beliefs have property A;* (2') *Positive religious beliefs that have A are (probably) such that if they have any epistemic explanation, it is negative;* (3') *Positive religious beliefs that (probably) have negative epistemic explanations if they have any are (probably) false;* so (4') *S's positive religious beliefs are (probably) false.*

Two comments enable us to round out the argument. One is that a properly basic positive religious belief, on the doctrine recited earlier, *need* not have a positive epistemic explanation because it need not have *any* epistemic explanation at all. (It will have none, presumably, if it has no *grounds*, for if it is properly basic, and it has *any* epistemic explanation, then its epistemic explanation will concern grounds rather than evidence.)

The other comment has to do with linking the premises thus far to the conclusion that (6) *Insofar as S has positive religious beliefs, S is irrational or unreasonable.* Now (6) divides into (6a), which concerns positive *basic* religious beliefs, and (6b), which concerns positive *nonbasic* religious beliefs.

To get from (4') to (6a) one needs something like: (5) *If S's basic positive religious beliefs have either no epistemic explanation or a negative epistemic explanation, then S, insofar as S has such beliefs, is irrational or unreasonable.* This, in turn, involves two claims:

> (5a) *If S has positive basic religious belief that P, and S's belief that P has no epistemic explanation at all, then S is unreasonable in believing that P.*

And:

> (5b) *If S has positive basic religious belief that P, and S's belief that P has a negative (and no positive) epistemic explanation, then S is unreasonable in believing that P.*

What (5a) asserts is that the possession of groundless basic positive religious beliefs is unreasonable. The obvious question to raise is whether this is not equally so with respect to groundless basic negative religious beliefs and groundless basic nonreligious beliefs. If not, why not? It is hard to see what might justify us in holding (5a) but rejecting (5a)'s analogues with respect to basic negative religious beliefs and basic nonreligious beliefs, short of having reason to think that all or most positive religious beliefs are false; but then, of course, direct assessment of those beliefs would be required. Then the strategy that (1'–4') outlines will not be available as an escape from the task of direct assessment, since it will presuppose that such assessment is not only possible but actual (and has yielded negative results for positive religious beliefs, or positive results for negative religious beliefs, across the board).

One could argue, of course, that sets of positive religious beliefs typically are incompatible with other sets to which they are logically contrary, and among incompatible sets of positive religious beliefs, only one set can be true, whereas sets of negative religious beliefs can all be true. Whether this is right or not depends, of course, on just how the sets in question are constructed. Consider, for example, nontheistic sets of religious beliefs S_1, S_2, and S_3; if *God exists* is true, then each of S_1, S_2, and S_3 will be false, even if they are negative and non-identical. One could construct values for S_1, S_2, and S_3 that fit this description by selecting only the (different) non–theistic-relevant negative beliefs from Jainism, Theravada Buddhism, and Advaita Vedanta, respectively.

One can argue that if sets S_4, S_5, and S_6 of propositions are made up of logically contrary positive religious beliefs, the probability of any one of them being true if we consider no relevant evidence is no better than one in three. But for any discipline or area of reflection, the same argument can be offered. There is nothing distinctive, in this regard, about positive religious beliefs as compared to positive economic beliefs or psychological beliefs or biological beliefs or the like.

To accept both (5a) and its analogues concerning groundless basic negative religious beliefs and basic nonreligious beliefs would be to decry all basic beliefs as unreasonable – to hold that any epistemic cluster that contains underived beliefs of any sort is for that reason one its owner unreasonably embraces. What might justify *that* assertion, I have no idea.

Similarly, to get from (4') to (6b), one will need (5'), which is identical to (5) save that "nonbasic" replaces "basic." And (5') will involve (5a'), which is identical to (5a) save that "nonbasic" replaces "basic," and (5b'), which is identical to (5b) save for the familiar substitution, with this result:

> (5a') If S has positive nonbasic religious belief that P, and S's belief that P has no epistemic explanation at all, then S is unreasonable in believing that P.
> (5b') If S has positive nonbasic religious belief that P, and S's belief that P has a negative (and no positive) epistemic explanation, then S is unreasonable in believing that P.

Obviously, one could know that, with respect to some person S/belief state/positive nonbasic religious proposition triad, an instantiation of (5a') or (5b') is true without possessing the results of any attempts to assess P. One need only know that S has no reasons or evidence for P, and accepts P (in the case that instantiates [5a']), as a result of entirely nonepistemic factors or (in the case that instantiates [5b']) for epistemic considerations that are not P-preferring. Equally obviously, if one knows that the analogues of (5a') and (5b') are instantiated with respect to some person S_1/ belief state/nonbasic negative religious proposition triad, or some person S_2 /belief state/nonbasic nonreligious proposition triad, one will have just the same reason for thinking S_1 or S_2 unreasonable that one has for thinking this about S.

If there are epistemic obligations concerning the acceptance or rejection of existential propositions, or of propositions generally, and of accepting them in such a way that they are nonbasic within one's epistemic cluster, then presumably they go along the following lines. Regarding belief that P, one can believe that P, believe that *not-P*, and suspend judgment regarding P. *Belief that P* is a concept that pairs with *two* others to complete a conceptual circle that exhausts the relevant alternatives; in that respect, it is like *being good*, which pairs with a pair of concepts – *being evil* and *being morally neutral* – to complete a conceptual circle that exhausts the alternatives rather than like *being true*, which pairs with a single concept – *being false* – to complete its circle. Evidenceless and groundless regarding nonbasic proposition P, one's epistemic duty, if such there be here, presumably is to suspend judgment regarding P. Structural propositions, necessary among one's beliefs if they are to be organized and rich in explanatory power, will typically be held as basic, and their holders will typically lack grounds for holding them. Although (5a') and (5b') may well be true, they do not seem to offer much support for the line of reasoning expressed by (1'–4') to religious belief in a way that has application of the results for which a critic hopes.

To see this, it remains to consider the pattern of reasoning that (1'–4') represents. I take it as fairly obvious that there is no good reason to think that *belief* itself is a natural kind, nor any more reason to think this about *religious belief, belief not produced by following a scientific method, belief associated with a prescientific worldview,* or the like. Since arguments of the form *All observed X's have A and most observed X's that have A also have B, so probably most X's have B,* where X ranges over concrete objects and X *has A* is not tautologous, are probably most forceful when they deal with natural kinds, arguments of the (1′–4′) pattern would seem at best not to be the strongest of their type.

The two features that seem to strike many critics of religious belief most forcefully are (alleged) *empirical falsehood* and (alleged) *untestability,* the suggestion being that religious claims possess one or the other of these epistemic liabilities. *Zeus causes thunder* and *It thunders when the gods are angry,* perhaps, represent the former sort of religious claim; *God is trinitarian* and *All that exists besides God depends on God for its existence* may represent the latter sort.

Some have proposed that religion be divided from science on the basis of the empirical falsifiability (in principle) of scientific claims and the lack of falsifiability (in principle) of religious claims. According to this criterion, however, *Jesus Christ was God Incarnate* is a scientific claim, since it entails *Jesus was a historical person,* which in turn is falsifiable in principle though true in fact. So far as I am aware, what historical claims a fairly orthodox Christianity is committed to are true, and while that obviously does not entail the truth of Christian theology, it does rebut the charge that all religious claims are either empirically unfalsifiable or else empirically falsified.

Further, of the religious propositions that have been empirically falsified, it is true, on the whole anyway, that their falsification has been complex rather than simple. If it is claimed that observable object X has observable property A at time t, and at t one observes that X lacks A, then X *has A* has suffered *simple* falsification. If it is claimed that observable phenomenon Y is best explained by positing the existence of B (and B is either not observable or else is observable but its existence has not been observationally confirmed), whereas one can explain Y at least equally well by describing the activity of D (and D, if not also D's activity, has been observed), then (in the absence of some other powerful consideration in its favor) Y *is best explained by positing B* has suffered *complex* falsification. Thus, *The little people cause milk to sour* suffered complex falsification relative to Pasteur's discovery that *Bacteria cause milk to sour.* Generally speaking, religious claims, when they have suffered empirical falsification, have suffered from its complex variety.

One could argue thus: Most of those positive religious beliefs that are empirically falsifiable and have been tested have turned out to be false, so if claim R is an empirically falsifiable religious claim, then probably R is false. But one could also argue to this effect: Most of the positive religious beliefs that are empirically falsifiable and required for the truth of some variety of monotheism that have been tested have turned out to be true, so if claim R_1 is an empirically falsifiable religious claim required for the truth of monotheism, then probably R_1 is true. Both arguments could be correct; their conclusions are not incompatible. In order to rebut this second argument, one would have to see whether the claim that comprises its antecedent is true. And that would require direct assessment of religious claims and historical evidence rather than resting one's case only on indirect assessment.

Sometimes, and more often than contemporary doubts about the cognitive status of religious claims would lead one to suppose, one can see that within a particular religious conceptual system, some proposition P is essential to that system (its falsehood will entail that the system itself is fundamentally in error) and complexly empirically falsifiable; call such propositions as these *accessible central claims. There has been a Hebrew people, Jesus lived in Palestine about 3 B.C. – A.D. 27,* and *Mohammed was a real person* are examples of accessible central claims. They are easily ignored, since they are plainly true and their truth does not entail the truth of Judaism, Christianity, or Islam. But they are relevant as fairly clear counterexamples to the thesis that religious conceptual systems bear no relationships to empirical data.

It is also worth noting that various ethical views – some of them highly plausible – have been associated with (or were part of) prescientific views. Unless moral principles and rules are properly produced by, or are the result of, the application of scientific method (which is false if by "scientific method" one means something like "those methodologies peculiar to one or more of the natural or social sciences"), the fact that an ethical view is part of a prescientific understanding of the world, or is produced by no scientific method, would seem to have little to do with whether that view is likely to be false. The same applies to religious claims.

While there are, of course, plenty of suggestions we have left uncanvassed, the results are not encouraging for finding plausible versions of the (1′–4′) argument that will serve the discreditor's strategy. If this is correct, one may wonder why the assumption that some version of the sort of indirect assessment of religious claims this argument expresses must be correct and even readily available enjoys such currency. The answer is simple: It is widely assumed (and seldom argued) that (save for religious perspectives that can be viewed as prescientific explanations of observable phenomena, and so can easily be falsified) there are no ways of directly rationally assessing religious beliefs. This is dubious, and the way to argue against it would be to argue for or against particular religious claims. Without showing that such arguments for or against religious claims always fail – either one after the other in an impressive and exceptionless array, or else from some grand and patently correct a priori stance – it is hard to see how one could establish the imperviousness of religious belief to rational assessment. (If it is only religious *believers* that are supposed to be impervious to argument, and not religious *claims*, then *even* if this is so, it is also true – to something like the same extent – regarding voters, consumers, and proponents of secularist ideologies.) Since only the latter, grand a priori strategy (i.e., direct rational assessment) would avoid the consideration of religious beliefs, and since such a priori strategies characteristically appear to make wide-ranging assumptions about the nature of thought, language, concepts, conceptual systems, language games, cultures, or reality at least as difficult to test as are many religious doctrines, it is hard to see exactly what *justifies* the common assumption that religious beliefs are impossible to assess rationally.

CONCLUSION

The preceding two sections have considered the discreditation, respectively, of psychological belief and of propositional belief, which begins with the claim that a belief possessed by some person is nonepistemically explicable and ends with the claim that that person is unreasonable or that that belief is (probably) false. Obviously, only certain strategies of discreditation were discussed, and those only partially. But if the examples of discrediting strategies were representative, and the remarks made about them were correct, what, if anything, follows?

It seems clear that the sheer fact that a person's belief is nonepistemically explicable entails very little, if anything, about the person's reasonability in holding it or the probable falsehood of the belief in question. Nor does the fact that a basic belief is held without reason or grounds seem to speak against the rationality of its believer – not at least with respect to the sort of propositions we called *structural*. It does not follow that one cannot rationally assess competing structural beliefs – that is another, and given the present argument an entirely open, question. It does seem correct that the more restrictive axioms of the ethics of properly held basic beliefs are ill-suited to deal responsibly with the acceptance of structural propositions. And at least some religious propositions – *God exists* among them – seem to be of that sort. Of course that raises the question of what, exactly, a structural proposition is – which, again, is another topic.

If the argument of this chapter is correct, this shift from considering whether some particular (and perhaps idiosyncratic) person is reasonable in accepting some proposition, in cases where this is an interesting and debatable matter, to considering whether (on the whole) this proposition can be accepted without rendering oneself unreasonable seems to be an issue one usually cannot rationally resolve without engaging in some sort of direct assessment of the proposition believed; and the strategy of trying to escape this by considering whether a person's acceptance of that proposition can be nonepistemically explained seems, on the whole, not a profitable enterprise. Further, often at least, it can be countered in one or another of the ways we considered in the preceding two sections. So I am inclined on the whole to view as futile the attempt to settle interesting debates about whether a person is reasonable in accepting a proposition by arguing that his acceptance is nonepistemically explicable.

If anything, things are worsened, so far as I can see, by attempts to argue from the fact that a person's belief is nonepistemically explicable to the conclusion that it is probably false. For, again, this argument has force only if the fact that this person's acceptance of it is nonepistemically explicable is not idiosyncratic, and this is establishable, often at least, only by appealing to the results of a direct assessment of the proposition believed (or by offering a judgment on this matter without benefit of any assessment, which, of course, is worthless). Nor is the nonepistemic explicability of a person's belief that P sufficient to discredit the person, let alone P, and the sorts of properties that are often alleged to accompany nonepistemically explicable beliefs seem either in fact not to accompany them or to accompany only a basically irrelevant and uninteresting subset of them or not to be such as to make falsehood of the propositions whose belief they accompany probable.

A final comment: These remarks, at best, scratch the surface of a difficult and complex topic. It is a topic on which, so far as I am aware, not a great deal has been written. My hope is that what I have said here may stimulate sufficient interest in the topic for others to provide further exploration of the issues I have been able only to highlight.

Part IV

The religious challenge

8

Self-authentication and verification

SUBJECTIVE EXPERTISE

It is sometimes suggested that those who have had religious experiences are the real experts as to what those experiences show – as to what they are evidence for. Others interested in such matters had best sit at their feet.

Obviously, anyone interested in whether religious experiences are evidence for religious belief has reason to be grateful for descriptions of such experiences offered by those who have them. These descriptions are grist for the philosopher's mill. (I do not suggest that in this lies their only or primary value.) But this says nothing regarding expertise as to what the experiences are evidence for.

It seems clear that there is something such persons (ordinarily, anyway) *are* experts about – namely, what it is like to have religious experience of the sort they have had. This, of course, is not surprising. Because he did it, Bill Russell is an expert on what it was like to be the center who led the Boston Celtics to nine NBA championships. Jimmy Carter and Ronald Reagan are experts on what it is like to be president in a way that Rodney Dangerfield and Bill Cosby are not. Those who have ridden an elephant are experts about what it is like, relative at least to those who have not ridden an elephant. One can think of exceptions: If A has done or experienced X (ridden a bike or seen a sunset from Pikes Peak or visited Europe or had a migraine headache or whatever) and B has only read a lot about doing or experiencing X, but A is really stupid, has a bad memory, and paid little attention while he was doing or experiencing X, whereas B is very bright, has a good imagination, and has carefully watched others do or experience X, maybe B will know more about what doing or experiencing X is like than A does. *A, but not B, has done or experienced X does not entail even A is more expert than B relative to what it feels like to do or experience X.* Still, ordinarily, A will be more expert about doing or experiencing X than B is if A has done or experienced X and B has not.

The fancy way of putting this is that the person who has a religious experience of a certain sort is likely therefore to have an expertise he or she would not otherwise have regarding that experience's *phenomenology* – about "what the world looks like from within the experience" or "what the content of the experience is" or the like. But that, by itself, is not expertise about whether the world *is* as it seems "from within the experience" or whether the experience's content correctly represents things. Of course, the person might also have expertise about that, but not simply by virtue of having had the experience.

SUBJECTIVE BIAS

If some have claimed that religious experiencers (REs) – people who have had religious experiences – are thereby made experts about the reliability or veridicality of those experiences (about whether or not they correctly represent the world), it should be noted that others have claimed that REs are about the last people one should expect to have any such expertise. They have argued that those who have such experiences – experiences that often are emotionally powerful and that sometimes result in instantaneous conversions or redirections of a life – are in no position to evaluate objectively the cognitive significance of such experiences. Further, particularly in the traditions that center on enlightenment experience, the investment in having such experiences (walking for years in a loin cloth from one end of India to the other, begging one's bread, or spending years learning the meanings of ancient arcane texts under the relentless guidance of demanding gurus, or a near lifetime of good works – in each case, instead of devoting oneself to seeking pleasure, wealth, and power), plus the status given to those who allegedly have had them (being elevated to a semidivine status where others bow in your presence or dare not even look you in the face), is just too great for anyone who claims to have had any such experience to be trusted to be at all rational in his reasoning or judgment regarding its cognitive significance. There is some reason, then, to look twice at the claim that a person who has had a religious experience is even *as* qualified as someone who has not to tell what evidence, if any, that experience provides. It depends on various things – what each person knows, what degree of objectivity she can obtain, how clearly she thinks, and the like. But then possession of experience is not sufficient for possession of evidential expertise.

In fact, some REs think and write poorly when they try to assess their experiences, and some think and write well. The class of REs contains both geniuses and frauds. Shankara, Ramanuja, and Madhva, for example, fall into the former category. I leave my readers to choose their own examples of the latter.

My suggestions thus far, then, have been these: (i) that being an RE does not make one an expert as to the *reliability* of one's religious experience or about *what it is, and is not, evidence for;* (ii) that being an RE ordinarily does make one something of an expert as to the phenomenology of one's religious experience – more expert, anyway, than one would have been had one not had the experience in question; (iii) that being an RE neither guarantees nor precludes one's becoming good at seeing what sort of evidence one's religious experience does, or does not, provide. But I have not yet *argued* in much detail for (i).

SELF-AUTHENTICATION

It will be useful to look more fully and carefully at the notion of *self-authentication* – of a religious experience being self-authenticating regarding a religious belief. Self-authentication is, as it were, a three-term relation; there is a person to whom an experience authenticates, an experience that does the authenticating, and a belief or proposition that is authenticated. "Belief" in this context plainly refers to *what is believed* – to what bears truth-value, or is *either true or false*. It does not refer to the believing or accepting of something. In other language, it is propositional belief rather than psychological belief that we are concerned with. Further, the belief or proposition in question is evidenced or authenticated in a particularly strong way – in such a way, in fact, that the person cannot be mistaken in accepting that belief or in believing that proposition.

Formally, the idea can be put in this fashion: Person S's experience E is self-authenticating regarding proposition P if and only if S has E, and it is logically impossible that S have E and P be false, and S rests S's acceptance of P on S's having seen both that S had E and that it is logically impossible that S have E and P be false.

It is plausible that there are experiences that satisfy these conditions regarding persons and beliefs. Suppose that Wendy, perhaps feeling philosophical, reflects that, in contrast to Santa Claus and unicorns but like salamanders and her dog, she exists. Reflection, after all, is a kind of experience, and if Wendy reflects at time t that she exists at t (a reflection that, she notes, includes her believing that she exists), then she is fully justified if she also notes that her reflecting that she exists is impossible unless she does exist; Wendy's experience of believingly reflecting on the fact of her existence is such that it is logically impossible that she do so and her belief be false. So (prosaically enough, and in nonimmortal prose) if she rests her belief that she exists at t on the experience of believingly reflecting that she exists at t, her experience of believingly reflecting that she exists at t will be self-authenticating regarding her belief that she exists at t. It seems the notion of a self-authenticating experience, unlike that of a round circle or a bad Boston Celtics victory, is not self-contradictory or without positive instances.

If we ask, then, what sorts of beliefs there are that can receive self-authentication from experience, it seems clear that among them are my belief that I now exist, my belief that I am now conscious, my belief that I now have at least one belief, and the like. Perhaps if I believe that I am now in pain, then it is true that I am now in pain (though I can be wrong about the pain's cause and its location). Assuming that some experiences are self-authenticating with respect to some beliefs, presumably these are the sorts of beliefs that self-authentication might secure. At best, the content of such beliefs is very modest. Security from every possible error is purchased at the price of slender content. The criterion for self-authentication will "allow in" Wendy's belief that she exists. It may also "allow in" Wendy's belief that she is in pain, or is now conscious. It will not "allow in" her belief that her dog exists, because she can believe that he does even though he does not, and she can believe that she experiences him when in fact she does not.

SELF-AUTHENTICATION AND RELIGIOUS BELIEFS

As a matter of fact, no religious tradition is only or mainly composed of claims that a believer cannot be wrong about or that evidentially rest on experiences such that it is logically impossible that a person be wrong about whether she has them or not. Indeed, so far as I am aware, strictly speaking, *no* religious belief is one that is self-authenticated to anyone. Consider two sample cases: experience of God and attainment of Nirvana (where the latter includes a recognition that a person is but a series of transitory states). It is logically possible that Wendy have an experience that she believes to be an experience of God, but which is not – because God does not exist or because God does exist but is in fact not the object of that experience (*God exists* does not entail *Anything someone takes to be an experience of God really is an experience of God* any more than *Kate Jackson exists* entails *Anytime anyone thinks she sees Kate Jackson, she does see Kate Jackson*). It is logically possible that Wendy have an experience that she thinks is an attainment of Nirvana, but is not – because there is no such thing as attaining Nirvana, or because there is but Wendy has not done it. (*Nirvana can be attained* does not entail *Anyone who thinks that he has attained Nirvana has attained Nirvana.*)

Of course some beliefs that are entailed by religious beliefs may be self-authenticated beliefs. Thus if *Andrew believes that he is a sinner* is true, it follows that *Andrew exists* is true, and if Andrew has this latter belief, as is likely, then Andrew believes a proposition that both is entailed by a proposition whose acceptance is a matter of religious belief and can be self-authenticated. But the interest for present purposes of the notion of self-authentication lies in the suggestion that there are religious beliefs that are self-authenticated, not that there are self-authenticated beliefs that are entailed by religious beliefs.

SELF-AUTHENTICATION AND FULL CONFIRMATION

The concept of a self-authenticating religious experience apparently wields perennial fascination. Unaffected by the slender rational credential of this concept, philosophers as well as nonphilosophers yield to this fascination. In what follows, I shall say a bit about why they do, and a good bit more about why they should not.

The attractiveness of the concept is not far to seek. If an experience of mine is self-authenticating, then there is something it authenticates to me. Analytically, we noted earlier, there is a self-authenticator (the experience), a self-authenticatee (the subject), and a self-authenticated (the belief confirmed to the subject of the experience). So where we allow S to range over persons, E over experiences, and P over propositions.

(1) A self-authenticating experience occurred

entails:

(2) Person S had an experience E that authenticated (confirmed) P to S.

Further, if an experience of mine is self-authenticating with respect to one of my beliefs, then (I take the idea to be that) it, by itself, fully confirms that belief. Other experiences might also confirm it; they might confirm it even better to someone else. But my experience fully (and perhaps irrevocably) confirms it to me. So (1) also entails:

(3) Person S had an experience E that confirmed P to S in such a manner that S need not (now, or perhaps ever) consider any other experience (or anything else) in order to tell whether P is true.

Now an experience of which (3) is true is very convenient to have if I wish to know whether P is true; having such an experience tells me in no uncertain terms and (assuming a reliable memory) for all time P's truth-value. If P is a proposition about whose truth-value I deeply care and if what I very much want is that P be true, then I will naturally highly prize any experience of which (3) is true. If P is *God exists*, and some experience of mine is self-authenticating with respect to P, then whatever I may be obligated to do for *their* sake, I do not for my own sake have to answer the skeptic, the natural atheologian, the agnostic, the chronic doubter, or even the epistemically weaker believing sister. (Or, if you like, if P is *God does not exist*, and some experience of mine is self-authenticating with respect to P, then whatever I may be obligated to do for their sake, I do not for my own sake have to answer the skeptic, the natural theologian, the agnostic, the chronic doubter, or even the epistemically weaker unbelieving brother.) Epistemic certainty about crucial matters – not merely psychological certainty that I happen to have, but epistemological certainty that I have *sufficient reason* for having – is a precious commodity. The notion of a self-authenticating religious (or, for the unbeliever, irreligious) experience provides promise in this regard; if an experience satisfying this concept can be found, such certainty will have been found – an authentic if epistemic Holy Grail. So two questions arise: (Q1) Is the concept of a self-authenticating religious experience consistent? (Q2) Has the concept of a self-authenticating religious experience any instance? Should the answer to (Q1) be negative, the answer to (Q2) obviously also will be. But an affirmative answer to (Q1) will not by itself entail an affirmative answer to (Q2), nor will a negative answer to (Q2) entail a negative answer to (Q1).

The obvious way to argue that (Q1) at any rate deserves an affirmative answer is to provide a logically consistent account of the locution "self-authenticating religious experience." I know of only one attempt to prove that (Q1) has an affirmative answer in a manner independent of providing any particular specification of the locution. In "Religious Experience and Rational Certainty" Robert Oakes argues in effect as follows. Consider the claim:

(O) If God exists, God can make *Person S had a self-authenticating experience of God* true.

If the antecedent of (O) is necessarily or contingently false, (O) – read as a material implication – is true. If the antecedent of (O) is necessarily or contingently true, the consequent must be false if (O) is false. But the consequent of (O) is false, presumably, only if *Person S had a self-authenticating experience of God* is contradictory. This proposition is contradictory only if (a) the concept of a self-authenticating experience of God is contradictory or (b) the concept of someone's having a self-authenticating experience of God is contradictory or (c) the concept of God's causing someone to have a self-authenticating experience of God is contradictory. Since there is no reason to think that (a), (b), or (c) is true, there is no reason to think *Person S had a self-authenticating experience of God* is self-contradictory, and so no reason to think (O)'s consequent false. Since (O)'s consequent is true unless it is contradictory, and since it is reasonable to suppose a proposition consistent unless we have evidence to the contrary, it is reasonable to think (O)'s consequent true; in which case it is reasonable to suppose that (O) is true. So it is reasonable to conclude that (O) is true.

There is some interest in this (as it were) a priori argument that the concept of a self-authenticating experience of God is consistent. Its obvious defect is that it proves, so to say, everything or nothing. To see this, throughout the a priori argument substitute for the locution "a self-authenticating experience of God" the locution "a self-ardulating frenescence of fridity," and run through the new a priori argument that results. One has an a priori argument "proving" that patent nonsense is logically consistent. Since what is logically consistent is possibly true, and nonsense is not, this conclusion is false. The patent difference between the locutions is that we are likely to at least believe we can attach a consistent (if intuitive or preanalytic) sense to the former but have no such belief with regard to the latter. To make this appeal is, of course, to consider some particular (if intuitive or preanalytic) concept of self-authentication. The question now is whether this concept really is as consistent as it appears. So much for the purely a priori route to (O). Thus far, (Q1) and (Q2) have received no answer whatsoever.

It may be unfair to ascribe the a priori argument just rejected to Professor Oakes, who after all offers his own analysis of the relevant concept. If so, we now make amends by turning explicitly to that analysis.

Oakes defends the view that there is a consistent concept of experiential self-authentication:

> We can now define 'self-authenticating' religious experience as veridical experience of God which is sufficient to guarantee that the person having that veridical experience could never (in principle) have any justification for questioning its veridicality. Hence, since it is a *logically necessary* condition for self-authentication that the experience in question be veridical, it is simply irrelevant to suggest that any putative experience of God *might* be delusive.

Schematically, then, we are offered this definition:

(A) Experience E of person S is self-authenticating with respect to proposition P if and only if that S has E is sufficient to guarantee that S could never (in principle) have any justification for questioning that E authenticates P.

That E authenticates P to S entails (according to Oakes) that E provides S with perpetually sufficient evidence for P. (What "sufficient evidence" amounts to is, of course, itself no easy matter; my only concern here is to stress that authentication for Oakes is, so to say, a triadic *evidential* relation between a person, an experience, and a proposition.) Apparently, given what follows, the locution "could never, in principle" is to be understood in terms of logical necessity. With these matters in mind, we can revise (A) in terms of:

(A1) Experience E of person S is self-authenticating with respect to proposition P if and only if, given that S has had E, it is logically impossible that S ever justifiably doubt that E is sufficient evidence for P.

This phrasing reads E's "veridicality" as tantamount to E being sufficient evidence for P. If one views E's veridicality as tantamount simply to P's *truth*, we can simplify (A1) to read:

(A2) Experience E of person S is self-authenticating with respect to proposition P if and only if, given that S had E, it is logically impossible that S ever justifiably doubt that P is true.

I suspect that Oakes intends (A2), though my critique will apply, *mutatis mutandis*, to (A1) or (A2). Now no doubt this unpacking of Oakes's definition would have to progress further. Presumably, for example, S must *know* that E authenticates P (rather than P's denial or some claim different from P that does not entail P). But it will be enough for my purpose to dwell simply on the elements first emphasized.

In appraising the thesis that religious experiences sometimes at least are self-authenticating with regard to properly selected religious beliefs, it seems appropriate to deal with two different issues. One concerns whether S's experience E, which is, at time t, conclusive evidence for P, can also place S in an epistemic position so secure that S need never again consider any *P*-relevant evidence, even rendering it some-how epistemically inappropriate for *S* to do so. The other is whether any experience can be, as it were, even momentarily self-authenticating with regard to some properly selected claim. An experience that along the lines of (A), (A1), or (A2) is self-authenticating at all is, so to speak, self-authenticating now and will be self-authenticating later. In what follows, I discuss these issues in the order in which I mentioned them earlier and offer reasons for doubting that any experiences self-authenticate any religious beliefs at all, later or now. The first set of arguments defends the claim that the concept of a self-authenticating religious experience (even if logically consistent) has no extension. The second set of considerations contends that the concept is not con-sistent after all.

I begin by noting that I am not at all clear what the exact force or content is of the locution "can never (in principle) have any justification for questioning" the veridicality of the relevant experience. The idea seems to be this. If an experi-ence *E* of mine is self-authenticating with respect to some proposition *P*, then, having had *E* at *t*, it is in some sense epistemically inappropriate of me to doubt, at *t* or any later date, that *E* does authenticate *P*, and so somehow epistem-ically inappropriate of me ever to doubt that *P* is true. But what exactly is one to make of this suggestion? Consider the claim *I am now in pain*. Here is a proposition that, it is plau-sible to contend, is sometimes justified to me by actually self-authenticating experiences. Suppose, at *t*, I have an ex-perience *E* such that *E* is self-authenticating to me with re-spect to *I am in pain at t*. Am I then doing something epistemically inappropriate if I wonder, at *t* + *1*, whether I really was in pain at *t*? Waiving doubts about personal iden-tity, about the reality of time, and about whether it was exactly at *t* that I was in pain (when, precisely, now was), supposing it was a clear pain that I had (not an ache, a throb, or a mild hurting perhaps not intense enough to really be a pain), could not my memory falter so as to make doubt ap-propriate? (A mere fiat that it will not, or that if it does the experience is not self-authenticating, will not help here.) Could I not just be confused, or momentarily impressed, by some argument that attempted to prove no one ever felt pain, or lots of other things time and ingenuity might suggest? In sum, I simply do not know how to unpack the locution in question in any way that renders it convincing, save perhaps by reference to the truth of the claim alleged to be evidenced by a self-authenticating experience.

But perhaps this is simply Oakes's intent. Perhaps the idea is that (along the lines suggested by [A2]) since *E is self-authenticating to S with respect to P* entails both *E is veridical* and *P is true*, if *S* comes to believe that *P* is not true, *S* is mistaken (since *P* is true) and of course if *S* comes to doubt that *P* is true, S doubts the truth of a true claim. But is *S*, in doubting *P*, doing something epistemically inappropriate? Let us grant, for the sake of the argument, that if *E*, at *t*, is self-authenticating to *S* with respect to *P*, then should *S* at *t* doubt that *P*, *S* acts with epistemic impropriety or without epistemic justification. What if *S* at *t* + 1 doubts that *P?* Even if *E* is a numinous experience, *P* the claim *God exists*, *P* true, and *E* caused by God, it yet may be that, through reflecting on the problem of evil or the varieties of religious experience (or whatever), *S* may mistakenly but not unreasonably believe himself to have found evidence that *E* was not veridical. *S* might then come, not unreasonably, to doubt, or even disbelieve, *P*. Unless one assumes – quite without justification – that (1) *P* is true, (2) *S* at *t* has sufficient experiential evidence for *P*, and (3) *S* at *t* believes *P* on the basis of *S*'s evidence for *P* together entail (4), at any time after *t*, *S* has sufficient evidence for *P*, there seem simply to be no conditions under which the relevant locution, with anything very like Oakes's intended connotation, applies to any epistemic circumstances in which any of us might find ourselves. But (1–3) do not entail (4).

A further point by now stands out in sharp relief. In order for *S* to know that one of *S*'s experiences is, in Oakes's sense, self-authenticating, *S* must know that it is veridical. So one cannot appeal to the fact that an experience is self-authenticating in order to prove, or provide independent evidence, that it is veridical; for *X is self-authenticating* assumes *X is veridical*. Being self-authenticating is a complex property with being veridical constituting one member of the complex. Thus, while *E is self-authenticating with respect to P* entails *E is veridical with respect to P*, in order to prove an experience self-authenticating, one must prove it veridical.

I have been seeking, quite without success, an answer to the question "What sort of experience could I have that would render it logically impossible that I ever thereafter be justified in doubting the proposition for which it provides sufficient evidence?" Oakes makes the answer deceptively easy: "Since it is a logically necessary condition for self-authentication that the experience in question be veridical, it is simply irrelevant to suggest that any putative experience of God might be delusory." The argument is something like the following:

(1) Necessarily, if *E* is self-authenticating, *E* is veridical.

Hence:

(2) *E is self-authenticating to S with regard to P and P is false* is self-contradictory.

Thus:

(3) If *S* believes his experience *E* is self-authenticating with respect to *P*, *S* is inconsistent if *S* doubts that *P*.

Then, from some such claims as:

(4) *S* had a putative experience of God.

and:

(5) Putative experiences of God are self-authenticating

we need to be able to derive something like:

(6) *S*'s experience of God is veridical

in order for the argument to succeed.

But of course "*S* believes his experience *E* is self-authenticating with respect to *P* and (in fact) *P* is false" is not contradictory, nor is "*S* believes his experience *E* is self-authenticating with respect to *P* and (although *P* is true) *E* does not authenticate *P*." Thus even if one believes that an apparent experience of God is self-authenticating regarding *God exists*, of course one can be mistaken about the experience being self-authenticating and about its being veridical. Given (1–3) plus the fact that someone has an apparent experience of God, one cannot derive (5) or (6) or (6) via (5), since nothing in (1–4) supports (5). Even if some apparent experiences of God are veridical – even if some are not only veridical but self-authenticating relative to *God exists* – it does not follow that all are.

Prior to Oakes's suggestions, our question was, How can one tell whether an apparent experience of God is veridical? He proposes the answer "By discovering whether or not it is self-authenticating," where *X is self-authenticating* entails *X is veridical*. But then for this to be helpful one must be able to discover that an apparent experience of God is self-authenticating without having first to discover, as before, whether it is veridical or not, and one cannot do this. What was sought was some way of being rightly assured that an experience is self-authenticating. How one tells whether one is, or merely mistakenly believes oneself to be, "self-authenticated to" remains a mystery. Further, while one started out with the hope of discovering conditions under which *S had a numinous experience* could be said to be, or not to be, evidence that God exists, we end up with an alleged definition of "self-authenticating experience" on which one could tell that one's experience of God was self-authenticating only after one had answered the more interesting question of whether it was veridical. Oakes's effort, then, is a failure. This is not, I suggest, Oakes's fault. No other effort toward the same end could succeed. For the end is that of providing a notion of self-authentication that is helpful in dealing with the overall question "Is there any experiential evidence for any religious beliefs?" And Oakes's effort failed because it seemed clear that no experience could meet the high conditions required for being self-authenticating, and even if one did it could be known to do so only after the substantive questions had already been answered. So far as I can see, there is every reason to expect that every effort whose end is the one Oakes adopts will share his effort's fate.

Perhaps the bankruptcy of the self-authentication thesis – the thesis that religious claims are confirmed by self-authenticating experiences – can be seen from another perspective. I suggested earlier that the proposition expressed by *I am in pain now* on an occasion of its sincere utterance was a plausible candidate for being a claim with regard to which an experience could be self-authenticating. Why is it a plausible candidate? In part, at least, because of the restricted scope of the claim. It is explicitly indexed temporally. Its subject term refers to exactly one being, and only one state of that being is under discussion. That state is minimally dispositional. There is nothing I need be or do at $t + 1$ if it is true that I am in pain at t, except for such things as it being the case that if asked, "Were you in pain at t?" I will (if I am sincere and no memory problems arise) answer in the affirmative. Being in pain at t is ephemeral in a way in which believing in God at t or being a physical organism at t is not. Roughly, the less dispositional a conscious state is, the better candidate it is for being a state about which its subject has incorrigible knowledge. Even if there is no conscious state about which its subject has incorrigible knowledge, one can make a better case for incorrigible knowledge of minimally if at all dispositional states (e.g., *being in pain* or *having a twinge*) than one can for complexly dispositional states (such as beliefs or hopes).

Connected with this matter is the fact that I can be in pain without there being any physical basis for my being in pain. (Or, for contingent identity theorists, that I am in the mental state *being in pain at t* does not entail that there is some physical state such that [a] is not identical to any mental state and [b] is the cause of my being in pain at t.) So the failure of a well-trained technician working with however sophisti-

177

cated tools to discover such a basis is no evidence (for me, at any rate) against my report that I am in pain. Even if there is evidence that my report is insincere because (a) other sincere reports of pains have correlated with, say, meter readings of sort M, and (b) the meter hooked to me at t gives no M-type reading, this will not prove to me that I do not feel pain. Rather, if I am at all clearheaded, it will prove to me that the correlation between M readings and pains is imperfect. Nor in so concluding am I being disingenuous, since in order to take the aforementioned correlation seriously I must also take seriously the truth of first-person pain reports known to be true independently of there being any known (though perhaps imperfect) correlation between pain states and M readings. But without further digressions into the cluster of issues surrounding private states and privileged access and the like, and whatever one's views concerning them, it remains true either that *I am in pain now* has no special status and cannot be self-authenticated, or that it has a special status but not quite that of being sometimes self-authenticated, or that it is sometimes self-authenticated and can be such in part (and perhaps as a necessary condition) because it concerns only the "current content of one's own immediate awareness," as one common phrase has it.

The claim *I am in pain* has minimal ramifications. Given that I know it to be true, there is little else I can rightly claim to know about the world because I know it to be true. And if this is not so, that fact reflects negatively on the claim that an experience can even momentarily self-authenticate the claim to me. Roughly, the fewer ramifications a claim has (the smaller the range of types of claim there are that are true if it is), the more plausible a candidate for being at least momentarily self-authenticated the claim is. As a Cartesian will understand *I am in pain*, my knowing it to be true will not, by itself, yield me the knowledge that there are other minds, an external world, a past, a future, a more than momentary present, or a Deity. It will, allegedly, allow me to know that I am an enduring being and a mental substance; it is just those matters that have raised the most difficulties for the

Cartesian position – it is very difficult to see that one does know *I am an enduring subject* and/or *I am a mental substance* simply because one knows *I am in pain now,* and in order to make the inference plausible Descartes had (surreptitiously) to introduce various matters in fact not "present to direct awareness." Otherwise, at best he would have had to remain exactly at the place one of his own *cogito* passages describes, namely, knowing now simply that *I exist now* is true.

On the other hand, if I claim *I have a pen in my hand at t* to be true, it cannot be that the conditions for its truth are all "present to me" at *t.* For pens and hands are physical (and hence enduring) objects – if not substances, then continuants. They have dispositional as well as episodic properties, and nonephemeral biographies. So other experiences are relevant to this modest claim, and confirmation of the claim is inherently open-ended. Its ramifications range beyond "present awareness" in both space and time; for this reason, it is a less plausible candidate for self-authentication than is *I am in pain now.* No matter how much confirming evidence one has, it is always overturnable. Hence no experience can be self-authenticating with regard to such a claim. Similar remarks apply to religious claims. If *God exists* is true now, it was true yesterday and will be true five minutes hence, since *God exists* entails *There is an everlasting being.* It also entails *There is a Creator and a Providence.* If not even *There is a pen in my hand now* can be self-authenticated, much less can *God exists.*

Any experience *E* that is self-authenticating with regard to *P* is also self-authenticating with regard to any proposition *P* entails. For any proposition *P* such that *S*'s experience *E* is self-authenticating with respect to *P,* given that *S* has had *E,* it is the case that for *S* the book on *P* is closed; even if there is further evidence for (or against) *P, S* will not need to refer to that evidence in order to know that *P* is true. But so far this does not sort out self-authentication cases from ordinary cases. The book on *I have a pen in my hand now* is de facto closed for me; there is no need for further evidence, even though lots more evidence for (and no doubt some against) that claim could be marshaled. Self-authentication is not necessary for knowledge or for reasonable belief. I can reasonably believe, and even know, *I have a pen in my hand* to be true, quite without canvassing "all the possible evidence" (if talk of such makes sense) or even all the evidence I could in fact think to check. And I can know this claim to be true even though I am never in a position in which it is inappropriate for me to check further evidence or reflect further on evidence already to hand. It is this supposed inappropriateness or at least nonnecessity in any circumstances of ever "checking again" that is an essential element in self-authentication. Self-authentication is valued because it gives freedom from (de facto, or only appropriate?) doubt. But for claims of a scope wide enough, and ramifications rich enough, to be religiously basic, further application of these beliefs (and so further relevant data, pro or con) is likely to be always possible, now and later. So further checking will be possible. Why it should not also be appropriate is opaque. To make the application at all is to risk failure in the effort; failure will be counterevidence.

If a self-authentication of C by some experience E renders E's subject insensitive to evidence against C – unable to weigh C-relevant evidence fairly unless the evidence is pro C – freedom from doubt begins to look like slavery to dogmatism. More fundamentally, where C is not a necessary truth or belief-entailed, it is altogether unclear that one could have an experience that so evidenced C that even though lots more evidence for C might become available, it was logically impossible that one (with epistemic propriety? at all?) come to revise one's view of C's truth-value, or even the security of one's grasp of what that truth-value was. It is always epistemically appropriate to weigh further evidence fairly, and with awareness it (logically) "can go either way."

Of course, the more ramifications a proposition has, the greater its opportunities for being false, and the more one knows if one knows it to be true. The more the ramifications a proposition has, the less plausible is the claim that it is self-authenticated. Concerning *God exists*, John Wisdom once remarked, "To this question every incident in the history of the world is relevant – whether it is the fall of a sparrow or the coming of a harvest, the passing of an empire or the fading of a smile." The remark is accurate in spirit if not in letter. So in the case of *God exists*, self-authentication claims are at their lowest level of plausibility. Perhaps only the importance of the claim, and the "electric" quality of some numinous experiences, could disguise this fact.

Nor are things different with regard to other religious experiences and claims. *Atman is Brahman*, in its doctrinal setting, entails such claims as *Brahman exists* and *No proposition stating that there are relations between things is true* and *No proposition that distinguishes between two things, or between a thing and its states or properties, or between the subject of a conscious state and the object of that state (or perhaps, makes any distinctions at all) is true*. (The last two claims, I take it, express part at least of what *All is one* means.) Further, *Atman is Brahman* presupposes, in its doctrinal setting, claims about reincarnation and liberation and the character of life as experienced under ordinary conditions. *I have attained Nirvana* presupposes very similar, if not identical, claims and, in its doctrinal setting, entails such claims as *There are no substances and no continuants* and *Nothing is either eternal or everlasting* and (perhaps) *The relation between toothache and sufferer is that of member to class*. Nor is the fundamental point that with regard to such claims as those under discussion, allegations of self-authentication are at a minimum of plausibility affected if one substitutes other analyses of these claims. For on any analysis of these claims that takes their doctrinal settings seriously, similar results will follow. Not to take these settings seriously is simply not to discuss the religions in question in a manner relevant to our inquiry, which concerns the possibility of religious claims being self-authenticated.

By now, the moral of our story should be clear. If we restrict the scope of a claim C radically enough so that *S's experience E is self-authenticating with respect to C* has (for an appropriate value of *E*) some plausibility, C's scope is so restricted that it, by itself, gives us almost no information. Its content, so to say, is so thin that it is not (religiously or otherwise) especially interesting; at any rate, one could not base a religion or a philosophy or even plans for a picnic on what it epistemically contains. Increase the scope of a claim – more carefully, enrich the meaning attached to a sentence so that it expresses more and wider claims – and one correspondingly trims down the plausibility of any allegation of self-authentication. Come to propositions of the wealth of ramifications possessed by basic religious claims, and self-authentication is just out of the question.

One final point. Talk of degrees of plausibility attaching to allegations of self-authentication ought not to obscure the fact that self-authentication itself is an all-or-nothing affair. Like such properties as *being perfect, being prime,* and *being pregnant, being self-authenticated* is not a property a claim, or *being self-authenticating* a property an experience, or *being self-authenticated to* a property a person can have to some degree. Like existence itself, these are all-or-nothing matters.

If the overall argument of this chapter is correct, then however much one may understand and empathize with those who wish to find once-and-for-all experiences that finally settle (for themselves at least, but in a fully rational manner) questions of the truth of falsity of basic religious claims, the search for this epistemic Holy Grail is hopeless. It is not that there might be self-authenticating religious experiences, but alas happen not to be; it is that the very concept of such experiences will not bear examination. Like those who wished to square the circle, those who seek (and those who claim to find) such experiences necessarily fail. *Necessary* failures are not tragedies. The result is that with regard to self-authentication, at least, religious beliefs are no worse or better off than beliefs of any sort. There is nothing tragic, and there ought to be nothing even surprising, about that, though perhaps there is something disappointing in it. What would be unfortunate is that we never realize the epistemic Holy Grail of religious self-authentication is not elusive, but inconsistent, or that one suspect, but never face up to, the inconsistency.

9

Religious practices and experiential confirmation

Two quite opposite traditions dominate contemporary discussions of religious experience. One says that there is only one sort of religious experience. Under the varieties of descriptions and reactions, doctrines and practices, ideals and institutions, there lies the pure essence of religious experience, which provides a, if not the, basis for a perennial philosophy. The other tells us that each religious tradition has its own type of religious experience, so that cross-traditional comparisons of religious experiences are possible only in terms of highly abstract and typically misleading comparisons. Such descriptions are of little worth; it is specific descriptions that are worthwhile. One can say that a Theravada Buddhist having an enlightenment experience and a North American Protestant being converted to personal faith in Jesus Christ are both having religious experiences. But it is what makes Theravada enlightenment itself, not what it shares with conversion to Christ, that makes it interesting to Buddhist monks, and what is specific to Christian conversion that makes it of interest to Protestants. When students of religious studies write about these experiences, the terms they use to describe both Theravada enlightenment and evangelical salvation tend to have one sense when applied to the one and another sense when applied to the other. Where apparently significant agreement occurs, there is in fact only unrecognized ambiguity. The one-type-of-religious-experience view does allow that religious experience provides evidence for religious belief, and the one-type-of-religious-experience-per-religious-tradition view does not. Obviously, the former perspective is, as it were, a one-type view *simpliciter*, and the latter perspective is a many-type view.

We find, then, deep disagreement as to how religious experiences, however carefully described by their subjects, should be treated. The first step toward a fully defensible view of religious experience is to note that while the two perspectives just outlined are mutually exclusive (they cannot both be true), they are not exhaustive (both can be false). The second step is a matter of discovering that both are false.

THE ONE-TYPE-OF-RELIGIOUS-EXPERIENCE VIEW

The one-type-of-religious-experience-grounds-perennial-philosophy perspective allows that religious experience can provide evidence for religious belief. What belief it provides evidence for will depend on what version of the view one is considering, and there is more than one variety. In order to develop and defend this one-type view, one must decide which the one type is. It is typical to do this by choosing (typically without argument) the religious perspective that one thinks is true, taking the sort of religious experience that favors that perspective as the one sort there is, and then claiming that descriptions of religious experience that do not agree with the preferred description are misdescriptions. One can responsibly take this line only if one first shows (without appeal to religious experience) that the sort of religious experience one prefers is the veridical sort. Even were that done, one would have to show (what seems absurdly implausible) that experiences that seem to differ greatly in both structure and content really are identical. However popular it is in some circles, there is little to be said for the one-type-of-religious-experience line.

ON THE NOTION OF A "PURE" EXPERIENCE

The one-type view typically embraces the notion of a pure experience. Then it is alleged that experiences occur that have neither content nor phenomenology. Obviously the question arises as to what would distinguish between having an experience possessed of neither content nor structure, and so altogether without phenomenology, and simply not having an experience at all. One answer sometimes offered is that one sort of experience that lacks content and phenomenology does occur – namely, dreamless sleep – and the difference between this experience and waking experiences is that one has to wake up from the former but does not have to wake up from the latter. But of course this does nothing to show that dreamless sleep is not a matter of "not having any experiences at all." Waking up need not be waking up from any experiences at all, contentless or otherwise. One who doubted that there are real unicorns would not reasonably be reassured by being told that if there are unicorns one can ride them. No reason whatever is provided by this sort of answer as to what there might be that prevents "experience lacking any content or phenomenology" and "there not being an experience going on" from referring to exactly the same cases.

CONCEPTS AS VEILS

Those who favor the one-type line tend to talk about concepts as veils between experiencer and reality. Concepts are supposed to create separating layers between subject and experience that need to be removed so that the experience can be seen for what it really is. (The standard problem, standardly ignored, of how one can be rightly confident that concepts are adequate for showing that "conceptual understanding" is unreliable but not for anything else of course arises with this view, which is self-defeating unless the problem is successfully faced.) Behind such talk lies the assumption that pure experience, experience unsullied by our conceptual contributions, lies there to be discovered. Such alleged pure experiences are central in some religious traditions and irrelevant or peripheral in others. Thus offering a philosophical account on which pure experiences are taken to be the universal type of religious experience makes a very strong claim to the effect that those traditions in which such experiences are central are on the right track, and those in which they are not central have gone significantly astray. At least this is so if one supposes, as is often done, that pure experiences are veridical or give particularly reliable and important information or insight. One could, of course, hold that all religious experience was really pure experience, disguised or plain, and that all pure experience was illusory or deceptive, nothing more than an empty hoax. Both of these perspectives are mistaken if religious experience is not essentially pure experience.

It is often supposed that if one can imagine (or by meditative technique learn to produce the result) that the alleged layers of conceptual interpretation are lifted off the raw data of experience itself, one will come to have the notion of a pure experience. One question to ask here is, why suppose that anything whatever remains? In the case of tasting a lemon drop, remove the sense of a smooth hard round object on my tongue and a lemon taste, and nothing whatever is left. In the case of sensing the presence of a holy God while partaking of the Eucharist (or taking Communion, or sitting at the Lord's Table), remove the sense of a holy presence, and your religious experience is gone. Neither tasting a lemon drop nor sensing a holy presence inherently is a matter of *interpreting X as Y* or *applying a concept to X*, which can then be followed by *encountering Y itself* or *experiencing X itself*. A vivid imagination might feel the pressure of a tooth on the tongue and interpret this as tasting a lemon drop, or feel a flutter in the diaphragm and apply the concept *presence of a holy being* to it. But without powerful argument for thinking that this is always what happens in such cases, it would be highly implausible to offer this as a descriptive analysis of the experiences in question. Even a hard-nosed skeptic can do his pious colleagues the courtesy of supposing that they can distinguish the phenomenology of a sense of the presence of God from the phenomenology of being nervous or having heartburn.

The proponent of the one-type-of-religious-experience-per-tradition, or many-types, line claims that concepts are constitutive of experiences and invalidly infers that experiences are somehow imprisoned by the concepts that partially constitute the experiences. Nonetheless, this view will rightly insist that, for example, *seeming to have been enlightened* is not a concept that one can prize off an experience and then find the real experience underneath; if it seems to one that one has been enlightened, then such things as feeling enlightened and believing that one has been enlightened are not extrinsic to the experience itself. So feeling and so believing involve having and using concepts, in particular the concept of being enlightened. Hence having and using concepts is not extrinsic to having the experience in question. Similar comments apply to any religious experience. Thus insofar as "pure experience" is not a misleading name for not having any experience, any really contentless experience it referred to would not be a matter of becoming enlightened (or otherwise having a religious experience).

"MYSTICAL" EXPERIENCES

One typical sort of description of a mystical experience tells us that the experience is "pure" or "contentless." Whatever else is meant by so describing an experience, presumably there being any distinct objects or elements in the experience is ruled out. Such experiences, so to say, are alleged to be blank or seamless or divisionless or homogeneous or such as to give rise to no distinctions. Hence, it is argued, no concepts apply to such experiences, for where concepts apply there are distinctions to be made. A proponent of the one-type line typically argues that since pure experiences are not even in part constituted by concepts – since they are somehow free of concepts altogether – they are not imprisoned by any concepts. Experiences that lack divisions do not live in conceptual prisons.

Two faults devastate such reasoning. One is that experiences to which no concepts applied could not be the things about which the one-type proponent's claims are made. The very nature of such supposed experiences would prevent its being true of them that they occur, or have this or that significance, or are those experiences that are intimately related to becoming enlightened – for any of that would entail the applicability of concepts to those experiences. The other is that "contentless experience," understood literally, is a contradiction in terms, and understood nonliterally refers to experiences to which some sort of description is applicable and hence (on the perspective held by the one-type view) in which some distinction is present.

Concepts are often thought of as necessarily connected to, because abstracted from, sensory experience. As our discussion of ineffability attempted to show, this way of thinking suffers from both an impoverished view of the range of concepts and an overmodest perspective on the power of concepts. The concept of a pure experience is a concept. One who reports to the effect *My current experience is seamless* applies several concepts to an experience, and removing the words "my" and "current" reduces the list but does not reduce it to zero. Given the previous long discussion of ineffability, we need not enter again into the ways in which this fact is devastating to the notion of a pure experience.

There is an appeal to meditation that is relevant here; the contention is that in meditation one can observationally or phenomenologically discern that there are layers of conceptual interpretation superimposed on an experience that in itself is featureless. But suppose that one has a sequence of experiences of the following sort. In experience number one, a complex set of concepts is applied. In experience number two, a less complex set is applied. Then the sequence continues as long as you like, provided it ends in an experience to which only such concepts as *is an experience, is seamless, has color properties, does not seem to be of any physical object or (other?) person,* and the like, apply. What, exactly, *follows* from there being such a series? Of course meditators are taught to interpret such sequences as showing that persons and physical objects are only phenomena or appearances or at most constructs out of something simpler, and that all there really is, is an unindividuated stream of being. But our question is not "How are people taught to interpret it?" but "What reason is there for interpreting it that way?" One could see this series as the progressive loss of perception and knowledge, a regression from experiencing the world in its rich complexity to seeming to experience only a sort of grainless tapioca. Why is this interpretation worse than the opposite?

Besides the claim that one who follows certain meditative paths and is erudite in meditational technique can have experiences in which one, as it were, observes conceptual layers being peeled off of one's experiences until one reaches a state of seamless consciousness, there is also the claim that the experience of infants is seamless as is that of adults who are asleep or on drugs or otherwise have escaped from the alleged clutches of conceptual operations. The obvious question regarding the first sort of consideration is whether infants are a sensible model for epistemological perfection. Drug experiences vary greatly in their content and structure and are hardly typically seamless; neither are dreams. Moreover, it is unclear why dream or drug experiences should be granted much by way of positive epistemological status.

The obvious reply to this response seems to be the claim that reality just is a seamless stuff – that it is infant (and similar) experience, assumed to be without structure or distinctionful content, that corresponds to, or properly grasps, the state of things. But then some reason should be provided for this claim, and the appeal to infant and similar experience in *its* defense is no longer open once the claim has been made that the reason for regarding such experience as reliable is that it corresponds to, or is a grasping of, what really is there. That would be analogous to saying, "Of course I'm not lying; just ask me." (I waive the question of whether infant experience *is* seamless.)

CAUSAL POWERS AND PURE EXPERIENCES

Perhaps the idea is that experiences lacking content and phenomenology can have causal powers that distinguish them from other experiences and, as it were, give them a toehold on existence. It is dubious that causal powers can be possessed by anything that does not possess them by virtue of its having other properties that are not causal powers. Lead, paper, and turnips have whatever causal powers they have by virtue of their mass, chemical composition, and the like. The thoughts *Two is greater than one, Entailment is transitive,* and *Lincoln was a later U.S. president than Washington* have their causal powers by virtue of being mental states that have the content and phenomenology they possess. A mental state without content or phenomenology would have its causal powers by virtue of whatever properties it had, content and phenomenology aside. What properties are they? Perhaps simply *being a state of consciousness?* But then the question arises again as to whether anything can be a state of consciousness without having other properties. *Being a state of consciousness* is an indeterminate property, and an item has an indeterminate property only by virtue of the determinate properties it possesses. Reference to causal powers of an item is entirely vacuous without reference as well to the non–causal-power properties on which causal-power properties ride piggyback.

One could grant that conscious states that lack content and phenomenology have non–causal-power properties by virtue of which they have their causal powers, but admit that one had no idea of what these properties might be. But, one could go on, we know what causal powers these states possess. This, of course, raises the question as to *how* we know this. Not by observation of the states; a state lacking content and phenomenology is not something one could notice oneself having. Not (in many of the traditions that favor such states at any rate) by noticing that I am not now having any states, for (in the view of these traditions) that would be the same as my not existing at all, in which case my observational powers would be thoroughly limited. Presumably, then, it is by inference that we know of the existence of these contentless and phenomenologyless states. The argument for them will be that things occur that we cannot explain by reference to physical states, or to contentful mental states, and that could not be explained by any causal power that any physical states or contentful mental states might have. So they must be explained by noncontentful mental states.

These mental states, on the line being pursued, will not have structure or content, so it is dubious that we can be conscious of them. One might introduce the notion of an unconscious mental state and suggest that *these* are the relevant possessors of causal powers. There is an ambiguity in "being conscious" that should be noted. In one sense, a conscious state is a state of consciousness. In another sense, it is a conscious state that we are conscious of. If *being a conscious state* is a sufficient condition of *being a mental state*, then it makes sense to use "mental" instead of "conscious" to express the former notion, and unconscious states will be mental states of which we are not conscious. In any case, the claim that there are unconscious states – states of consciousness that we are not conscious of and whose noncausal properties we are ignorant of, but whose causal powers we must refer to in order to explain certain phenomena – is vacuous without being replaced by a particular version of the theme. In order for us to have a hypothesis at all, we must be told what their existence would explain and what properties they have by virtue of which their existence is explanatory. A general statement to the effect that there are unconscious states is not logically incoherent, but it also does nothing to entail that there are any "pure" experiences. Neither does reference to specifically conceived unconscious states.

In any case, while the one-type-of-experience perspective is of interest as a sharply contrasting view to the one-type-of-experience-per-tradition view, it cannot adequately account for the data noted in Chapter 1 or survive the critique of the varieties of ineffability. An experience can no more be ineffable than can God. An experience to which *no* concept applies, of which *no* description is true, is impossible for reasons discussed earlier in detail. There can be experiences in which one "relaxes one's mind" and entertains neither visual or other imagery on the one hand nor propositional content on the other. Such experiences contain no informational content. To take them as revelatory of the nature of things is like discovering that the square root of nine is the color red; you can *say* that you have done so, but nothing consistent corresponds to the claim. Since the experiences in question have no informational content, they can have no informational content that is true. Perhaps the idea is that, as it is in itself, reality is *like* those experiences by way of being seamless or distinctionless. Then the experiences in question only serve as one term of a proposed analogy (a dubious one insofar as one can be aware of having an experience of letting one's mind relax, for such a state has phenomenological content, is not propertyless, and is nonrepresentational and so does not represent reality as seamless). Dubiousness aside, the analogy provides no experiential evidence for the claim *Reality is seamless,* which then requires support from some other source.

One might suggest that the same sorts of descriptions that might apply to a self-authenticating experience also might apply to a pure experience if the latter is coherently conceived – some such description as *It seemed that I became enlightened* or *There appeared to be no distinctions* might do in this regard. Of course such experiences then are not pure, and even about them as "impure" experiences three things should be noted. First, these descriptions must be merely phenomenological if self-authentication is involved. Second, it does not follow from the self-authenticated phenomenological claims, if there are any, that one *was* enlightened or that there *are* no distinctions. Third, *There appeared to be no distinctions* amounts to *No distinctions appeared.* If one is describing purely private psychological states, perhaps this justifies concluding *There were no distinctions within the experience* (with the proviso that the experiencer may nonetheless be distinct from the experience). But if one wishes to make or to infer some claim beyond the fact of one's having had a seamless experience – a claim, say, that no distinctions are real or that nothing really bears any relation to another thing – that

goes enormously beyond what has been experientially confirmed. Our previous discussion of ineffability has this cognitive import regarding experience: Experiences have some
content or other. Content inherently is describable; to have
an experience is to conceptualize.

THE ONE-TYPE-OF-EXPERIENCE-PER-TRADITION VIEW

The subject of a religious experience, typically at least, is
something of an expert on what it is like to have the sort of
experience that she has. Of course other things besides experience may affect the content of the description of an experience by its subject. Considerations of prestige and
acceptance may lead a subject to offer the type of descriptions best accepted in her tradition. She may overdescribe
the experience, or underdescribe it; she may claim that the
experience had properties that it lacked or lacked properties
that it had. It is typical that a religious tradition, as it were,
supply forms for its adherents to use in reporting their religious experiences. Still, subjects of religious experience, even
if they are members of these traditions, tend not to use these
forms to report eating breakfast, getting the mail, or taking a
walk. Nor does everyone who has a religious experience
belong to a religious tradition or, member or not, use traditional language to describe her experience.

In some circles it is in fashion to hold that religious experience is so much a product of religious concepts and beliefs
that it cannot possibly be evidence that such beliefs are true.
If religious experience inherently is hostage to religious belief, its testimony on behalf of the fine character of its warden
should be seen as unbridled self-interest. To a large extent,
the source of this perspective lies in a vaguely conceived but
widely influential assumption regarding the nature of human experience, namely, that the subject of experience
(some kinds of experiences, or all – but if only some kinds,
one needs deep reasons for this restriction if it is not to be
simply arbitrary) is active in *producing* experience as much as

undergoing it. Hence, it is claimed, experience can best be seen as more a reflection of the subject than a revelation of any object of the experience.

Such views usually are traced to Immanuel Kant's *Critique of Pure Reason*, where Kant claims to show that certain basic concepts, which he calls categories (for example, *substance*, *event*, and *cause*), are applicable in such a way as to yield knowledge only of items that possibly are sensed. His arguments basically are of two sorts. He claims that attempts to apply basic concepts beyond the approved range permit us to develop antinomic argument pairs. An antinomic argument pair is a brace of arguments of the following sort: (i) Both arguments plainly are logically valid; (ii) both arguments rest on, or presuppose, some highly plausible version of the principle of sufficient reason; (iii) each premise of each argument seems plainly true; (iv) the conclusion of one argument is the logical contradiction of the conclusion of the other. Kant's famous examples of such arguments seem to most philosophers less impressive than criterion (iii) suggests. It is quite unclear that Kant presents, or that there are, any genuine antinomic argument pairs.

The other main sort of argument for the restriction of basic concepts to the approved scope contends that such propositions as *The shortest distance between two points is a straight line* and even $7 + 5 = 12$ are necessarily true but not true by definition. Their necessity, it is alleged, can only (or at least best) be explained by holding that what such propositions are true of are our spatial and mathematical constructions. Similarly, the nondefinitional necessary truth of *Nothing can be red all over and green all over simultaneously* as well as the most basic principles of physics can only (or at least best) be explained by holding that what such propositions are true of is our sensory constructions. As one might expect, Kant's remarks concern a deep and complex issue, the nature of necessity, which he construes as nonverbal, nonconventional, and nonempirical, and yet (except for logical necessity) as complexly dependent on human nature. Kant's account has won relatively few advocates. If true mathematical propositions are true with logical necessity, Kant's more important examples fail him, for then their truth can be known by our seeing that their denials are self-contradictory. Even if *A straight line is the shortest distance between two (Euclidean) points* lacks a formally contradictory denial – even if the result of properly symbolizing it and then affirming its contradictory does not yield a proposition of the form *P and not-P* – it does not follow that the proposition is not true with logical necessity. The denial of the proper symbolization of *If Sally draws a square, then Sally draws a figure* is not of the form *P and not-P*, but plainly the proposition is a logically necessary truth. Not all logical necessity is discernible by eliciting formally contradictory structures from the denials of properly symbolized, necessarily true propositions, using logical techniques currently at our disposal. Even if *A straight line is the shortest distance between two (Euclidean) points is true*, but not a logically necessary truth, discovering its truth may be a matter of learning something mind-independently true about the structure of Euclidean space.

In the *Critique of Pure Reason* Kant argues for more than the restricted application range of basic concepts (which, roughly, is what he calls, "transcendental idealism"). He also contends that their proper applications within the sanctioned range do yield knowledge (a position that he calls "empirical realism"). It is arguable that his powerful defense of empirical realism, plus the weakness of his case for transcendental idealism, justifies the removal of the adjective in front of "realism."

It is plain that it is not the arguments for transcendental idealism that constitute its broad attraction. The general idea is that somehow we contribute so much to our experience that experience yields only knowledge of itself. It does not yield information concerning something that exists whether experienced or not or at least not of something *as* it exists whether experienced or not. This notion is a sort of philosophical chocolate that attracts thinkers who otherwise would not be expected to have similar diets. Here are some contemporary expressions of it relevant to our current interests:

> The most refined mysticism, the most exalted spiritual experience is *partly* a product of the social and intellectual environment in which the personal life of the mystic has formed and nurtured. There are not experiences of a sort which are independent of preformed expectations or unaffected by the prevailing beliefs of the time. . . . Mystical experiences will be, perforce, saturated with the dominant ideas of the groups to which the mystic belongs, and they will reflect the expectations of that group and that period. (Rufus Jones)

> All "givens" are also the product of the processes of "choosing," "shaping," and "receiving." That is, the "given" is appropriated through acts which shape it into forms which we can make intelligible to ourselves given our conceptual constitution, and which structure it in order to respond to the specific contextual needs and mechanisms of consciousness of the receiver. . . . This means that the mystic . . . is also a shaper of his experience. (Steven Katz)

RELATIVISM DECLINED

The viewpoint under discussion grants that there can be no such thing as a conceptless experience – neither an experience to which no concepts apply nor an experience whose having does not require the possession of concepts by its subject. The fact is that the religious experiences people describe themselves as having plainly involve the use of concepts by subjects of these experiences. On the view that such experiences cannot be evidence for religious belief, presumably one's concepts (or beliefs) either *block out* what is there to be experienced (as a person traumatized by dogs may not see the retriever lying on the rug) or else *create* the experience (so that its occurrence just tells us about the experiencer). A halfway view on which *some* concepts are simply created and forced on an experience whose content is *partly* determined by what is there to be experienced leaves open the possibility that there be verification and disconfirmation procedures by which one can tell, at least to some degree, what exists and what properties it has, and that appeal to experience plays a large role in this telling. Chapters 10, 11, and 12, in effect, define and defend this possibility. It is just this possibility, in religious contexts, that the view in question is intended to rule out altogether.

Further, the hypothesis is not that any old concept or belief can produce any old experience. This view is no more plausible than the view that *all* of one's experiences are caused by one's concepts and beliefs. The view that all of our experiences are created by our beliefs is self-defeating. Let the one-type-of-religious-experience-per-religious-tradition view be *the Thesis*. Either one accepts the Thesis or one does not. If one does, then according to the Thesis one will have experiences that "confirm" that belief. If one does not, one will have experiences that "disconfirm" the Thesis. Even conceptual experience will be a wax nose that one's beliefs and concepts twist into their own preferred shape. So ends rational discussion, including any attempt of the defenders of the Thesis to provide any grounds for thinking the Thesis true. But that is not at all what defenders of the Thesis want or accept. So the question arises as to how one introduces limits that allow the view to escape the conclusion that all experiential evidence (including whatever evidence reflection concerning the Thesis might turn up) is worthless. If religious beliefs cannot be evidence because in some fashion or to some unacceptable degree (how measured?) religious beliefs produce religious experiences, what exactly prevents one who buys this much from buying the analogous claim regarding each type of experience other than religious, however many types there may be?

To say that experience is imprisoned by concepts is to accept some such view as the following. Suppose, not implausibly, that there are things that exist independently of any human being experiencing them. These items will have properties, and so to experience these items will be to experience items that have properties. Since even very modest objects have an infinite number of properties, it seems not mere humility to suggest that our experience of mind-independent items will not be a matter of our experiencing them in all of their propertied splendor. Insofar as we experience things that exist independent of our experience, presumably we will fall between the extremes. We will not experience *all* of anything's properties. But if we experience *none* of an item's properties, it seems not extravagant to deny that we experience it at all. So when we experience something, we experience some of its properties. *John experiences X* entails *There is some property that X has, and that John experiences X as having*. This speaks to *a* necessary condition of experiencing something, not to the sufficient condition of doing so. We can know, in a nonimprisoned way, that what we seem to experience either exists or not, and that either it has the properties we seem to experience it as having, or it does not. Why (assuming possible experiential evidence to the contrary) cannot there seeming to be something be evidence that there is that thing, even in religious contexts? Is *conceptual* experience unimprisoned, but all other experience imprisoned?

The issue as to whether experience is imprisoned by concepts of course is not decided in the one-type-per-tradition view's favor by the fact that all experiences are conceptual. To say that experience is conceptual at least is to say that *John experiences X* entails *John applies concepts to X*. A definition of applying a concept to something will be helpful here. Let us say that concept *C* fits *X* if *C* is the concept of property *A* and *X* has *A*. To apply a property concept to *X* is for one to experience *X* as having *A*. If it indeed is true that *John experiences X* entails *John applies some concept to X that fits X*, then *experiencing X* requires *applying concepts to X*. It does not even follow from any of this that one is *active* in applying a concept to anything. It is consistent with all of the foregoing that the experiencer *recognizes* that an item has a property that it plainly has – recognizes that *is A* fits *X* – and applies concepts to *X* only in that sense.

Presumably, then, those who hold that concepts imprison experience will wish the application of concepts to be *creative, and so active,* on the part of the experiencer. It will not be the case that $X's$ *being A* causes Kim to apply the concept *being A* to X. Of course even this will not prevent its being the case both that John applies the concept *being A* to X and that X *is A* is true. Indeed, the item may nonetheless have the property that the application of the concept to it suggests, and there may be experiential evidence that this is so.

It is logically possible that whenever one is in the presence of any item whatever, one has an experience in which it seems that the item has each of a large set of properties, that the item indeed has all of the properties it seems to one that it has, that anyone who rightly believes the item has those properties properly can be said to know a good deal about the item, and yet that the item plays no role whatever in causing the experience. But it hardly seems sensible to call this a world in which concepts *imprison* experience, unless one has in mind "white collar" prisons, and one's being so favored epistemically is most naturally explained by the object playing a not insubstantial causal role in one's knowledge. Hence the sheer fact that having an experience of X involves applying concepts to X has no comfort to offer to imprisonment theorists.

Each person has various beliefs. For concepts to affect one's experience, on one variety of the view that they do so, will be for one's beliefs to affect one's experience. The suggestion that this occurs, without some specification as to how, is not worth much. One might, then, suggest this: Any property that any item is experienced as having is a property the subject's beliefs caused the subject to experience the item as having. Then, one might say, one's experiences are *totally imprisoned* by one's beliefs. Alternatively, one might say that some properties, or all properties, that some entities seemed to have were properties the experiencer or subject experienced them as having only because the subject had the particular beliefs that she had. Then one would need to say what properties or items were involved. Thus there are var-

ious possible degrees of imprisonment that one might ascribe to experience. Consider the strongest version of the
imprisonment theory as we have conceived it:

> (1) For any property anything seems to anyone to have,
> its seeming to have that property is caused by the
> beliefs that the experiencer has.

Whatever else one can say about (1), it is problematic in two
ways. For one, there are experiences that do not seem to
their subject to be experiences of anything that exists, if it
exists at all, independent of its being experienced. *Experience
E is caused by A* does not entail that *Experience E is an experience
of A*. A dream caused by eating too much pizza, a daydream
elicited by an odor like that of a familiar childhood place,
dizziness produced by overexertion, and a headache caused
by having struck one's head on a low beam, are not experiences, respectively, of pizza, an odor, overexertion, or the
beam. Experiences such as being in pain, itching, feeling
nauseated, feeling dizzy, losing one's balance, feeling generalized anxiety, experiencing generalized euphoria, and the
like, have no object, apparent or real. But these experiences
have a certain phenomenology, a particular content, that distinguishes each from the others. So if we want the strongest
version of the sort of thesis (1) represents, we shall have to
replace it by something like:

> (1a) For any experience that one has, the entire content of
> that experience is caused by the beliefs that the ex-
> periencer has.

The other problem can be noted once a further specification
of the view is provided. A view such as (1) or (1a) obviously
raises the question as to how the belief–experience linkage
goes. Perhaps the least implausible account is also the simplest: A belief that X exists produces an experience in which
it seems to the experiencer that X exists. On this account,
however, experiential disconfirmation seems impossible,
save in the case of logically incompatible beliefs, each of
which (simultaneously) produces an experience that pro-

vides evidence against the other belief. No view that makes experiential disconfirmation of beliefs an impossibility has much plausibility.

THE VIEW SHARPENED

The basic thesis of the view at hand can be stated more precisely if we approach it by stages. First, there are certain logically necessary conditions of a person's having an experience. One must exist and be conscious. There must be some experiential content. Second, there are certain causally necessary conditions of a human being's having an experience. The person's body must be alive and not comatose, in the presence of sufficient oxygen, and the like. There are other conditions that perhaps are logically, or perhaps causally, necessary. The experiencer must belong to a linguistic community and participate in a form of life and have something of an at least implicit worldview. The context of a religious experience – the set of conditions necessary to the occurrence of the experience – of course is much more detailed in any particular case than these general remarks suggest. There may be practices that one must engage in, and beliefs that one must have, in order to have any particular religious experience. These vary, of course, from one type of religious experience to another. Indeed, on the view that we are discussing, it is precisely that variance that makes an experience of one type differ in type as well as token from another. On that view, the particular practices, techniques, and beliefs that one must engage in, apply, and have in order to have a given religious experience together have this feature: Given them, the content of the experience *cannot* be other than what it is. It is not clear whether the claim is that it is logically impossible that an experience's content be other than what it is given these precedents, or merely causally impossible, so we will have to keep both readings in mind.

If it is logically impossible that the precedents be followed by, or give rise to, an experience with a content other than what it is, one thing that follows is this. Suppose that

Melinda is a devout, learned Theravada Buddhist. She wants to know the truth about matters religious, and seeks that truth with all her heart. Being a Theravada Buddhist, her religious beliefs do not include belief in a Creator and Providence. She does not so much disbelieve in God as she fails to regard whether there is a God or not as something of any religious interest or relevance, a perspective that monotheists will not share. She masters the practices and techniques, and has the beliefs, requisite to seeking Nirvana, and just as she seems about to reach Nirvana, she has a vision of God similar to that of Isaiah in the temple. As a result, she becomes a devout monotheist. On the stronger reading of the one-type-of-experience-per-tradition (and since there are many traditions, the many-type) view, this scenario is logically impossible. On that view it is logically impossible that Melinda's practices, techniques, and beliefs, being what they are, be followed by a numinous experience. But plainly the scenario described is not logically inconsistent; what it describes could occur without falsifying the principle of noncontradiction. But on the many-types view, it cannot describe even a miracle. Hence that view is false. If causal laws are necessary truths, then again the scenario described cannot occur; the description would be contradictory. Since the scenario plainly is not logically impossible, the stronger version (and the weaker version, too, if the relevant causal laws are logically necessary truths) of the one-type-per-tradition view is mistaken.

Similarly, on the stronger reading, it is logically impossible that religious experiences occur spontaneously, without the requisite engagement with practices, techniques, and beliefs. The same applies if causal laws are necessary truths. If causal laws are contingently true, then a miracle could occur, but one would be required in order that a religious experience occur without its characteristic precedents. Thus Katz's claim, however interpreted, entails that no spontaneous religious experiences occur. The stronger view entails that it is logically impossible that they occur. But it is not logically impossible that such experiences spontaneously occur, and in fact sometimes it appears that they do occur. So for another reason the stronger version of the view should be rejected.

Similarly, it follows from the many-types position (strong version) that it is logically impossible that drugs cause religious experiences (or experiences with corresponding phenomenologies) in cases in which the subject of an experience has not engaged in practices, techniques, and beliefs that would produce the experience. It is not logically impossible that drugs produce religious experiences in nonengaging drug users. So again the view is to be rejected.

If causal laws are contingent, then the scenario is logically possible. On the weaker version of the many-types view, one must add to it some such proviso as "miracles aside," and since every numinous experience, if monotheism is true, involves a miracle, this qualification makes the position vacuous. It then says that veridical numinous experiences do not occur, unless they do occur.

On the weaker version, without the proviso that renders it vacuous, it follows merely that spontaneous religious experiences never happen. In fact, they do sometimes happen. Hence the weaker version is simply empirically false.

IS THE VIEW JUSTIFIED IN ITS LIMITATIONS OF ITS OWN SCOPE?

It is not clear that there is any good reason to restrict what the many-types view says about the concept-imprisoned status of religious experiences to religious experiences alone. Why should it not be true of a scientist who has been trained to run a certain sort of experiment, is devoted to a theory that says that a certain event will occur under certain experimental conditions, and knows that her theory is false if that event does not occur, that she will have an experience in which that event at least seems to occur once she has created the relevant experiential conditions? How is it even possible, along the lines of the many-types view, that there be experiential refutation of anything a subject believes that is recognized by the subject as really being a refutation (or contrary evidence or counterexample)? After all, science too has its paradigms and practices, its societies and conventions, as much of the history and philosophy of science in recent decades have emphasized. Further, various cultures have various notions of commonsense beliefs and practices and expectations. Does this fact render their experiences of objects conceptually imprisoned and hence evidentially worthless?

It is not clear whether the intent of the many-types view is to say that it is the actual details of a subject's conceptual framework, or what seem to the subject to be such, that determine the phenomenology of his experiences. No subject has incorrigible knowledge of the details of the world-view that he in fact embraces; mistakes can be made about such matters. If it is the actual, not the mistakenly assumed, features of one's worldview that determine the phenomenology of one's experience, one could be surprised by that phenomenology and find that one thought that one's worldview had been refuted when it had not. But since on the many-types view no experiential confirmation of religious beliefs (from religious experience anyway) is possible, presumably no experiential disconfirmation of such beliefs is possible either.

LOGIC AND ALLEGED IMPRISONMENT

The principle of noncontradiction, stated regarding properties, says that it is logically impossible that anything whatever (including a property) have logically incompatible properties. The principle of noncontradiction, stated regarding propositions, says that it is logically impossible that a proposition be both true and false. It follows that if one believes of some item that it both has and lacks a property, or of some statement that expresses a contradiction that it is true, one believes falsely. The principle is true of things, and so of thought about things. These basic and homely truths are expressed in concepts, and having the conceptual experience of seeing that the principle of noncontradiction is true no doubt is at least in part constituted by concepts. Nothing in this entails that the principle of noncontradiction is not true or that the conceptual experience in which one sees it to be true is unreliable. That an experience is at least in part constituted by concepts – or by the application of concepts – thus does not *universally* condemn it. What is still unclear is why that fact should *ever* condemn an experience to the status of not being evidence for claims whose content is matched up properly with the content of the experience. If it is the case that if experiences meet certain conditions, then they are evidence for claims properly based on them, and it is the case that at least some religious experiences meet these conditions, then the fact that all experiences are such that their occurrence involves subjects having concepts that at least in part are constitutive of these experiences will not entail anything about those experiences being imprisoned by those concepts. The reasoning pursued in Chapters 10–12 contends that at least some religious experiences do occur in such conditions.

DOXASTIC PRACTICE PHILOSOPHY OF RELIGION

In the Madison *Capital Times Weekender* magazine for July 7–8, 1990, in an article by Thomas D. Elias, the following appears:

> Is Dolly Parton religious? Most definitely, she says. "I pray every day, throughout the day," she declaims. "I ask God to be my business partner, my photographer, my lawyer, my accountant, my producer. I ask him to be there every day and lead me. He lets me learn the lessons there are to learn. I always talk to God, and I always believe He will answer me. And He does. God has never spoken to me in a voice – I'd jump out of my skin if I heard Him say 'Yo, Dolly!' – but He answers me with a feeling inside. The world would be a better place if people stopped running from God."

It is not part of our present purpose to ask whether or not God is the cause of the feeling inside Ms. Parton, or to discuss whether or not her descriptions of the ways of God, at least relating to her life, are entirely accurate. My claim is simply this: Supposing (as seems likely) that Ms. Parton's perspective here is that of a large portion of American Protestant piety (and of other pietistic traditions), her feeling is not evidence that God exists. Her religious practice of course presupposes the existence of God, but it does not provide evidence that this presupposition is true. (Nothing that Ms. Parton says here supposes that it does provide evidence.) If one follows what some have called *doxastic practice philosophy of religion,* such feelings are evidence that God exists. This I deny.

A doxastic practice is a way of dealing with experience that interprets it as evidence for certain claims. We typically take our sensory experience to be evidence that we are surrounded by the physical objects that appear to occupy our immediate environment. This "taking" is a doxastic practice.

The defense of doxastic practice philosophy of religion goes as follows. If we do not suppose that there are physical objects, then our practice of taking particular sensory experiences as evidence for particular physical objects having certain properties (and hence for the existence of the particular objects) will no longer operate. If we do not suppose that God exists, then the pietistic doxastic practice of taking particular religious experiences (for example, Ms. Parton's feelings) as evidence of God's having done certain things (and hence for the existence of the God who so acts) will no longer operate. If we do assume that there are physical objects, then a given sensory experience will provide evidence for some such claim as *There is a blue cup on the card table,* and thereby *A blue cup exists* and *A card table exists,* and hence in their turn for *There are cups and tables* and so for *There are physical objects.* Similarly, assuming that God exists, religious experience provides evidence for such claims as *God led me to become a minister,* and *God made me see the folly of my addictions and gave me strength to overcome them.* Each of these claims, of course, entails *God exists.* So if religious experience is evidence for those claims, it is evidence for God's existence.

Our sensory doxastic practice is rationally pursued. The analogous pietistic doxastic practice is thus rational, though perhaps not obligatory, to engage in. Perhaps the sensory practice is pragmatically inescapable, whereas the pietistic practice is not. But in the relevant respect – namely, whether they are reasonably followed – they are alike. This, then, is the argument for doxastic practice philosophy of religion.

Various differences between sensory and religious experience were explored earlier in this chapter. For now, one difference deserves emphasis. For the relevant practices, while there can be, and presumably there are, a multitude of physical objects, there is, and presumably can be, only one God. For the typical pietistic tradition, at most only one God requires religious attention because *necessarily* there are not more gods than one. Thus while no particular physical item is presupposed by the practice related to our sensory experience, a particular divine being is presupposed by the practice related to religious experience.

To this fact another must be added. Within our sensory doxastic practice, sensory experience may provide evidence *against* the existence of any particular physical object that is said to exist, without this in any way calling into question the substantial support sensory experience provides for the claim that there are physical objects. The claim that there are physical objects allegedly presupposed by the sensory doxastic practice is in no wise threatened if the overall evidence tells me that there is no bear where I thought I saw one. But within a pietistic doxastic practice, no religious experience can count as evidence against the existence of God without its casting some question on the truth of, or providing some sort of evidence against, the presupposition of the pietistic doxastic practice.

The disanalogy that these two facts comprise is of crucial importance. Given the disanalogy, one practice can be rational to pursue, and the other not rational to pursue. Precisely this is true.

Within the pietistic practice, depending on the details, one may be permitted to falsify such propositions as *God forgave me for lying about the car* or *God led me to take that job*. If one prays for forgiveness for lying and does not feel forgiven, one may decide that one's repentance has been insincere. If the job turns out to involve cheating customers, one may conclude that one misread the signs. But that God has not forgiven a sin or led someone to take a job does not entail that God does not exist. No experience interpreted within pietistic practice is permitted to provide evidence that God does not exist. Nor is there any circumstance in which the nonoccurrence of an experience is permitted to provide evidence that there is no God. God always answers prayers, but sometimes the answer is no. No answer is a negative answer, and a negative answer presupposes an answerer as much as a positive answer does. But if the pietistic doxastic practice is such that neither the occurrence nor the nonoccurrence of any religious experience is permitted to count against the existence of God, then even if God does not exist one could not discover this by reference to religious experience, interpreted within that practice. If no experience could count as evidence against a belief, then none can count for it either. Within pietistic practice, no experience can count as evidence against God's existence. So, within pietistic practice, no experience can provide evidence in favor of God's existence.

The sensory practice is another matter. Within it, nothing is evidence for there being physical objects without first being evidence that some particular object exists. But for any sensory evidence that some particular physical object exists, there are sensory experiences whose occurrence, or nonoccurrence, would be evidence that the object in question does not exist. The sensory practice plays fair. The pietistic practice does not. Thus the one practice can yield evidence and the other cannot. This disanalogy is crucial and final.

Thus far, we have joined the defense of the pietistic doxastic practice in supposing that our sensory doxastic practice assumes that there are physical objects and that the pietistic practice presupposes that God exists. In fact, the sensory practice need not presuppose that there are physical objects.

It can remain neutral about that matter until the evidence is in. My seeing a tree can be evidence that there is a tree, and so that physical objects exist, without my having to make any prior assumptions about there being trees or physical objects of any sort. The pietistic practice, save insofar as it contains what at least appear to be direct experiences of God, cannot get off the ground without a prior assumption to the effect that God exists. The direct experiences of God need not be interpreted within a pietistic doxastic practice in order for them to provide putative evidence for God's existence; indeed, so interpreted, they do *not* provide any such evidence. So if religious experience provides evidence that God exists, it must do so outside the context of pietistic doxastic practice precisely because (as that practice actually operates) it does presuppose that God exists and makes no room for the possibility of experiential evidence against the existence of God. Only in a context in which, if God does not exist, that fact is experientially accessible, and in which, if God exists, that fact is experientially accessible can religious experience provide evidence that God exists. Otherwise, religious experience is no evidence regarding the existence of God, either pro or con.

Of course pietistic doxastic practice might just make its assumption and go on about its internal religious business. The contention here has been that no experience interpreted within it can, so read, provide evidence that God exists.

The argument offered concerning doxastic practice philosophy of religion can be summarized as follows: Both practices take a type of experience (sensory in one instance, religious in the other) to be evidence for a certain claim (that there are physical objects, that God exists); in this respect, they are analogous. (Whether religious experience is either *a* type or a *single* type of experience does not matter for our argument here; if it is not a single type, that is something for the doxasticist to worry about.) Even on the doxasticist's terms they are disanalogous in two respects: the religious practice assumes one God, whereas the sensory practice assumes many objects or at least does not assume merely one, and the religious practice does not allow there to be evidence against *God exists,* whereas the sensory practice does allow there to be evidence against *This object exists* for any physical object you like. The first disanalogy is important only insofar as it leads to there being the second disanalogy. Since a kind of experience can be evidence for the existence of something only if an experience of that kind can be evidence against its existence, sensory experience can be evidence for the existence of an object (and hence for the claim *There is at least one physical object*), whereas doxastically interpreted religious experience cannot be evidence against (nor hence for) God's existence. The obvious reply to this objection goes as follows. Typically, our evidence that there really was not a physical object though there appeared to be one rests on there really being an object that there appears to be. We learn that there really was not a bear where one seemed to be one last night when in the daylight we discover an oddly shaped bush just where the bear seemed to be. Not only is this typical, it is fundamental. Only in cases in which we have evidence that some physical object does exist have we evidence that some other object does not. But then we must assume that some object exists, whatever we do regarding evidence that some object does not exist.

The reply makes this assumption: if our sensory evidence that one object does not exist must involve sensory evidence that some other object does exist, then we must *assume* that some physical object exists. This is false. *Having evidence that X exists is one thing; assuming that X exists is another. The former does not entail the latter.*

The relevant facts are these. Sensory evidence that a particular physical object does not exist typically and perhaps necessarily requires that there be sensory evidence that some other object does exist. Evidence that there are not objects at all will be conceptual – arguments to the effect that there is some hidden contradiction in the concept of a physical object. Evidence that some particular object does not exist can be conceptual (that there be that particular sort of thing is logically impossible) or perceptual (that the object in question exists is incompatible with the properties possessed by one or more objects we have perceptual evidence in favor of). That sensory experience provides evidence in favor of the existence of a particular sort of object is possible only if there can be sensory evidence against there being that type of object. It does not require that we assume that there are physical objects of some sort or other.

One might object that sensory experience, interpreted within its doxastic practice, cannot be evidence against the claim *There are physical objects.* This leads to two responses. First, our epistemic practices regarding sensory experience could allow for two rules (or corresponding practices) that took these shapes: (i) Whenever there sensorially seems to be an X, presumptively there is an X; (ii) whenever there sensorially seems to be an X, and consideration Q applies, all presumption of an X is canceled. Consider the claim: (iii) Q always applies (or: we have better reason than not to suppose that Q always applies). Then it might empirically be the case that (iv) were (iii) so, we would not take sensory experience as evidence for there being objects. But suppose that (iii) is not so. Then (i) and (ii) could hold and it be true that we rightly take sensory experience to be evidence that there are physical objects. This remains true even if we add: (v) Were Q always to apply, then that fact would be evidence *against* there being objects, provided it is true that if there are physical objects, we will have evidence that they exist, and (vi) if it is true that if there are physical objects, then we will have evidence that they exist. Thus claims (i), (ii), (iv), (v), and (vi) can constitute a practice in which sensory experience is rightly taken as evidence that particular physical objects exist, and so that there are physical objects, perfectly compatibly with our having evidence that there are no objects. (One value for Q is "our having evidence that an evil deceiver causes our sensory experiences.") One can argue about whether (i), (ii), (iii), (v), and (vi) describe our actual practice. My point is that whether they do or not, a sensory doxastic practice could be developed that did not disallow our having evidence against there being any physical objects at all. The practice defined by following (i), (ii), (iv), (v), and (vi) is just such a practice; if (iii) were also plausibly accepted, we would have such evidence. If our evidence for (iii) were less strong than our evidence that objects exist, we might be rational in supposing that objects exist, and that we have evidence that they do, even while we accept (ii). But allowing for experiential evidence that God does not exist to be found within experiences interpreted by pietistic doxastic practice is not consistent with pietistic practice – not at any rate as I understand it and have seen it applied. Hence sensory and pietistic doxastic practices are crucially disanalogous to the evidential disadvantage of the latter.

The more important reply is that one need not presuppose that there is any particular physical object, or that there are any physical objects at all, in order for sensory experience to provide evidence that there exist particular physical objects, and so for one to have evidence that *There are physical objects* is true. One might argue that by accepting the simple idea regarding apparent experience of God, one is adopting a doxastic practice regarding those experiences. Perhaps so. But two points should be added. The first is that adopting the simple idea and applying it to apparent experiences of God does not involve one in assuming that God exists. The second point is that one needs to add the simple negative idea in order to yield a practice that permits evidence. Further, and most important for our purposes, one does not need to assume that God exists, or engage in any practices that have that assumption, in order to have experiential evidence that God exists. These claims are defended later in this book.

Part V

The argument from religious experience

10

The argument in
twentieth-century philosophy

In *Religion, Philosophy, and Psychical Research*, the philosopher Charles Dunbar Broad offered an argument that is very like the argument with which I began this book. Broad claimed that (a) people report experiences in which they seem to experience God, (b) these experiences occur cross-culturally, and (c) over time these experiences have a common core (there is a considerable agreement among those who have them as to how to describe what seems to be the object of their experiences). Broad's argument obviously embodies the positive idea. While Broad speaks of "mystical experience," a term that sometimes refers to apparent experience of God but typically refers to other sorts of experience as well, we will not use that term. Religious experiences other than apparent experiences of God will occupy our attention later. His argument does not pay any attention to the negative idea.

One can put Broad's argument in these terms:

(B1) People cross-culturally and over time report having experiences in which it has seemed to them that they experienced God.
(B2) If people cross-culturally and over time report having experiences in which it has seemed to them that they experienced God, then people cross-culturally and over time have seemed to experience God.

So:

(B3) People cross culturally and over time have seemed to experience God.

(B4) If people cross-culturally and over time have seemed to experience God, then there is experiential evidence that God exists.

So:

(B5) There is experiential evidence that God exists.

One might deny that the first premise is true. But it is not significantly controversial whether people in different cultures do report experiences that they take to be experiences of God – experiences that seemed to their reporters to be experiences of God. One might wonder whether these reporters of experiences use the word "God" in a sufficiently common sense so as to support the first premise, and there is a view of religious experience on which even data that appear to confirm the first premise on reflection cannot do so; we argued against that view in Chapter 9. But the first premise is by far less challenged than the fourth. The most frequent (and most interesting) criticism of Broad's argument claims that even if there is the sort of cross-culturally religious phenomenon as the first premise alleges, that still does not provide any evidence that God exists.

That argument, of course, is philosophical, not historical or anthropological. A modest look at part of the twentieth-century history of philosophical argument on this point will be useful in identifying what the basic philosophical issue raised by the fourth premise really is.

MARTIN'S OBJECTION

In his book *Religious Belief*, C. B. Martin challenges Broad's sort of argument by offering a counterargument. Sensory experience, he suggests, does well with regard to both simple ideas. Religious experiences, he thinks, stay shy of the second, negative idea. Hence they are evidentially worthless. He argues, in effect, as follows:

(M1) If people's seeming to experience God is evidence that God exists, then there is a way to test these experiences.
(M2) There is no way to test these experiences.

Hence:

(M3) People's seeming to experience God is not evidence that God exists.

Martin contrasts religious experience with sensory experience in that sensory experience is (a) public, (b) pluralistic (involving multiple sensory modalities), (c) very often, producible pretty much at will, and (d) predictable, whereas experiences that seem to be experiences of God, he says, are none of these.

Martin's argument for the claim that there is no way to test these experiences is at least not far from this:

(M2a) Experiences in which people seem to experience God cannot be checked in the ways in which sensory experiences can be checked.
(M2b) If experiences in which people seem to experience God cannot be checked in the ways in which sensory experiences can be checked, then there is no way to check these experiences.

Thus:

(M2) There is no way to check these experiences.

This argument relies on disanalogies between sensory and religious experience, and claims that these disanalogies rule out apparent experiences of God from possibly being evidence that God exists. We will call this "the sensory checking argument." Martin obviously focuses on the negative idea as well as on the positive. In Martin's view, seeming to experience X by itself does nothing by way of providing evidence in favor of the view that X exists. Even if a proposition of the form *Susan seems to experience X* is true, for Martin this does not even create *presumptive* evidence in favor of X existing. The positive idea has force only when filtered through the negative. Martin offers two sorts of argument, besides the sensory checking argument, in reply to Broad. One argument endeavors to show that *God exists* is what Martin calls a "low-claim assertion." The other argument also concerns checking experiences and rests on the claim that an experience is evidence only after being certified by another experience. We will call the former sort of argument "the reduction argument" and the latter sort "the series of checks argument."

MARTIN'S ATTEMPTED REDUCTION

Martin offers an argument intended to show that the actual content of religious claims is very much less than their apparent content. He distinguishes between *low-claim assertions* and *high-claim assertions*. The former assert something only about an individual's conscious states, and the latter assert something about matters independent of the subject's conscious states. Thus, *I am dizzy* is a low-claim assertion, and *My dog is a beagle* is a high-claim assertion. I suppose that *I am dizzy because my dog is a beagle* is a *mixed* claim. More important, *I see my dog* is a mixed claim, in that it is true only if my dog is there to be seen, and I see it. More generally, any claim of the form *X experiences Y* (where if Y exists, it does so independently of being experienced by X) will be a mixed claim; it will be true only if X has whatever conscious states she must have in order to experience Y, and X actually does experience Y, which of course requires that Y exist. Thus *Jane experienced God* will be a *mixed* claim. Martin does not consider mixed claims. He says: "We are tempted to think that the religious statement ['I have direct experience of God'] must be one sort or the other [a 'low-claim assertion' that is only about one's conscious states or else not a 'low-claim

assertion']. The truth is that *per* impossible it is both at once"
(p. 76).

The argument here seems to go as follows:

(1) A proposition asserted by Jane is a low-claim assertion if its truth conditions concern only Jane's conscious states.

(2) A proposition asserted by Jane is not a low-claim assertion if its truth conditions concern something that
exists independent of Jane's conscious states.

(3) If Jane asserts *I have a direct experience of God*, what she
asserts is true only if God exists.

(4) If God exists, it is false that God depends for existence on Jane's conscious states.

Hence:

(5) *I have direct experience of God* is not a low-claim assertion.

(6) There is no test for the truth of *I have direct experience
of God*.

(7) If there is no test for the truth of a proposition, it is a
low-claim assertion.

Hence:

(8) *I have direct experience of God* is a low-claim assertion.

Hence:

(9) *I have direct experience of God* is a low-claim assertion
and is not a low-claim assertion.

Being a *mixed* claim is one thing. Being *only* a low-level claim
and *not* being only a low-level claim is another. Martin claims
to have shown that the claim *I have direct experience of God* has
this pair of incompatible properties. More carefully, he claims
to show that it is no more than a low-claim assertion and that
hence it is a mistake to treat it (as monotheists do) as if it
were also a high-claim assertion. This claim, in turn, is based
on the view that an experience reported via *I seem to experi-*

ence God cannot be tested, and so (in spite of its structure) ought to be reported via something like *I had a godly experience* – reported, that is, as if it is only a private state that purports to give no information about anything other than the subject's condition. The crux of the argument is Martin's assertion that there is no way of testing such claims as *I have direct experience of God*.

MAVRODES'S RESPONSE

In yet another book, *Belief in God: The Epistemology of Religious Experience*, George Mavrodes suggests that (a) unless an experience is evidence even without its being checked, there is no point in checking, and (b) it is the possibility, not the actuality, of failing a test that is crucial.

Suppose that, prior to being tested, an experience reported via *I seem to see a car in the garage* provided no evidence for *There is a car in the garage*. Then why think that *after* being tested it *will* provide evidence? It is worth asking what, exactly, *testing* amounts to here. Essentially, to test the experience reported by *I seem to see a car in the garage* is to look again or take a picture or walk into the garage for a closer look or try to touch the car or the like. Suppose also that I look again, and again seem to see a car in the garage – one that looks just like the one I seemed to see before. On the assumption that no untested experience has evidential value, my new experience has no evidential value. Why, then, should the fact that my old experience agrees with my new one, which lacks evidential value, be anything in favor of my old experience?

Passing *that* sort of test is worthless. Suppose, then, that we drop the assumption that our untested experience is evidentially worthless. Then there is nothing to prevent my seeming to see a car in the garage being evidence for there being a car there, *before* any testing is done. Then if I seem to see a cow in the field as I ride in a train or bus, and do not have the chance to test my experience, I nonetheless can have evidence that there was a cow in the field. In sum: If one rejects the positive idea, or endeavors to restrict it in the way that assuming that no untested experience is evidence restricts it, one ends up with there being no experiential evidence at all. On these points, Mavrodes plainly is right. Thus the positive idea has its own force. It does not follow, however, that the negative idea is not equally important, or that one can avoid integrating both ideas into a single principle of experiential evidence.

None of this, of course, plays down the importance of testing. Often it matters considerably that one be able to look again, see if further experience supports one's initial conclusion, and the like. An important feature that talk of "testing" highlights is integral to the positive idea. At least seeming to see a car in the garage is *not* evidence that there is a car there if things seem so only under conditions where there would seem to be a car there whether there was one or not. No doubt there are circumstances in which this would be so, but in the absence of any reason to suppose that one is in such circumstances there is no reason to take that explicitly into account. Further, if it is possible that sensory experience count for the claim that there is a car in the garage, then sensory experience can count against there being one there. Similarly, seeming to experience God under conditions where one would seem to do so whether God exists or not will not provide evidence that God exists; and if religious experience can count in favor of the existence of God, then religious experience can count against it.

Nothing Martin says shows that religious experience does not provide evidence against the existence of God, because Martin leaves unclear *why* religious experience cannot be tested, or (to say the same thing in other terms) why it is logically impossible that religious experience provide evidence against the claim that God exists. He points to certain disanalogies between religious experiences and sensory experiences and assumes that these disanalogies entail the untestability of religious experience. He does not show that it is logically impossible that one sort of religious experience provide evidence against the reliability of another or that it is logically impossible that two religious experiences of the same sort speak with different evidential voices. It is only this *possibility* that is required. To test an experience is to see if the evidential promise it already shows is somehow misleading, and in order for me to have evidence that my right foot still has a big toe, I do not have actually to find something wrong with my experiential evidence for that claim, but only be able to detect deficiencies should there be any. The same holds for religious experience.

CONWAY'S ARGUMENT

In the *International Journal for the Philosophy of Religion*, David Conway offers an argument with the same sort of intent as Martin's argument and endeavors to provide a proof of the point that Martin left open. He suggests that experiences that are evidence for the existence of something can be used to check one another – if one both sees and hears the boiling kettle, one's visual experience and one's auditory experience serve as mutual checks without any unhappy regress occurring. One need not check experience *A* by appeal to experience *B*, which one checks by appeal to experience *C*, so that one goes on forever or else ends with an unchecked experience. If we call such mutually relevant experiences "reciprocally checking sets" we can put Conway's argument as follows:

(C1) If people's seeming to experience God is evidence that God exists, then experiences that seem to be of God occur in reciprocally checking sets.

(C2) Experiences that seem to be of God do not occur in reciprocally checking sets.

Thus:

(C3) People's seeming to experience God is not evidence that God exists.

There is an easy response to Conway's argument as stated so far. If there is not substantial disagreement about what properties one is justified in ascribing to the object of experiences that seem to be experiences of God – if, supposing these experiences to be reliable or veridical, God appears essentially the same to all of the subjects of religious experience – then there is no problem to be dealt with. There *could* be disagreement about this matter, and the fact that there is relatively little argues well for the reliability of religious experience. Similarly, if there are reports of sightings of an exotic animal in the neighborhood, and all the received reports agree that there is a feline, furry, black, and powerful creature not seen in the area until recently, the task of those assigned to capture the beast is easier than otherwise. What is crucial is *possible, detectable* disagreement, not *actual, detected* disagreement. So long as detectable disagreement among religious experiences is possible, Conway's argument fails. Such detectable disagreement is possible. Hence Conway's argument fails.

We can put the point in somewhat different terms. Suppose that in typical apparent experiences of God, God appears to have property *A*, whereas in a few God appears to have property *B*, where *God has A* and *God has B* are logically incompatible. Suppose further that *God has A* fits nicely into one or more coherent theologies whereas *God has B* does not. Then why would it not be reasonable to suppose that those experiences in which God seems to have *B* are flawed? If God's seeming to have *B* is essentially what those experiences amount to, then it is plausible to suppose them to be nonveridical. The absence of any such conflict among apparent experiences of God would involve these experiences, taken together, lacking an epistemic feature that otherwise would prevent them all from plausibly being taken to be veridical. We need only compare numinous experiences. Since it is logically possible that numinous experiences collectively are as described, it is possible to have experiential evidence that some apparent experiences of God are unreliable.

An interesting and different alternative is that religious experience be able to provide, not strictly evidence that God does not exist, but evidence that religious experience does not provide evidence that God exists. Suppose that (a) religious experience of kind *A* provided some evidence that *God exists*, (b) religious experience of type *B* provided some evidence for *Either God does not exist or religious experience does not provide evidence that God does exist*, and (c) *A*-evidence and *B*-evidence are of equal force (so far as anyone can tell), and there is no other type of religious experience. Then religious experience (on balance) would provide evidence neither for nor against the existence of God. But religious experience would satisfy the condition that a source of positive experiential evidence for a proposition be a logically possible source of negative experiential evidence.

There is a further interesting element in Conway's argument. The notion of God, he suggests, is the notion of an "absolutely elusive" being (p. 164). God "will be experienced only when he chooses to reveal himself" (p. 170). The problem with the notion of an absolutely elusive being is that there is always an all-too-easy explanation as to why she is not experienced – namely, that she does not want to be experienced. Conway argues, in effect:

(C2a) Experiences that seem to be of God occur in reciprocally checking sets only if there can be experiential evidence against God's existence.

(C2b) There can be experiential evidence against God's existence only if the notion of God is not the notion of an absolutely elusive being.

(C2c) The notion of God is the notion of an absolutely elusive being.

So:

(C2d) There can be no experiential evidence against the existence of God.

Thus:

(C2) Experiences that seem to be of God do not occur in reciprocally checking sets.

RESPONSE TO CONWAY'S ARGUMENT

It is important to sort out from the rest of Conway's argument what in fact is his most interesting and possibly telling point. Let us say that if experiences that seem to be experiences of God occur in different cultures can be compared – that we can tell whether the descriptions of God that the subjects of these experiences offer are mutually consistent (and redundant or complementary), or partly consistent and partly inconsistent – then these experiences are "accessible to comparison." Then consider this reply to Conway:

(RC1) If people cross-culturally and over time have experiences that seem to be experiences of God, and these experiences are accessible to comparison, then these experiences form an evidentially reciprocal set.

(RC2) People do cross-culturally and over time have experiences that seem to be experiences of God and these experiences are accessible to comparison.

Thus:

(RC3) These experiences form an evidentially reciprocal set.

(RC4) If these experiences form an evidentially reciprocal set, then they are evidence that God exists.

So:

(RC5) They are evidence that God exists.

What this reply does, of course, is to rely on the claim that (in principle at least) one can appeal to the whole set of experiential apples in order to see if some experiential apples are bad. The bad ones (if any) will be the ones that are in informational contrast to the majority, unless some good theory dictates otherwise (and then the majority will be in doubt). The reply trades (again) on the notion *apparent experiences of God that we have reason to think unreliable*. Conway's response, in effect, is twofold. One part of it insists that the relevant notion, strictly put, is this: *apparent experience of God that we have reason to think unreliable, provided we have any reason to think that any such experience is unreliable.* The other part is the claim that we can have no reason to think that any such experience is unreliable only if God is not absolutely elusive. If God is absolutely elusive, then there is no religious experience whose failure to occur would be evidence that God does not exist. The nonoccurrence of any religious experience can always be explained by reference to God's elusiveness. Then there can be no evidence from religious experience that God does not exist. The notion *Religious experiences whose failure to occur is evidence against God's existence* necessarily has no application if God is absolutely elusive, and necessarily if God exists, then God is absolutely elusive. Even if God exists, then, there can be no experiential evidence that God exists. This is Conway's basic point, and there is no reply to it in the (RC1–RC5) argument. The (RC1–RC5) argument is fully successful against Martin's critique. It indicates how apparent experiences of God can be tested. But it does not succeed as a reply to Conway. Conway does not see how religious experience could provide evidence that God does *not* exist and hence denies that religious experience can provide evidence that God *does* exist. Unless, then, one can do what the (RC1–RC5) argument does not – namely, develop out of the fact that religious experiences are evidentially reciprocal a way in which religious experience in principle could provide evidence *against* the existence of God – appeal to evidential reciprocality will not answer Conway.

A PHILOSOPHER'S STORY

Philosophers who are deeply skeptical of whether there is any way of making Broad's argument into anything intellectually respectable tend to think that once one takes the simple negative idea into account, it becomes obvious that the argument will not work. David Conway tells this story:

> Suppose that while walking down a quiet street one afternoon, I see before me an elfin sort of man, no more than two feet tall. I think it odd that no one else appears to notice such an unusual creature, but he speaks and tells me that he can

appear to one mortal at a time and even that only once every ten thousand years or so (emphasizing the last two words). Distrusting my eyes, I reach out to touch him, but he assures me that he is quite intangible even to the one person to whom he appears. . . . Finally, he tells me that his allotted time is up and that he must go, mentioning before he disappears that it is his nature to leave no trace whatever since his existence is never completely within our space-time framework.

Having told his story, Conway draws his moral:

The fact that no one else saw my little friend, that he left no physical evidence of his presence, and that the information he gave cannot be "checked out" are not evidence against his being there, because all of these are to be expected, given his "nature." So I have no evidence *against* my perception being a genuine [or veridical] one. My evidence for its being veridical is simply the experience itself. The encounter with the "little man" is only one of an indefinite number of experiences which could be made up which would be, in principle, uncheckable. In such cases, should we adopt the position that because nothing can count for or against our experience being veridical, we should accept it as veridical? To do so would seem to open the way for any sort of lunacy whatever, provided only that the "lunatic" experience is carefully enough guarded so that it is clear that we *could not expect* any checks or tests to be relevant. (Conway, p. 168)

"Checks" obviously means "religious experiences whose non-occurrence would be evidence that God does not exist." Conway is not the only philosopher who supposes both that there can be experiential evidence for God's existence only if there can be such checks, and that no such check is possible.

ROWE'S DEFENSE OF CONWAY'S TYPE OF POSITION

William Rowe defends a similar position, arguing as follows:

(R1) If people's seeming to experience God is evidence that God exists, then there are ways of telling genuine from delusive experiences of God and ways of

227

telling what condition one has to be in, in order to experience God.

(R2) There are no ways of telling genuine from delusive experiences of God and no ways of telling what conditions one has to be in, in order to experience God.

Hence:

(R3) People's seeming to experience God is not evidence that God exists.

Part of Rowe's argument is open to an easy response. It is easy to tell what condition I must be in, in order to experience God. God must exist, and cause me to experience God. Further it is easy to tell whether I am in that condition: If I am, I will have an experience of God, and it will seem to be an experience of God because it is. Otherwise, I will not be in such a condition.

What Rowe has in mind, however, clearly is something like this: A "reducing condition" of an experience cancels out, or at least negatively effects, that experience's evidential force; the reducing occurs relative to some experience as evidence for some statement that the experience otherwise would be evidence for. A "rebutting condition" is evidence against what the experience in question is evidence for; it may be stronger or weaker than, or of the same force as, the experiential evidence it rebuts.

Examples of (at least alleged) reducing conditions and rebutting conditions are needed. There are various social science explanations of religious experience. Psychology, sociology, and anthropology each offer their versions. It is often suggested that whatever reason we have for thinking that some such explanation is true is equally a reason for thinking that religious experience is nonreliable or not veridical. At the very least, they are often thought to remove whatever presumptive evidential force religious experience otherwise might have. They are paradigms of alleged reducing conditions.

Rebutting conditions are provided by alleged evidence

against the belief for which the experience provides presumptive evidence. Arguments that the concept of God is logically inconsistent, that the existence of evil is evidence against the existence of God, and any other standard antitheistic argument, is potentially a rebutting condition. By using these notions, we can put Rowe's argument in a more forceful manner:

(R4) If people's seeming to experience God is evidence that God exists, and if there are reducing conditions of these experiences, then there is also reason to think that we can discover them, and if there are rebutting conditions, then there is also reason to think that we can discover them.

(R5) Even if there are reducing conditions of apparent experiences of God, there is no reason to think that we can discover them, and even if there are rebutting conditions of apparent experiences of God, there is no reason to think that we can discover them.

(R6) People's seeming to experience God is not evidence that God exists.

A RESPONSE TO THE REVISION

There is no reason to think that if any of the conditions is successful as a reducer of evidence or a rebuttal to evidence, this cannot be discovered. Hence there is no reason to accept Rowe's argument. Thus a reply to that argument can be constructed. The reply to Rowe that is called for goes like this:

(RR1) If we can tell whether or not there are reducing conditions relevant to experiences that seem to be experiences of God, and if we can tell whether or not there are rebutting conditions relevant to experiences that seem to be experiences of God, then people's having experiences that seem to them to be experiences of God are evidence that God exists.

(RR2) We can tell whether or not there are reducing conditions relevant to experiences that seem to be experiences of God.

(RR3) We can tell whether or not there are rebutting conditions relevant to experiences that seem to be experiences of God.

Hence:

(RR4) People's having experiences that seem to be experiences of God is evidence that God exists.

A reducing condition of Sam's apparent experience of seeing spiders all over his bed is that Sam is having delirium
tremens. A rebutting condition of the experience is information that Sam's bed is in Aunt Agatha's house, and that
Aunt Agatha keeps an insect-free environment and lives in
a spiderless county. A reducing condition of Sandra's apparent experience of God is that Sandra has ingested some
mind-altering substance and is in a religious setting, especially if others similarly have ingested the substance in a
religious setting and appear to see God. A rebutting condition of Sandra's apparent experience of God is a plausible
argument to the effect that the concept of God is inconsistent or that the existence of evil is incompatible with the
existence of God.

Obviously, in all of these cases, other examples could be
given. What is important, however, is not to try to give lots
of examples. It is not even necessary that there *be* any examples. The two crucial points are these. First, *if* there are examples, it should be possible for us to discover them. If there
are conditions in which one would seem to experience God
"no matter what" (or in which one's seeming to experience
God is rendered more probable than not by nonreligious
factors), then in order for the reply to Rowe to succeed, these
must be discoverable. If there are reasons to think that God
does not exist, then in order for the reply to Rowe to succeed, these too must be discoverable. But there is no reason
to think that if there are such conditions, or such reasons, they cannot be discovered. Plenty of people think
they have discovered them (their views are discussed in
Chapters 4 and 10). Second, if there are not such examples,

then that too presumably is discoverable. What is sound in Rowe's position is not that there *must* be such examples; he does not even claim that there must be. It is only that any such examples there might be must not be necessarily beyond our reach. Rowe himself (mistakenly) thinks he finds a rebutting condition in the existence of evil. Many think that social science explanations specify reducing conditions. Philosophy of religion investigates just these issues, among many others. If there are rebutting or reducing conditions, we are not walled off from that fact. Hence, Rowe's argument fails.

The arguments we have considered, then, save perhaps for Conway's interesting argument, do not succeed. They represent much of the sort of objections usually raised against religious experience being evidence for anything significant. Martin's argument, part of Conway's argument, and Rowe's argument against Broad all fail. But there remains one argument that picks up on Conway's notion of an absolutely elusive being and Rowe's concern about telling genuine from deceptive experiences. I suggest the following argument as one that captures the spirit and sharpens the letter of the type of counterargument to Broad's argument that we have been considering. This argument captures what remaining force there is to Conway's and Rowe's contentions.

STILL ANOTHER ARGUMENT

Suppose that there is some condition that humans can be in such that if God exists, then anyone in that condition will seem to experience God. Then if one in that condition fails to experience God, it will follow that God does not exist. Call such a condition a "divine crisis condition": Anyone in such a condition will experience God (and hence seem to do so) if there is a God to experience. The argument goes like this:

(AA1) If people seeming to experience God is evidence that God exists, there is a divine crisis condition.

(AA2) There is no divine crisis condition.

Therefore:

(AA3) People's experiencing God is not evidence that God exists.

The argument states a crucial part of the negative idea in a clear and challenging manner. Like other views we have considered, it entails that religious experience is not even presumptive evidence for the existence of God unless it can be discovered to be mistaken in a certain way. We have argued that religious experience can meet the condition of being possibly and discoverably mistaken in other ways. But this argument insists on a new condition that religious experience must meet. It offers a new and powerful formulation of the negative idea. One who offers this argument is committed not only to:

(AA4) Religious experience E is evidence that God exists only if it is logically possible that E is not evidence that God exists.

And to:

(AA5) Religious experience E is evidence that God exists only if, were E to be non-veridical, then we could discover this.

But also to:

(AA6) Religious experience E is evidence that God exists only if there is some circumstance in which E's nonoccurrence would be evidence that God does not exist.

We shall discuss whether this way, or any of still other ways, of embodying the negative idea gives Conway and Rowe what they want.

11

The principle of experiential evidence

A principle of experiential evidence, if it is true, tells us when an experience provides evidence of the truth of a proposition. As we have seen, two simple ideas underlie the notion of experiential evidence: (i) If one seems to experience X, that is evidence that X exists; (ii) if one can have experiential evidence that X exists, one can have experiential evidence that X does not exist. Our task here is to develop these ideas in ways that take advantage of the argument whose course we followed in Chapter 10.

UNDERDETERMINATION

Sensory experience underdetermines the physical object claims based on it; the computer that I see presumably has a side opposite to the one I see, an inside as well as an outside, complexly curved innards as well as simple, flat outer surfaces, and the like. Presumably, it exists during my eyeblinks and inattention and while I am out of the office. To claim that something is a computer is to claim that it is more than I can see (hear, feel, etc.) it to be at any given moment. More so, of course, numinous experience underdetermines claims to the effect that God is omnipotent, omniscient, and perfectly good, that God can create without using preexisting materials, and the like. The "omni-" properties are linked to numinous experience by means of theory or theology, although such claims, as it were, move in the same direction as does the phenomenological content of strong numinous experiences. This underdetermination is a logically necessary feature of our experiences, and the fact that our experiences have this feature does not prevent those experiences from providing evidence for claims that meet the relevance conditions relative to those experiences.

TOTAL RELEVANT EVIDENCE

Several things are worth noting about experiential evidence. *Having evidence that X exists* is compatible with *being unreasonable in believing that X exists*, for it is compatible with having stronger experiential (or total) evidence that X does not exist than one has that X exists. We will use "experiential" in the standard way, so that what one might call "conceptual experience" (proving that the Pythagorean theorem is true, showing that $2 + 2 = 4$, making it clear that *There are no objective values and one ought to be tolerant* is self-contradictory, and the like) does not count as experience.

One's *total relevant evidence* regarding some proposition P is precisely all the evidence one has, experiential and nonexperiential, relative to whether or not P is true. There is always more relevant evidence than experiential. For example, a proposition can be *necessarily true* (it is if its denial is self-contradictory), *necessarily false* (it is if it is self-contradictory), or *logically contingent* (it is if it is neither necessarily true nor necessarily false). Thus *I seem to see my computer* is evidence that *My computer exists*, but if I had evidence that *There are computers* is subtly contradictory, this would cast doubt on my experiential evidence. In fact, my conceptual evidence is that *There are computers* is not logically contradictory (nor is it a logically necessary truth). Rather, it is a logically contingent claim. Conceptual evidence regarding its logical status (necessarily true, necessarily false, logically contingent) is relevant to the question of whether or not a proposition is true. Further, there is the question of a proposition's consistency with other propositions for which we have evidence. The final chapter of this book considers some salient conceptual experiences and some relevant matters regarding consistency.

One might argue that all that is required to make it possible for apparent experiences of God to be evidence that God exists is that apparent experience of God be intentional regarding God and that it be possible that some experience or other would provide us with evidence that God does not exist; the contrary experience need not be of the same kind as that which speaks in favor of God's existence. I will not so argue here. For one thing, it may be that the most plausible example of antitheistic experience is our encounter with evil and that there is no even possible experience of evil that does provide evidence against God's existence; it may be that philosophers such as Plantinga, Mavrodes, and Adams have done so well in providing answers to objections to God's existence that appeal to the existence of evil that negative evidence from the experience of evil is not available. It might even be that no such experience is logically possible. (I do not think that this is so, though I think that one has to go a long way to describe such logically possible experiential evidence.)

It may be that some development along the following lines would be sufficient for the overall argument of this book. Perhaps we need no principle of experiential evidence stronger than something like:

> (EP) If S's experience E is intentional regarding X, then E is evidence that X exists unless (i) S would seem to experience X whether X was there to be experienced or not; (ii) were E not veridical, S could not discover this; (iii) E is of a type of experience that is systematically misleading; or (iv) no type of experience could count against X exists.

I shall assume, however, that condition (iv) should be stronger.

What (iv) says is that we can satisfy the second simple idea in this way: If we can have one kind of experience that would provide evidence against the existence of some X, then we can have some other kind of experience that provides evidence for the existence of X (assuming that apparent experience of X is otherwise in order – that the notion of an X is not contradictory, that X is the sort of thing that can be experienced, and the like). Part of what makes this suggestion hard to deal with also plagues the second idea itself – namely, the notion of a *kind* of experience is not lucid. It is at its best when we consider such notions as *being a visual experience* and *being a tactile experience* as defining kinds of experience; once one ascends even to the level of *being a sensory perceptual experience*, it becomes unclear what falls within, or belongs to, the kind in question. So let us suppose that there are at least the following kinds of experience: visual, tactile, auditory, olfactory, gustatory, aesthetic, moral, and numinous. This leaves aside introspective experience; the notion of introspection is messy all by itself. Dream images, hallucinations, and mental imagery can have color properties and sound properties and even contain apparent tastes and smells, but these are not typically accessible to vision, hearing, taste, and smell as ordinarily conceived; they are *private properties*, one might say, as opposed to the *public properties* of the color of the wall, the taste of an orange, the sound of rain falling, or the smell of wet leaves. Now *being numinous* is not a visually (or otherwise sensorially) accessible property, and it is a property distinct from *being aesthetically beautiful*. It can contain, but it goes beyond, *being morally good*. *Being numinous* is a matter of *being awesome, being majestic, being overwhelmingly powerful, being fascinating but dangerous,* and the like. To have a numinous experience is to have an experience in which one at least seems to experience a being with such properties as these. These properties may, as it were, be conveyed by images or sounds that have public or private properties. But these properties are not strictly perceptual properties, either private or public, if "perceptual" means "(five) sensory." Perhaps, then, private experience that is quasi-sensory (visual mental images, silently speaking to oneself, deliberating about whether to take a trip, having a song run through one's mind, etc.) is one sort of experience, and experience of public, observable items is another. Numinous experience, though it might include private quasi-sensory or public sensory components, is not simply a matter of there occurring private quasi-sensory or public sensory experiences.

Two suggestions, then, come to mind. One is to say that numinous experience possibly is evidence that God exists only if there can be religious experience that speaks otherwise, thereby treating *religious experience* as a type of experience. The other is to treat *numinous experience* as a more restrictive type of experience and suggest that numinous experience itself, in principle at least, can provide negative as well as positive evidence regarding God's existence. A principle of experiential evidence that requires only that religious experience (of whatever sort) *possibly* provide evidence against *God exists* would incorporate a less stringent strategy than one that required that numinous experience itself must *possibly* provide evidence that God does not exist. A principle that required the latter would incorporate a more stringent strategy. The argument that must be met by anyone who claims that religious experience or numinous experience provides evidence that God exists goes as follows:

(1) One can have experiential evidence for God's existence only if there is some condition under which one's failing to experience God is evidence that God does not exist.

(2) There is no condition under which one's failing to experience God is evidence that God does not exist.

Hence:

(3) One cannot have experiential evidence that God exists.

The purpose of this chapter, then, is to see if one can successfully combine the negative and positive idea in such a way as to meet this argument. In so doing, we will incorporate the more stringent strategy just referred to.

DEVELOPING THE SIMPLE IDEAS

As we have noted, one important question to ask in developing these ideas is, what would cancel the apparent evidence that I have in favor of *X exists* if I have an experience in which it phenomenologically seems to me that I encounter an *X*? It is hard to be sure that one has all of the relevant cases in mind, but something like the following is right so far as it goes: (i) My seeming to experience *X* is not evidence that *X exists* is true if I would seem to experience *X* whether I actually was experiencing *X* or not; (ii) my seeming to experience *X* is not evidence that *X exists* is true if, even if *X* did not exist, I could not tell that *X* did not exist; and (perhaps) (iii) if the *type* of experience to which my experience of at least seeming to encounter *X* belongs were systematically misleading, I could not tell that it was. This leads to the following suggestion:

(EP) If *S* has *E* and *E* is intentional regarding *X*, then *E* is evidence that *X* exists unless *S*'s having *E* occurs in circumstances that satisfy (i), (ii), or (iii).

Whatever experiential evidence one has for a proposition of the form *X exists* presumably comes by virtue of one's having experiential evidence for a proposition of the form *X has A*, where *A* is some property other than existence, and where of course *X has A* entails *X exists*. At any rate, this seems the characteristic way of obtaining favorable experiential evidence regarding existential propositions. It is plausible to read the negative idea as requiring that it must be logically possible that experiential evidence against *God lacks A* occurs if one can have experiential evidence for *God has A*, where *A* ranges over any properties an experience might provide reason to suppose God possessed.

"CIRCUMSTANCE"

No doubt, the concept *circumstance* is less than lucid. What it amounts to here is something like this. If a proposition *P* is logically contingent and if P is true, then one's failing to experience X is evidence that X does not exist, then let us say that the circumstance or condition *P's being true* is a *falsification circumstance* or *condition* of X *exists*. Some of the more stringent versions of the principle of experiential evidence insist that there can be experiential evidence in favor of the existence of an item only if that item has some falsification circumstance. This, I think, gives to the notion of *circumstance* the precision it needs in the present discussion.

Using these terms, we can put some versions of the principle of experiential evidence along the following lines. In each case, one should read the principle in conjunction with (EP), given in the preceding section.

(P1) S's experience E that (phenomenologically) is of object O and occurs in circumstance C is evidence that O exists only if C is a falsification circumstance for O *exists*.

(P2) S's experience E that (phenomenologically) is of object O and occurs in circumstance C is evidence that O exists if and only if some circumstance C^* (C or some other) is a falsification circumstance for O *exists*.

(P3) S's experience E that (phenomenologically) is of object O and occurs in circumstance C is evidence that O exists only if either there is some circumstance that is a falsification circumstance for O *exists* or there is some item O^* such that O^* *exists* is evidence against O *exists* and there is some circumstance C^* that is a falsification circumstance for O^* *exists*.

(P4) S's experience E that (phenomenologically) is of object O and occurs in circumstance C is evidence that O exists only if there is some circumstance that is a falsification circumstance for O *exists* or there is an item O^* such that O^* *exists* is evidence against O *exists* and there is some circumstance C^* that is a falsification circumstance for O^* *exists* or there is an item O^* such that O^* *exists* is evidence against O *exists* and one can have an experience that (phenomenologically) is of

O^*, even though no circumstance is a falsification circumstance for either *O exists* or *O* exists*.

Save for the last, of course, each principle is more stringent than the one that follows it. The argument that derives from Conway's in effect holds that (P1) or (P2) is true and that no experience of God can occur under any circumstance that is a falsification circumstance for *God exists*.

DEVELOPING THE NEGATIVE IDEA: THE ALTERNATIVES

In the light of the negative idea, perhaps it is this principle of experiential evidence that should be pressed:

(P*) For any proposition *God has A*, where *A* is not "exists" and where *God has A* entails *God exists*, if one can have experiential evidence of kind *K* in favor of *God has A*, then one can have experiential evidence of kind *K* against *God has A*.

There is still a question as to how exactly the development of the negative idea should go. Roughly, the salient alternatives are these: Either it is the case that experience *E* of kind *K* can provide evidence for *X exists* only if it is logically possible that experience *E** (also of kind *K*) provides evidence against *X exists* or it is the case that experience *E* of kind *K* can provide evidence for *X exists* only if it is logically possible that experience *E** (also of kind *K*) provides evidence against *E provides evidence that X exists*. For obvious reasons, let the first of these alternatives be *the negative evidence alternative* and let the second be *the evidence cancellation alternative*.

The evidence cancellation alternative is already built into our progressively developing principle of experiential evidence. Conditions (i), (ii), and (iii) in (EP) concern evidence cancellation conditions of experiential evidence. Hence, it is the other alternative, the negative evidence alternative, that deserves attention here.

The abstract general rationale for the negative evidence

alternative goes like this. Suppose that (P*) is true. Suppose also that a proposition of the form *If God exists, then God has A* is a necessary truth. It then follows that if *The object of this experience has A* can be supported by experience, then *The object of this experience lacks A* in principle can be supported by experience; it will be logically possible that the negative proposition be experientially supported. To the degree it is so supported, the proposition *The object of this experience is not God* also will be supported.

Consider, for example, that the proposition (H) *If God exists, then God is holy* is arguably a necessary truth. If one can have experiential evidence for *God is holy*, and thereby for *God exists*, then (given the truth of [P*]) it follows that there can be experiential evidence, not against (H), but against *The object of this experience is holy* and so against *The object of this experience is God*. If there also is reason to think that *If the object of this experience exists and is not God, then that is evidence that God does not exist* or *God and the object of this experience probably do not coexist*, then experiential evidence for *The object of this experience is not God* will also be evidence that God does not exist.

Suppose that David has two religious experiences. One experience at least seems to be of a being that is immensely powerful and holy. The other experience at least seems to be of a being that is immensely powerful and obviously not holy. It might well be that the phenomenologies of these experiences provide support for the claim that if there is any real object of these experiences, they have the same object. Then David would have some experiential evidence against the claim that God is the object of those experiences, and some evidence for the claim that there exists an enormously powerful being who is not God. This, of course, by itself would not be evidence that God does not exist, though the addition of further considerations might yield that result.

If *God has A* is contingent, then things may be just as (P*) suggests. But presumably an experience of God in which God appeared to have essential divine properties could provide evidence that God exists. Indeed, if there are no such experiences, it is not clear that there is much by way of experiential evidence for God's existence. Thus a relevant principle of experiential evidence should apply to cases in which apparent experiences of God occur in which God at least seems to have properties essential to divinity. Perhaps, then, we should blend (P*) into:

> (P**) For any proposition *God has A*, where *A* is not "exists" and where *God has A* entails *God exists*, if *If God exists then God has A* is a necessary truth, one can have experiential evidence of kind *K* in favor of *God exists* only if one can have experiential evidence of kind *K* against *The object of a kind K experience has A* and hence against *The object of a kind K experience is God*, and if *If God exists then God has A* is contingent, one can have experiential evidence of kind *K* in favor of *God has A* only if one can have experiential evidence of kind *K* against *God has A*.

Suppose one holds the principle of existential accessibility:

(PEA) If something exists, then there can be experiential evidence that it exists.

Suppose that one also holds that something exists about which it is necessarily true that there is no circumstance in which one's failing to experience it would be evidence that it did not exist. Assuming that one's confidence in the principle of experiential accessibility remains unabated, one presumably will hold it true that:

> (N) If it is a necessary truth that even if something *X* exists, there is no circumstance such that one's not experiencing *X* in that circumstance is evidence that *X* does not exist, then that there is no such circumstance does not prevent experiences, if any, that seem to be experiences of *X* from being evidence that *X* exists.

More generally, one might be attracted to:

(N1) For any criterion Q, if it is true that even if X exists, X does not satisfy Q, then there being experiential evidence that X exists does not depend on X's satisfying Q.

If it is true of X that even if X exists, there is no circumstance such that if one in that circumstance failed to experience X, then that is evidence that it does not exist, one may infer from that fact plus (N), or plus (N1), that there being no such circumstance does not prevent apparent experiences of X being evidentially favorable regarding X's existence.

Recognition of (N) and (N1) should be built into the notion of experiential disconfirmation. If one can disconfirm a proposition of the form *O has A* by not observing O in circumstances in which it would appear if it existed, or by observing O and noting that it lacks A, or by observing O^*, which has B, and remembering that a good theory entails *If O^* has B, then O lacks A*, then *O has A* falls within the scope of experiential disconfirmation.

EXCEPTIONS

Generally, what falls within a proposition's experiential disconfirmation scope also falls within its experiential confirmation scope, and conversely, but there are exceptions. *Someone or other will be alive tomorrow* is the sort of proposition that one can experientially confirm tomorrow, but its contradictory cannot be experientially confirmed tomorrow, or today either, unless one can infer it from something one does experience plus a good theory. Similarly, *No one will be alive tomorrow* can be disconfirmed tomorrow but not confirmed tomorrow, or today either, unless one can infer it from something one does experience plus a good theory. The exceptions are special cases, isolated from other cases by themselves containing reference to something that is a necessary condition of confirmation or disconfirmation. The cases that interest us are not exceptions, save on a certain view.

Some varieties of theism entail that it is a necessary truth that *If any human beings exist, then God exists,* this being a more specific case that falls under the alleged necessary truth that *If anything contingent exists, then God exists.* On this view, it would be logically impossible for anyone to have experiential evidence that God did not exist, unless He did exist, and impossible for anyone who knew the propositions in question to be necessary truths rationally to suppose themselves possessed of sufficient experiential evidence against God's existence to make it rational to suppose that He did not exist. Even if this were so, it would be possible to have some experiential evidence against the existence of God.

If it is widely agreed that there is a general parity between experiential disconfirmation and confirmation – that save for special cases, they share the same scope or have the same propositional extension – there is not the same degree of agreement in how to shape the concept that defines that parity.

It of course is not necessary for a proposition to come within the scope of experiential disconfirmation that it actually be disconfirmed, as if experiential disconfirmability entailed falsehood. Nor is it necessary that a proposition that falls within the scope of experiential disconfirmation have evidence placed against it, as if experiential disconfirmability entails dubious epistemic character. It is accessibility to experiential disconfirmation, *should there be any,* that is essential; it is not essential that there be any, although it is essential that it be logically possible that there be some.

If *O has A* – I shall treat this propositional function as if it were a proposition, simply for ease of expression – can be refuted, if at all, only by showing that it is logically impossible that *O* have *A,* then *O has A* does not fall directly within the scope of experiential disconfirmation. It might nonetheless be the case that *If O exists, then O has A* was a necessary truth, that something as strong as *If O* has B, then O lacks A* is true, and that *O has B* is experientially confirmable; then *O has A* falls indirectly within the scope of experiential disconfirmation. I am treating *O has A* (as one would expect) as entailing *O exists*.

Concerning Conway's pragmatic argument, one should note that there exist a variety of principles of experiential evidence to serve as barriers to lunacy, and that if Conway's favorite candidate for epistemic sergeant at arms is not selected, other strong candidates are available.

THREE DOCTRINES OF EXPERIENTIAL DISCONFIRMATION

Three brief doctrines of experiential disconfirmation, each to be explained, go as follows:

(PP) *S*'s experience *E* that is intentional regarding *O* provides evidence that *O* exists only if *O exists* falls within the scope of *polar disconfirmation*.

(PC) *S*'s experience *E* that is intentional regarding *O* provides evidence that *O* exists only if *O exists* falls within the scope of *collegial disconfirmation*.

(PL) *S*'s experience *E* that is intentional regarding *O* provides evidence that *O* exists only if *O exists* falls within the scope of *lateral disconfirmation*.

The general ideas behind these principles are as follows.

Polar disconfirmation

The proposition *O has A* comes within the scope of *polar disconfirmation* if and only if there is some condition *C* such that *O*'s not being experienced in *C* is evidence in favor of *O does not exist*. I suggest that it is polar disconfirmation that Martin, Conway, and Rowe need to make their cases against Broad's argument.

Collegial disconfirmation

The proposition *O has A* comes within the scope of *collegial disconfirmation* if and only if it is logically possible (if the proposition *O exists but lacks A* is contingent) that an experience occur that provides evidence for *O lacks A* or (if the proposition *O exists but lacks A* is contradictory) it would be logically possible that an experience occur that would provide evidence for *O lacks A* were *O exists but lacks A* contingent.

It will be necessary to provide a better explication of collegial disconfirmation, and I shall do so shortly. This introduction provides only a rough idea.

Lateral disconfirmation

The proposition *O has A* comes within the scope of *lateral disconfirmation* if and only if it is logically possible that there be an experience that provides evidence for *O* has B* (where, of course, *O** is different from *O*) and the truth of *O* has B* is evidence against the truth of *O has A*.

We have seen that a principle of experiential evidence corresponds to each of these notions of disconfirmation. Strictly, of course, one can hold each by itself, embrace all three, or hold any two together. The notion of collegial disconfirmation requires clearer statement.

COLLEGIAL DISCONFIRMATION
MORE FULLY CONSIDERED

Suppose that *If God exists, then God is holy* is a necessary truth. Then it is logically impossible to experience anything that is both not holy and God. But were it possible that a being be God and not holy, it would be possible to experience it. Is there some elegant way of turning these materials into a circumspect variety of collegial disconfirmation?

The proposition *O has A* comes within the scope of collegial experiential disconfirmation if and only if, should *If O exists, then O has A* be contingent, it is logically possible that one have an experience that provides evidence for *O lacks A*, and, should *If O exists, then O has A* be logically necessary, it is logically possible that one have an experience that provides evidence for O^*, *which has some property that it is reasonable to think that only O has if O exists, lacks A*, where O^* lacks A entails O^* *exists*. Thus, for example, if one finds a being O^* that is very like O but that lacks some property essential to O, and it is unlikely that both O and O^* exist, then one has evidence that O does not grace us by its presence. Thus, if *If O exists, then O has A* is a necessary truth, *O has A* is available only if we bring lateral confirmation within the scope of collegial confirmation.

With this in mind, then, imagine an Old Testament-style conversation between God and a Hebrew leader, say Abraham. Abraham wonders whether God, strictly speaking, is omnipotent. The answer, perhaps not entirely without some tongue-in-cheek flavor, is that of course God is omnipotent; after all, the philosophers have declared that *God is omnipotent* is a necessary truth. (We shall suppose that Abraham has been favored with prepublication copies of various later works in philosophical theology.) But Abraham presses: Is the Divine Person, Blessed Be He, with whom he converses, strictly omnipotent? The reply is surprising: For complicated reasons, which Abraham may have if he wants them, the Divine Person, Blessed Be He, who graciously grants the interview finds (as He knew He would) that if He creates certain tiny inert particles out of preexisting materials, then He can immediately annihilate them if He wishes, but if He creates them by sheer fiat without using preexisting materials, He cannot destroy them for three seconds, even though it is not logically impossible either that they be destroyed right after they are created or that God destroy them right after He creates them. This is the only limit on divine power (or, if this limit entails others, this limit and the other limits it entails are the only limits on divine power). Being omniscient, God knows how to handle this limit without any dangers arising in terms of providential care for God's people, and the same holds for all other good purposes. So Abraham's informant on this account, strictly speaking, is not omnipotent, and thus, strictly speaking, is not God. It is not clear to me that if the theology behind this story is logically consistent, and were the experience actually to occur and to be known to be veridical, it would follow that religious monotheism would be endangered, although philosophical monotheism would have to be readjusted somewhat. Strictly, what would follow on the assumptions just outlined is that Abraham's informant is not identical with the God of the philosophers, and hence that *that* God does not exist.

A numinous (uncanny, majestic, powerful, and awesome) being need not be holy (not at least in a sense that includes being righteous or good). One might have a numinous experience whose phenomenology includes the sense of power and knowledge that typically underdetermines claims to experience an omnipotent and omniscient being, but altogether lacks holiness or also contains an aura of unholiness. Suppose that instead of having an experience of the sort described earlier, one has a series of experiences. In one experience, one seems to see a burning bush and upon seeming to investigate has an experience whose phenomenology resembles that described in Exodus until it is interrupted by a horrifying laugh and a voice that tells us that God is an illusion; the experience then ends with a vision of people being tortured by an evil presence that seems to enjoy his evil activity. In another experience, things start out as in Isaiah's vision in the temple, but end again in a torture chamber. Similar experiences, so far as one can tell, copy the phenomenologies of numinous experiences that have played central roles in the world monotheisms, but then trail off into dismal scenes of people being viciously maimed and slaughtered, injured and tortured, by an evil being who enjoys his work.

Although a writer more skilled than the present author could make the envisioned series of experiences more vivid, presumably the basic idea is clear – one has a series of experiences that mimic those central to world monotheisms, save that they end in a radically different manner. Suppose further that the series includes experiences whose phenomenologies are characterized by explanations of how the various numinous experiences were produced, which explanations are true only if the experiences are nonveridical. Thus the content as well as the tenor of the experiences that constitute what we might call a series of antimonotheistic numinous experiences seems to go against the truth of monotheism.

Two things should be noted here. First, the notion of such a series of numinous experiences is not contradictory. Second, the occurrence of such a series would provide some countertheistic evidence. How much, of what quality, and with what result of course would depend on the details. Hence numinous experience, in principle, can count against the existence of God. Indeed, we have seen two ways in which numinous experience might provide evidence against the existence of God.

A BRIEF REVIEW

As noted, then, three versions of a principle of experiential evidence can be formulated as follows.

> (PP) S's experience E that is intentional regarding O provides evidence that O exists only if O *exists* falls within the scope of polar disconfirmation.
>
> (PC) S's experience E that is intentional regarding O provides evidence that O exists only if O *exists* falls within the scope of collegial disconfirmation.
>
> (PL) S's experience E that is intentional regarding O provides evidence that O exists only if O *exists* falls with the scope of lateral disconfirmation.

The strongest version of a principle of experiential evidence, constructed from these materials, would conjoin these three versions. The weakest version would disjoin them. If (PP) is a conjunct in the *correct* version, Broad's argument and its more sophisticated successors fail, since they do not satisfy (PP). The simple argument that this is so follows:

> (1) One's experience that appears to be an experience of X is evidence that X exists only if sometime one's

failure to experience X would be evidence that X did not exist.

(2) There is no time at which one's failure to experience God would be evidence that God does not exist.

So:

(3) One's experience that appears to be an experience of God is not evidence that God exists.

The crucial epistemological premise in this argument is premise (1), which is tantamout to requiring that existential propositions for which there can be experiential evidence fall within the scope of polar disconfirmation.

AN ARGUMENT FOR (2)

The argument for (2), if one is needed, goes like this. A being is *omnicompetent* if and only if it is omnipotent, omniscient, and morally perfect. Then:

(2a) If God exists, then God is omnicompetent.
(2b) If God is omnicompetent, then She can prevent any person from experiencing Her at any time.

Hence:

(2c) If God exists, then She can prevent any person from experiencing Her at any time.
(2d) If God prevents any person from experiencing Her at any time, then God is not wrong in preventing that person from experiencing Her at that time.
(2e) If God exists, then God is not wrong in preventing any person from experiencing Her at any time.

So:

(2f) If God exists, then God can prevent any person from experiencing Her at any time, and God is not wrong in preventing any person from experiencing Her at any time.

(2g) A person justifiably can infer from his not experiencing God at some time that God does not exist at that time only if it is the case that if God exists, then God could not prevent him from experiencing God at that time, or if it is the case that if God exists, then God would be wrong in preventing him from experiencing God at that time.

So:

(2h) A person cannot justifiably infer from his not experiencing God at some time that God does not exist at that time.

(2i) A person's failure to experience God at some time is evidence that God does not exist at that time only if he can justifiably infer from his not experiencing God at that time that God does not exist at that time.

Hence:

(2j) A person's failure to experience God at some time is not evidence that God does not exist at that time.

This establishes the other premise – the one besides a version of (PP) – that is necessary to show that if (PP) is the correct version of the principle of experiential evidence, or must be a conjunct in that version, then a Broad-type argument fails.

Collegial disconfirmation of *O exists*, at least in one of its varieties, occurs if we find experiential evidence that a being very like *O* nonetheless lacks at least one of *O*'s essential properties. Lateral disconfirmation occurs if we find that a being *O** that may be extremely unlike *O* is such that *If O* has B, then O lacks A* and we have experiential evidence that *O** has *B*. If, say, one conjoins (PC) and (PL), for the strongest principle of experiential evidence these materials will yield without our using (PP), then so far as I can see a properly revised version of Broad's argument can succeed.

I offer two arguments for favoring some mix of these principles that does not include (PP). Since the conjunct of (PC) and (PL) is the strongest remaining principle if we eliminate (PP), I shall take my argument to be an argument for favoring that conjunct. By "the conjunct of (PC) and (PL)" I mean this principle:

(PCPL) *S*'s experience *E* that is intentional regarding *O* provides evidence that *O* exists only if *O* exists falls within the scope of both collegial and lateral disconfirmation.

I will assume here that the task of constructing logically consistent descriptions of possible disconfirming experiences that show that a Broad-type argument satisfies (PCPL) is a matter of time and ingenuity, and faces no difficulty in principle. One factor that might not unreasonably predispose one to favor (PCPL) is that typically our confirming and disconfirming experiential evidence regarding propositions of the form *O exists* comes in terms of propositions of the form *O has A* or *What I took to be O turns out to lack A* or *O* has B, and if so then there cannot be an O that has A or O* has various of the properties of O, but lacks a property O must have, and it is not likely that there be two things with the properties that O* has*, and the like. This fact, plus the considerable strength of the test provided by falling within the scope of (PCPL) might just be enough to carry the argument for a Broad-type argument not needing to satisfy (PP) so long as its premises fell within the scope of (PCPL).

I offer two arguments against (PP). One is a priori; the other is a posteriori.

THE A PRIORI ARGUMENT

(PP) entails that, even if God exists, even veridical experiences of God do not provide evidence that God exists. Thus it is true that:

(PPG) If (PP) is true then if God exists, God's being experienced cannot (and so does not) provide evidence that God exists.

This goes against the not implausible idea that anything that exists, unless it has special properties that make it impossible that it be experienced, is such that it can be experienced, and that if it can be experienced, its being experienced is evidence that it does exist. Consider the following argument:

(1) God exists. (assumption for conditional proof)

(2) If X exists and it is not logically impossible that X be experienced, then it is logically possible that X be experienced.

(3) If X can be experienced and it is not logically impossible that X's being experienced provides evidence that X exists, then X's being experienced provides evidence that X exists.

(4) If God exists, then it is not logically impossible that God be experienced.

(5) It is logically possible that God be experienced. (1, 2, 4)

(6) It is not logically impossible that God's being experienced provides evidence that God exists.

Hence:

(7) God's being experienced provides evidence that God exists. (3, 4, 6)

(8) *God exists* entails *God's being experienced provides evidence that God exists.* ([1, 7] by closing conditional proof)

Hence:

(9) It is false that *God exists* is compatible with *God's being experienced cannot provide evidence that God exists.*

Setting (1) aside, I find each premise a plausible candidate for being a necessary truth. The only role that (1) plays is setting the stage for a conditional proof, and the assumption that (1) states is dismissed in one's moving by conditional proof from (7) to (8), and (9) follows from (8), assuming the consistency of (8)'s antecedent. Together with (PPG), our conclusion (9) entails not-(PP). So that is one argument against (PP).

Perhaps the argument bears brief review. If (PP) is true, the claims (1) *God exists* and (not-7) *God's being experienced cannot (and so does not) provide evidence that God exists* are logically compatible. Each of (2–6) is a necessary truth. Whatever (1) *God exists*, plus (2–6), entails, (1) alone entails. Now (1) plus (2–6) entails (7); so (1) entails (7). If (1) entails (7) and (1) is not a contradiction, then (1) cannot be compatible with (not-7). Indeed, if (PP) is true, *God exists* not only is compatible with but entails (not-7), assuming that if (PP) is true at all, it is necessarily so. So if our a priori argument is sound, *God exists* does not entail (not-7) and so (PP) is false.

AN A POSTERIORI ARGUMENT

Suppose that there exist items of the following sort: (a) They emit light at a very low level; (b) any attempt to detect their presence other than through the human eye or a light meter that functions at a range of light sensitivity analogous to that of the human eye disperses them (destroys them or sends them out of detectable range, as you prefer); (c) the light they emit runs from one to five photons, and only if four or five photons are received by the receptor is their presence detected; (d) the process of sending the photons is indeterministic – not probabilistic, but random. Call these entities (after my colleague who suggested them to me) *dretskes*.

On one account, the features mentioned are essential properties of these entities. Anything that lacked any of (a–d) would not be an entity of this sort. These are *essentialist visual dretskes*. It is necessarily false of essentialist visual *dretskes* that given ordinary conditions and competent observers, their being there entails that they will be seen. Yet sometimes one can see them, although one cannot predict when one will see them and there are no conditions under which failing to see them is evidence that they are not there.

On another account, (a–d) are contingently true, and what

they are true of (of course) are *nonessentialist visual dretskes.*
The analogous claims are true of them, though contingently
so. I will not explore this avenue.

It seems to me that one could have evidence that there are
dretskes, even though the experiences that provide such evidence violate the claim that evidence is available only in
terms of experiential evidence that falls within the scope of
polar confirmation.

Obviously, once the idea is there, one could talk about
essentialist auditory *dretskes,* and so on through the sensory
modalities. But there is no need to multiply counterexamples
beyond necessity. I offer the following argument:

(1) Were the claim that only experiences that fall within
the scope of polar disconfirmation are capable of providing evidence for existential propositions true, it
would be logically impossible to have experience that
provided evidence for the existence of *dretskes.*

(2) It is not logically impossible to have experience that
provides evidence for the existence of *dretskes.*

Hence:

(3) The claim that only experiences that fall within the
scope of polar disconfirmation are capable of providing evidence for existential propositions is false.

So, again, (PP) is false. My suggestion is that we replace (PP)
with (PCPL), which is a strong principle of experiential evidence. With it, we are not helpless against the lunacies Conway fears. The question remains as to how, exactly, a revised
Broad-type argument will look. The next chapter considers
that matter in some detail.

12

The argument triumphant

The groundwork having been laid, it is time to offer the core argument of the book. I shall do so in some detail – more detail, perhaps, than is strictly necessary, given previous discussions – in an effort to make its meaning and force as clear as I can. I begin by dealing with a final objection.

There is a disanalogy between explanation of at least apparent experiences of physical objects and at least apparent experiences of God that is worth pursuing. It is a disanalogy that seems to tell against the possibility of religious experience's providing evidence for religious belief, and we shall consider it before developing an argument from numinous experience. In the case of offering a physiological explanation of one's seeing a giraffe, the giraffe plays a role in the explanation. The explanation begins, "Light waves bounce off the giraffe," and ends with an account of the motions of internal visual machinery. (The step to the visual experience itself is controversial, and I leave that aside here.) Conversely, one can begin with the experience of at least seeming to see a giraffe, and (typically) trace it back to the giraffe. Whatever there is by way of an account of the motions of internal machinery in the case of one's having a numinous experience, there of course is no physical causal chain that one can follow link by link to an end held by God's hand.

256

We are used to following causal chains and finding physical objects at their end – seeing where the light is coming from, following the leak to its source, discovering what is causing the odor, finding the source of the buzzing noise, and the like. This is familiar ground. There is nothing like it in the case of numinous experience. It would be foolish to expect there to be anything like it.

The point the critic finds relevant is this: The physiological explanation of visual experience refers to the object sensed, whereas the social science explanations of religious experience do not refer to any numinous being. When it is possible to give a physiological explanation of one's at least seeming to see a giraffe without referring to a giraffe, that is evidence that one only seems to see a giraffe. Analogously, then, if one can give a social science explanation of one's at least seeming to experience God without that social science explanation referring to God – as of course it will not – then that is evidence that one only seems to experience God. Since one can always offer a social science explanation of a numinous experience without referring to God, one can always have evidence that the one having the numinous experience *only* seems to experience God. But a numinous experience about which there is evidence that one's having it is *only* a matter of its seeming to one that one experiences God is not much by way of evidence that there is a God to experience.

Arguments by analogy are tricky. One must always be alert to relevant differences. The argument just recited is not sufficiently alert. It is a necessary truth about physiological explanations that what they refer to can be found at the end of a causal chain whose links are physical. That, I take it, is the nature of physiology – not merely what one should expect, but what necessarily is the case so long as physiology is not made into something it currently is not. Whether social science explanations also refer to what can be found at the end of a causal chain whose links are physical depends on whether materialism or physicalism – the two terms generally used to refer to the view that all that exists is a material thing or a property of a material thing or a relation between material things – is true. That issue we cannot try to decide here.

It is clear (though sometimes denied nonetheless) that insofar as one can distinguish between social science and superstition, and between bad social science explanations and good ones, we need to refer to mental states, and to some mental states as being in better cognitive order than others.

Minimally, a mental event is an event *correctly described as mental*. Perhaps we can explain this notion as follows: x is correctly described as mental by description D if and only if D is true of x, and D *is true of x* entails *x is a conscious state*. Roughly, x is a conscious state if and only if S *is in x at time t* entails *S is conscious at time t*. This very rough characterization of the notion of a mental state leaves open the question whether an event that is mental can also be physical.

Presumably anything that is material is essentially so, and the same goes for anything immaterial, and for anything mental. If God exists, then God is immaterial and mental. (A Platonic Form, a number, a Fregean concept, and the like, if they exist, are essentially immaterial, but not mental.) Hence, if God exists, God is essentially immaterial and essentially mental, and so necessarily immaterial and necessarily mental. Mental states, of course, are also essentially, and hence necessarily, mental. No mental state is necessarily identical to a physical state. If it is possible that a mental state be identical to a physical state, the identity is contingent.

A "physical event" is a change in the properties of some physical object. A "physical chain" is a sequence of physical events that comprises two or more nonsimultaneous members such that each later member in the succession is at least partly caused by an earlier member. (If two or more physical events are simultaneous at time t_1 and cause one or more physical events at time t_2, we can treat the events at time t_1 as a *single complex* event, and those at time t_2 as another *single, complex* event.) To "trace back a physical chain" is to begin with an experience that is caused by a physical event and proceed to the object whose change of properties was the first event in the sequence. In particular, one takes the physiological explanation of one's sensory experience and uses it either as a recipe for the discovery of the causing object or (if that will not work) for inferring from that explanation to some other method of finding the object that has this feature: If the explanation is true, then the method will work.

This account does not assume that sensory experiences themselves are physical events. It does assume that a sensory experience either is a physical event or has a physical as well as a mental component (in which case it is the physical component that appears in a physical chain) or has a physical correlate (in which case it is the physical correlate that appears in a physical chain).

Finally, a "physical experiential chain" is a physical chain that goes backward from an experience that at least seems to its subject to be of some (mind-independent) item to some physical object. It is a physical chain that begins with an experience; if the experience is veridical, one can trace back a physical chain to an object that the experience seems to its subject to be an experience of. The case of one's having perceived an object that of course existed when one perceived it, but no longer exists and hence can no longer be discovered at the end of a physical chain, will be dealt with, although implicitly, in the way the relevant principles are stated below – see (PC**)

Obviously, no veridical numinous experience will be a member of a physical experiential chain. God is not at the end of any physical chain. God is not a physical object, and even if God can change, such changes are not physical events. An omnipotent God can cause physical chains and bring about physical events without God's belonging to such chains and without anything happening to God being a physical event. Even if numinous experiences have physical components or correlates, the apparent object of such an experience is not part of a physical chain.

The notions of a physical event, a physical chain, a physical experiential chain, and tracing back a physical chain are relevant to testing the veridicality of sensory experiences. Perhaps, for example, it is true of any sensory experience *E* and physical object *O* that

> (PC) If one has a sensory experience *E* that at least seems to be of an item *O*, and one cannot trace physical causal chain back from *E* to *O*, then that is a reason to suppose that *E* is not an experience of *O*.

Or, if that is not so, perhaps it is at least true that

> (PC*) If one has a sensory experience *E* that at least seems to be of an object *O*, and one cannot trace a physical causal chain back from *E* to *O*, then unless there is some explanation of this inability that itself makes essential reference to *O*, then that is a reason to suppose that *E* is not an experience of *O*.

Or, to speculate even more cautiously, perhaps the truth is that

> (PC**) If one has a sensory experience *E* that at least seems to be of an object *O*, and one cannot trace a physical causal chain back from *E* to *O*, then unless there is some explanation of this inability that is compatible with *O*'s being part of the cause of *E*, then that is a reason to suppose that *E* is not an experience of *O*.

But of course the corresponding claims regarding numinous experience have not the slightest plausibility. They would be plausible only if the notion of tracing a physical chain back to God (God being the physical object change in which is the first member of the relevant physical chains) was a sensible notion; and it is not. The relevant parallel claims regarding numinous experience are as follows:

> (NC) If one has a numinous experience *E* that at least seems to be of God, and one cannot trace a physical causal chain back from *E* to God, then that is a reason to suppose that *E* is not an experience of God.

(NC*) If one has a numinous experience E that at least seems to be of God, and one cannot trace a physical causal chain back from E to God, then unless there is some explanation of this inability that itself makes essential reference to God, then that is a reason to suppose that E is not an experience of God.

(NC**) If one has a numinous experience E that at least seems to be of God, and one cannot trace a physical causal chain back from E to God, then unless there is some explanation of this inability that is compatible with God being part of the cause of E, then that is a reason to think that E is not an experience of God.

But only if (N) or (N*) or (N**) or something very similar were true would the fact that one cannot trace a physical causal chain from an experience to God be any reason to think that the experience was not an experience of God, and none of them is true. Alternatively, one might reject (NC) but embrace (NC*) and note that *Necessarily, if God exists then God is not physical* provides the explanation referred to in (NC*). One might accept (NC**) and refer to the same explanation as the one that (NC**) requires.

There is one epistemological consequence that follows from our discussion. Attempting to follow a physical experiential chain, and finding that one does not thereby discover the relevant physical object, under relevant conditions, can provide evidence that one's sensory experience was not veridical. This means of checking our experiences is not available regarding numinous experiences. Whether this is of any particular epistemological importance depends on whether there are sufficient checks on numinous experience in order for it to be evidence.

THE ARGUMENT FROM NUMINOUS EXPERIENCE

Within Judaism, Christianity, Islam, and Bhakti Hinduism one finds descriptions of what Rudolf Otto called numinous experiences. Using "seems" in that sense, noted earlier, in which to say "I seem to experience an *O*" neither contrasts appearance to reality nor expresses an insecure opinion, but reports how things appear, so to say, "from within" the experience reported – using "seems" phenomenologically – the subject of a numinous experience seems to experience a being that is awesome, majestic, unique, righteous, over-powering, holy, intensely alive, and the like. Alternatively, the subject seems to experience a being to whom reverence, awe, recognition of one's guilt, humility, gratitude, and wor-ship are appropriate responses. The varieties of numinous experiences, even if we limit our attention to instances cen-tral to the monotheistic traditions rather than considering as many sorts as does Otto, are of course richer than this brief characterization suggests. But numinous experience is as fla-grantly subject-consciousness-object in structure as is sen-sory experience.

I do not assume that there is any experiential modality peculiar to having numinous experiences. It may be that such experiences in some manner supervene on visual, auditory, and so on, experiences or on moral or aesthetic experiences. The phenomenology of such experiences no doubt deserves detailed analysis. But for present purposes I shall only note that, as seems patent from the reports their subjects offer, they are subject-consciousness-object in structure and seem to be of a mind-independent object.

Not surprisingly, then, the core premise of an argument based on numinous experience can be cast in these terms:

(PN) For any subject *S* and experience *E*, if *S*'s having *E* is a matter of its (phenomenologically) seeming to *S* that *S* experiences a numinous being *N*, then if *S* nonculpably has no reason to think that (i) *S* would seem to experience *N* whether or not there is an *N* that *S* experiences, or (ii) if *E* is nonveridical, *S* could not discover that it was, or (iii) if *E* is of a type *T* of experience such that every member of *T* is nonverid-ical, *S* could not discover this fact, then *E* provides *S* evidence that there is an *N*.

The argument triumphant

There are various similarities and differences, analogies and disanalogies, between sensory and numinous experience. Sensory content differs from numinous content, somewhat as visual and auditory experiences differ in content. This is of particular interest here only if it has consequences of epistemic significance. Both sensory and numinous experience have a subject/consciousness/object structure. Not everyone, it would appear, has numinous experience, whereas in at least some of its modalities everyone has sensory experience. At least not infrequently, its descriptions suggest, having numinous experience involves having imagery (visual and auditory), whereas (veridical) visual and auditory experiences do not; they involve seeing the visually accessible, and hearing the auditorially accessible, properties of objects that are not images. Imagery mediates numinous content rather than being its main focus. What other similarities and differences are there?

Among the epistemically most interesting are these: First, suppose S_1 has veridical sensory and numinous experiences. If S_1 veridically senses an O, and S_2 is placed similarly to S_1, then S_2 (barring special considerations) also senses an O, but if S_1 at time t and in place A has a veridical numinous experience of N, S_2, who is also in A at t, may not experience N. In the case of sensory experience, veridicality entails publicity; in the case of numinous experience, it does not. This point is to be distinguished from a denial of the necessary truth that (regarding either sensory or numinous experience) if S_1 and S_2 are alike in *all* relevant respects, if one has an experience of O or N, so does the other.

Second, sensory experience comes in modalities and numinous experience does not; correspondingly, sensory experience is associated with sensory organs whereas there is no set of "numinous organs." Thus, whereas one modality of sensory experience can be appealed to in checking another, the analogous move is not available regarding numinous experience.

Third, if S senses an O, then often S is in a position to draw predictive conclusions from *There is an O* and if these conclusions are falsified, *There is an O* is falsified, whereas if S experiences N, S seems not in a position to draw predictive conclusions from *There is an N*, which could be falsified. (If eschatological predictive conclusions follow, this may satisfy a verificationist theory of meaning, but it does not help with present theory assessment.) On a confirmationist view, the predictions being accurate will confirm *There is an O*; on a falsificationist view, their being accurate will prevent *There is an O* from being epistemologically condemned, and not failing severe tests is a high virtue in a proposition whose truth would have explanatory value. *There is an N* seems ineligible for this predictive sort of confirmation though it may possess this type of virtue.

Fourth, psychological and physiological explanations are sometimes offered to "explain" both particular perceptual and particular numinous experiences. If one has good evidence that a person does not see a Great Dane that is plainly there to be seen, one may discover that he was badly bitten when young and has a canine phobia that simply blocks dogs out of his perceptual world. If a person has ingested (say) peyote and later has a vision of a numinous being, then (while the role of physiological, psychological, and environmental factors in such cases seems quite complex and not very well understood) perhaps one can explain the vision by reference to the ingestion. The person (likely) would have the vision even if there is no numinous being, or even if no such being causes any experience of the person in question. It is the availability of this sort of explanation that centrally calls into epistemological question the evidential worth of drug-related religious experiences. Were one to offer an epistemologically discrediting psychological or physiological explanation of all sensory experience (and so all sensory evidence) – one that entailed that beliefs based on such experience or evidence were never thereby rendered more reasonable than their contradictories or contraries – one would thereby call into question the very psychological or physiological theory on which the plausibility of the evidence-canceling explanation was offered. But a psychological or physiological explanation that "explained away" all numinous experience and evidence would in no obvious way thereby undercut its own credibility.

The first two dissimilarities – those concerning publicity and comparing different modalities – are epistemologically important because of the possibility of one's comparing sensory notes gleaned from one sensory observer with those gleaned from another and of comparing (say) visual with tactile data to provide relevant tests for object claims. Numinous experience lacks publicity and multiple modalities. Unless there are tests that have a function for numinous experience similar to the epistemological service these features provide for sensory experience, this dissimilarity will be of negative relevance to numinous experience as evidence.

The third dissimilarity seems to me not relevant to whether numinous experience is evidence. One could not offer an argument based on numinous experience that if God exists then all experience is nonveridical, for that argument would invalidate its own evidential resources. But perhaps a revelation that all sensory experience was nonveridical need not have that effect, and in any case a theology that one had excellent reason to accept, and entailed that sensory experience was systematically misleading, would not thereby become self-defeating. But this fact does not call sensory evidence into question. Why, then, should the fact that one can specify explanations that would (in principle) "explain away" numinous experiences without undercutting sensory evidence be any more significant than the fact that one can specify explanations that would (in principle) "explain away" sensory experiences without undercutting numinous evidence? The relevance of questions about whether numinous experiences are "psychologically explicable" lies elsewhere than in the fact that the theories that would generate such explanations could not "explain away" sensory experience without undercutting their own evidential support.

NUMINOUS EXPERIENCE AND TESTABILITY

Are there, then, ways of testing numinous experience? In particular, would there seem to be an *N* whether there was one or not, and are there analogues to publicity and multiple modalities? It is (as noted) true that one is at least more likely to have had a numinous experience (or its counterfeit) if one has ingested certain substances and is in a religious setting (seated in a high-ceilinged chapel, say, before stained-glass windows, with Handel's *Messiah* being played on a good pipe organ). Depending on what credence is to be given to various psychological theories, one may be somewhat more likely to have numinous experiences if one has had certain past experiences (say, loss of one's father when one was young) or if one suffers from certain maladies (e.g., reference is often made to the alleged epilepsy of the apostle Paul when his experience on the road to Damascus is being discussed). Then the facts that one has never ingested such substances, has a healthy father, and shows no traces of epilepsy will bar the attempt to "explain away" one's numinous experience by appeal to these explanations, and it will also be the case that (i) were one in any of these conditions, one could know it, and (ii) if one knew that one were in one of these conditions, and knew that there was a reliable theory that said that if one was in one of these conditions then one would (probably) have a numinous experience, one would know that it probably would seem to one that one experienced a numinous being, whether one did experience an actual numinous being or not. The stronger the theory that if a person is in state *A*, then it will seem to her that she is experiencing a numinous being, the better the position of the person who knows she has not been in *A* and could tell whether she was in *A* or not will be regarding the claim that were she in a condition where she would seem to experience a numinous being whether she actually did so or not, she could discover that she was in that epistemic condition.

So far as I am aware, there are no especially plausible or persuasive psychological theories that link up being in some psychological or physiological state A as cause to numinous experience as effect, save perhaps for those that link drug intake with the having of such experiences. So I am inclined to think that if one knows that one has ingested (say) nothing stronger than aspirin within (perhaps) the last seventy-two hours, and one has a numinous experience, one can nonculpably assume that (so far as condition [i] goes) one's seeming to experience a numinous being is evidence that one is experiencing such a being. But if there exist such theories, then one can learn them and (if the theories are worth much) find out whether one is in the conditions they specify, and if one is not and one has a numinous experience (or knows of someone else who has one and is not in the conditions they specify) then one – so far forth – has evidence that a numinous being exists. Obviously, one can also refer to such matters as food deprivation and sleep deprivation in these contexts. It is perhaps worth noting that sensory experiences of various sorts can also be drug-induced, and that the fact that alcohol consumption can produce hallucinations of insects does not serve to call entomology into question.

One can, of course, compare the description of one numinous experience with the description offered of another, and one can compare descriptions offered at one time and place with those offered at another time and place, descriptions offered within one culture with those offered within another, and descriptions offered within one religious tradition with those offered within another. Similar comparisons are often available for sensory descriptions and are highly useful, as when an astronomical theory is tested by its retrodictions concerning past events through records kept by past astronomers over centuries in various cultures.

There seems in fact (and perhaps surprisingly) to be considerable agreement in such descriptions of numinous experiences, once one allows that different metaphors, similes, symbols, and even literal ascriptions may vary greatly from one culture to another even while predicating roughly the same sort of characteristics. So there are cross-cultural and cross-traditional as well as cross-spatiotemporal comparisons to be made in the case of numinous experience, and if the important epistemological point behind the publicity and multiple modality of sensory experience is that it provides experiential testability for claims based on sensory experience, there seems to be considerable experiential testability for claims based on numinous experience, even though it lacks publicity and multiple modalities. Hence there is significant similarity regarding testability.

The second condition in principle (PN), as related to numinous experience, requires that S be able to discover that S's experience is nonveridical, if it is. Notoriously, there is widespread skepticism – or perhaps failure of nerve – about whether any religious belief can be in any fashion an object of any rational assessment (unless perhaps it is negative). The tendency is strong to put religious belief "beyond the pale of reason." For all that, arguments concerning whether there is any successful version of the problem of evil, or of one of the theistic arguments, continue relatively unabated. Should some devastating antitheistic argument ever succeed, then (I suppose) (ii) would be satisfied. Alternatively, one could discover that a particular numinous experience was nonveridical, or was at least reasonably believed so, by discovering that the numinous experience in question conflicted in its putative information content with the information content of most others in a context in which there was no good reason to overturn majority testimony.

Suppose that there are propositions known or reasonably believed to be true that have the form *Necessarily, if there is a numinous being, then it has property A* and that an experience occurs that in other ways seems to be of a numinous being but nonetheless represents its putative numinous object as lacking A by virtue of possessing some property B, where *being B* is incompatible with *being A*. Then presumably that numinous experience is nonveridical in at least that respect, and if all numinous experiences represent their putative object as being B they are all at least in part nonveridical. (This will assume that the evidential credentials of *If there is a numinous being, then it has A* do not include essential reference to numinous experience.) In these ways, then, condition (ii) in (PN) seems discernibly satisfiable.

It is perhaps easiest to consider other ways one might meet condition (ii) of (P*) as applied to numinous experience by considering also condition (iii) – that if numinous experience as a type of experience is nonveridical, this should be discoverable. Suppose that one of the attempts to disprove theism by appeal to evil has at least apparent success. One would then have reason to be highly suspicious of numinous experience in the presence of strong reason to think monotheism false. Or suppose that one discovered a contradiction in the concept of a numinous being, or at least had good reason to think one had. Then one would have good reason to suppose that numinous experiences are all nonveridical. Or suppose that there was good reason to accept some variety K of religious experience other than numinous as veridical, where if K-type experiences are veridical, then monotheism is false. Or suppose (as many believe) that some purely secular explanation of the occurrence of numinous experience is known to be "sufficient" in some sense that precludes any reason to think that it is caused by anything numinous.

What condition (iii) of (P*) as applied to numinous experience requires is that there be a way, in principle, to discover that numinous experience, as type (or, if one prefers, in all of its tokens) is nonveridical, if indeed it has this inelegance. It seems that, in principle, there are a variety of ways – namely, those just mentioned – in which one could discover this.

It is not required, of course, that one actually discover that numinous experience is nonveridical, or that one find good reason to suppose that it is, or the like. That would absurdly require that numinous experience is evidence only if we know that we have good reason to think that it is not. What is required is that one be able to specify one or more ways in which the global nonveridicality of numinous experience might be discovered, if that is the truth of the matter regarding such experience. We have noted several possibilities in that regard. These same possibilities (in addition to those previously noted) apply to condition (ii), which requires that were a particular numinous experience not veridical, this could be discerned.

Our concern here has been, so to say, with the "stronger" or "closer to maximally numinous" of numinous experiences. Roughly, such experiences have this feature: If they are veridical, they are experiences of God. Even such experiences as these underdetermine the theistic claims based on them, which is not surprising since (as noted) sensory experiences underdetermine the claims typically based on them. Viewed analytically, theological traditions wed numinous content with metaphysical constraints (e.g., explanatory adequacy) to yield claims about omnipotence and omniscience. Obviously, this story is very complex, and I will not deal with it here. But there is at least no a priori reason to think that there is no nonarbitrary way to "fill in" the conceptual distance between experience and doctrine.

EXPLANATIONS AND NUMINOUS EXPERIENCES

There are various social science explanations of religious doctrines, institutions, rites, and experiences. That there are such explanations is not by itself reason to think that numinous experiences – at least ones that occur under conditions that are not ruled out by considerations specified in (PN) – are not protheistic evidence. Since this is not exactly universally accepted, it is appropriate to argue again for this claim, even if briefly.

Suppose that one accepts psychological explanation A of religious experience, where A fits the pattern *Whenever psychological factor FP is present in a person S, S is likely to have a numinous experience under circumstance C,* and a sociological explanation of the form *Numinous experiences occur with greater frequency in societies in which social factor FS is present than in those in which FS is absent,* and an anthropological explanation of the form *Numinous experiences are frequent in cultures in which anthropological feature FA is present and rare in cultures in which FA is absent.* Suppose that Kim lives in a society that exhibits *FS*, a culture blessed with *FA*, and that Kim plainly manifests *FP*. Even if Kim is found in circumstance *C*, of course Kim may not have a numinous experience. But suppose Kim does; Kim has numinous experience *EK*.

Call the psychological, sociological, and anthropological explanations formally characterized earlier explanations *EP*, *ES*, and *EA*, respectively. To whatever degree either *EP*, *ES*, or *EA* has plausibility, and is not reducible to the others (or any other), it is also plausible that appeal to *FP* or to *FS* or to *FA* by itself is not sufficient to explain Kim's having numinous experience *EK*. Suppose *EP*, *ES*, and *EA* are the only plausible relevant theories going in their respective social sciences, and that *EP* requires reference only to *FP*, *ES* only to *FS*, and *EA* only to *FA*, in proffering an explanation of *EK*. Then reference only to *FP* is sufficient in psychology for explanation of *EK*. The same goes for reference only to *FS* in sociology, and *FA* in anthropology, as one explains *EK* in these disciplines; *EA* is sufficient in anthropology, *ES* is sufficient in sociology. Suppose that no other social science is relevant to numinous experiences, and combine *EP*, *ES*, and *EA* into one social science explanation *SE*. Then *SE*, we can say, is social science sufficient regarding *EK*. But that *SE* is social science sufficient and true does not entail that Kim does not meet all the conditions relevant to (PN) regarding *EK*, and so *EK* can be evidence that *N* exists, even though *SE* is sufficient and true. Meeting (PN) is sufficient for *EK*'s being evidence that a numinous being exists.

SE seems clearly not to exhaust what needs to be said regarding even the necessary conditions of *EK*. There are presumably physiological states of Kim such that, were Kim not in them, Kim would not have *EK*; and if physiology is construed as part of psychology, physics is not, and presumably there are physical (in the sense of "studied by physicists") states such that, were Kim not in them, Kim would not have *EK*. Combine the physiology/physics explanations, and any other natural science explanation relevant to Kim's having *EK*, into explanation *NE*, which is sufficient in natural science regarding *EK*. Regard *SE* as reducible, or as not reducible, to *NE*, as you like. There is no incompatibility between *NE*'s being natural science, and *SE*'s being social science, sufficient regarding *EK,* and Kim's meeting all of the conditions that *PN* specifies she must meet if *EK* is to be evidence that a numinous being exists. And again, if Kim has a numinous experience in conditions that meet (PN)'s requirements, then so far forth Kim has evidence that God exists.

THE ARGUMENT COMPLETED

The argument thus far has been conducted in terms of the principle of evidence (PN), namely:

> For any subject *S* and experience *E,* if *S*'s having *E* is a matter of its (phenomenologically) seeming to *S* that *S* experiences a numinous being *N,* then if *S* nonculpably has no reason to think that (i) *S* would seem to experience *N* whether or not there is an *N* that *S* experiences, or (ii) if *E* is nonveridical, *S* could not discover that it was, or (iii) if *E* is of a type *T* of experience such that every member of *T* is nonveridical, *S* could not discover this fact, then *E* provides *S* evidence that there is an *N.*

The preceding chapter favored a higher standard that is arrived at by supplementing (PN) with the requirement sanctioned by (PCPL):

> *S*'s experience *E* that is intentional regarding *O* provides evidence that *O* exists only if *O exists* falls within the scope of both collegial and lateral disconfirmation.

The proposition *O has A* comes within the scope of *collegial experiential disconfirmation* if and only if, should *If O exists, then O has A* be contingent, it is logically possible that one have an experience that provides evidence for *O lacks A;* and, should *If O exists, then O has A* be logically necessary, it is logically possible that one have an experience that provides evidence for *O*, which has some property that it is reasonable to think that only O has if O exists, lacks A,* where *O* lacks A* entails *O* exists.* Thus, for example, if one finds a being *O** that is very like *O* but that lacks some property essential to *O,* and it is unlikely that both O and O^* exist, then one has evidence that O does not grace us by its presence. For any proposition of the form *God has A*, where A is not "exists" and where *God has A* entails *God exists*, if *If God exists, then God has A* is a necessary truth, one can have experiential evidence of kind K in favor of *God exists* only if one can have experiential evidence of kind K against *The object of a kind K experience has A* and hence against *The object of a kind K experience is God*; and if *If God exists, then God has A* is contingent, one can have experiential evidence of kind K in favor of *God has A* only if one can have experiential evidence of kind K against *God has A*.

The proposition *O has A* (where A may or may not be "exists") comes within the scope of *lateral experiential disconfirmation* if and only if it is logically possible that there be an experience that provides evidence for O^* *has B* (where, of course, O^* is different from O) and the truth of O^* *has B* is evidence against the truth of *O has A*.

Lateral experiential disconfirmation and collegial experiential disconfirmation may (or may not) amount to different portions of a single continuum; how that turns out does not affect the present argument. They were, as the previous chapter makes clear, suggested by somewhat different examples.

The previous chapter argued that it is logically possible that there be experiential lateral disconfirmation of *God exists* and that it is logically possible that there be collegial experiential disconfirmation of *God exists*. At the least, one could have experiential evidence against this proposition. Further, we controversially assumed it to be essential that such evidence itself come from numinous experience that was at least of something like the strongest sort. If this assumption is false, then the argument that numinous experience is evidence for *God exists* is easier to make – it can be conducted along the lines of some of the weaker principles of experiential evidence discussed earlier. But here the stricter conditions will be assumed.

The final version, then, of our principle of experiential

evidence, stated so as to apply explicitly to numinous experience, goes as follows:

(PN*) For any subject S and experience E, if S's having E is a matter of its (phenomenologically) seeming to S that S experiences a numinous being N, then if S nonculpably has no reason to think that (i) S would seem to experience N whether or not there is an N that S experiences, or (ii) if E is nonveridical, S could not discover that it was, or (iii) if E is of a type T of experience such that every member of T is nonveridical, S could not discover this fact, then E provides S evidence that there is an N, provided that (iv) *O exists* falls within the scope of both collegial and lateral disconfirmation.

The argument goes as follows:

(1) If persons have numinous experiences under conditions that satisfy all of the conditions specified in (PN*) – if numinous experiences occur that are not prevented from being evidence by their failing any of the tests that (PN*) includes – then there is experiential evidence that God exists.

(2) Persons do have numinous experiences under conditions that satisfy all of the conditions specified in (PN*) – numinous experiences occur that are not prevented from being evidence by their failing any of the tests that (PN*) includes.

Hence:

(3) There is experiential evidence that God exists.

The principle of experiential evidence appealed to in step (1) has been defended in detailed arguments. Of course, for all that, it may be mistaken. If it is shown that it is, then of course it must be revised and the success of the argument will then rest on its fate in the hands of the revision, assuming that it is correct. That numinous experiences *can* satisfy all of the conditions specified by a properly constructed principle of experiential evidence has also been defended in detailed arguments, and I have nothing to add to them here. I think that it is fairly clear that actual numinous experiences have occurred under conditions that do not fail the relevant tests, but of course a defense of that claim would require an interesting foray into matters of religious history and biography. Plainly, the argument is valid: Steps (1) and (2) entail step (3). So far as I can see, then, a properly revised version of Broad's argument, relying on a principle of evidence considerably more complex than any to which he explicitly appealed, in fact succeeds.

Part VI

Enlightenment and conceptual experience

13

Are enlightenment experiences evidence for religious beliefs?

There are religious experiences other than apparent experiences of God. Two sorts interest us here. One sort is viewed as providing evidence regarding the nature of the person or self. The other sort is viewed as providing evidence of the existence of qualityless Brahman, a God-beyond-God, experience of which "trumps" or "sublates" strong numinous experiences. Each type of experience is discussed in turn. The relevance of the first sort to our fundamental question as to whether apparent experience of God provides evidence that God exists is indirect: The Jain doctrine of persons might be too thick, and the Buddhist doctrine of persons too thin, to be compatible with typical monotheistic doctrines regarding persons. A typical monotheistic account of what a person is views a person as a mental substance whose existence is logically contingent and existentially dependent. Regarding any actual person Kim, the view is that *Kim does not exist* is false, but not self-contradictory, and *Kim was created, and is sustained in existence, by God* is true. According to Jainism, persons do not depend for their existence on the existence of anything else; each person is a mental substance that exists on its own. According to much of the Buddhist tradition, a person at a particular time is only a bundle or heap of momentary, transitory states; over time a person is a series of such bundles. A typical monotheistic concern with the Jain view will be that at most a person can exist independent of everything *save God* so that Jain persons are thicker than is consistent with monotheism. A typical monotheistic concern with the view frequently held within Buddhist contexts is that nonsubstantive persons may not possess sufficient identity at a time, or sufficient continuity over time, for typical monotheistic doctrines of responsibility, forgiveness, and retribution to be applicable, so that Buddhist persons are thinner than is consistent with monotheism. Exactly how all of this actually works out is beyond our current concerns. What will be argued here is that the introspective experiences referred to in defense of the Jain and Buddhist doctrines do not provide evidence for those doctrines – not merely that they provide *insufficient* evidence but that they provide *no evidence at all* – so that the conclusions defended in this book are not affected by appeals to introspective evidence in favor of the claims about persons that were just briefly rehearsed.

The view that certain esoteric religious experiences provide evidence that only qualityless Brahman exists, and that the evidential force of these experiences overrides that of strong numinous experience, is a more direct challenge to our project and will be directly met.

INTROSPECTIVE RELIGIOUS EXPERIENCES

Some religious experiences at least seem to have the subject herself as their object, as the item referred to by the subject term of a statement for which the relevant experience provides evidence. There is a temptation to think that these religious experiences are more reliable, easier to interpret, more likely to be veridical, and so forth, than experiences that do not reflexively refer back to their subject. Such experiences often are referred to as introspective.

PSYCHOLOGICAL CLAIMS VERSUS RELIGIOUS CLAIMS

A particularly interesting and religiously important example of religious claims partially based on appeal to experience concerns competing doctrines regarding the nature of the self. These doctrines, as well as other religious doctrines based in whole or in part on religious experience in the sense that such experience allegedly provides evidence for the doctrines, contrast sharply with merely psychological claims. The claim to feel peaceful, calm, free from desires, secure, or blissful can be important to the individual who makes it; having the experience that supports the claim may be crucial to the continued or restored health of the person who makes it. But these are matters of psychology, not of religion. Even if a religious tradition holds that enlightenment experience always includes the element of blissful feeling, not every feeling of bliss is part of an enlightenment experience. A person who has a sense of calm well-being while inhaling gas as a root canal procedure is in process has not thereby achieved Nirvana, *kevala,* or *moksha.* Religious claims do not reduce to claims about the momentary psychological states of the subject or subjects of certain sorts of experience.

Jains believe that a person is a mental substance, a subject of self-consciousness who exists over time and is not made up of the experiences she has. On a Jain account, *Sharon is daydreaming about writing a mystery novel* ascribes a psychological state to an enduring mind; it does not say that "Sharon" names a collection and "daydreaming" refers to a part of the collection. Typically, Buddhists believe that a person at any given time is just a bundle of psychological states and over time is a series of such bundles. (Sometimes a person is also said to contain physical states, but I leave this aside here.) On the Jain account, a self is noncomposite and enjoys numerical identity over time. On the typical Buddhist view, no noncomposite item has numerical identity over time. The difference between Jain and typical Buddhist teaching regarding the nature of a person or self is deep and uncompromising. By itself it refutes the silliness that all religions teach the same thing. Since both Jain and Buddhist confidently appeal to religious experience to confirm their very different views on this matter, and since the dispute is cross-cultural and also occurs outside the context of religious disputes, it is an especially interesting example.

Two arguments, then, constitute the next sections of this

chapter. One – *the specific argument* – deals with the dispute concerning the nature of persons or selves, especially as it occurs between Jainism and Buddhism as both traditions appeal to religious experience as alleged evidence for their contrasting doctrines. The other – *the general argument* – underlines some basic and salient properties of religious doctrines and religious experiences, reflection on which makes plain that the results of the specific argument are not atypical.

THE SPECIFIC ARGUMENT

If the core of Jain doctrine is true, then there are everlasting or eternal souls. They are simple, not composite – individuals, not heaps. If one has experiential evidence for this Jain doctrine, then one at least has experiential evidence for the claim:

(J) An individual endures through time.

By assuming that this individual is typical, the subject of an experience confirming (J) can infer to a universal claim about the durability of all individuals.

If the core of Buddhist doctrine is true, then (save for Nirvana) everything is impermanent. No individual endures; only heaps endure. A heap need not endure; a composite might exist only at a moment. But if anything endures, at a given time it is a composite of transitory simple items that exist at that time, and at any later time at which it exists it is a composite of items that are numerically distinct from all of the earlier transitory simple items. Composites can in turn be composed of composites, but higher-order composites of lower-order composites finally reduce to first-order composites. A first-order composite at a time comprises transitory simples that exist at no other time. So whatever endures is a heap. If one has experiential evidence for this Buddhist doctrine, then at least one has experiential evidence for the claim:

(B) No simple individual endures through time.

It might seem that the Buddhist claim, involving a universal negative, is problematic regarding experiential confirmation, and that the Jain claim is much simpler to confirm experientially. This disparity is only apparent, as we shall see. Plainly (B) goes beyond any one experience at any time. If it is true, never anywhere is there any individual that retains numerical identity over any time. An experiential step toward, or at least not away from, (B) would be an experience correctly reportable in terms of:

> (B1) I now experience no individual that has retained numerical identity over time.

Of course the Jain claim is that there are many souls, all of whom are everlasting or eternal. Thus the Jain claim goes beyond anything that a single experience of a single person at a time could justify. An experiential step toward, or at least not away from, (J) would be an experience correctly reportable in terms of:

> (J1) I now experience an individual that has retained numerical identity over time.

What is requisite can be made still more explicit via:

> (J2) I now experience an individual such that an individual that previously existed still exists and is numerically identical to this individual.

Of course any experience that confirmed this claim would disconfirm (B). If one has experienced something that has endured through time, then of course it is false that nothing does endure over time.

Plainly, (J2) is a claim whose truth conditions extend beyond any single time. But the same thing applies to (B1). What is requisite can be made more explicit via:

> (B2) I now experience no individual such that an individual that previously existed is numerically identical to this individual.

Plainly, (B2) also is a claim whose truth conditions extend beyond any single time. Having an experience that confirmed (B2) would not disconfirm (J). That one is not now experiencing anything that endures through time does not entail that there is nothing that endures through time.

If one prefers, one has:

(B3) I now experience one or more individuals, none of which is numerically identical to any previously existing individuals.

(J3) I now experience one or more individuals, at least one of which is numerically identical to a previously existing individual.

It is having experiences of these sorts (perhaps among others) that will be relevant to having experiential support, respectively, for (B) or (J).

Apparently, episodic memory must play an essential role in any experience of which (B3) or (J3) is a report; in each case, the claim can be known only if something is known about the past, namely, that (for [J3]) *at least one,* or else (for [B3]) *none* of the individuals remembered to be experienced (by myself or another) is now being experienced. Unless one is to infer the claim about the past from such general claims as *Some individuals endure* (in the case of [J3]) or *No individuals endure* (in the case of [B3]), presumably the element of past-tense knowledge required if an experience is to be correctly reported by (B3) or (J3) must be provided by memory – one's own memory or memory expressed by the testimony of others. After all, it is precisely these general claims for which such experiences as those expressed by (B3) and (J3) are supposed to provide evidence. It will be highly inconvenient if they do so only after these general claims already are known in some other manner or else simply must be assumed. If the claims must be known to be true in some nonexperiential manner, then the experiential evidence will be unneeded. If we must simply assume their truth, then experiential evidence for them will be unavailable.

As both (J3) and (B3) seem to require an experiential confirmation that requires appeal to memory, whatever must be the case in order for memory sometimes to be reliable has to be allowed for in both Jain and Buddhist metaphysics. It seems obvious that one can remember only what one somehow participated in, and one can learn from the memory of others only by testimony. Presumably Buddhist and Jain ontologists will agree that

> (BJ) Reliable memory occurs only if something endures through time.

This entails:

> (JB) Reliable memory occurs only if something retains numerical identity over time.

The Jain candidate for such retention of numerical identity is a person considered as an individual; the Buddhist candidate is a person construed as a heap.

Strictly, then, what would seem to lend support to the Buddhist claim would be an introspective experience correctly reportable via:

> (B4) No individual that I now introspectively experience has numerical identity to any individual that I remember having introspectively experienced.

One would also need evidence that one's own experience was fully typical in this regard. A priori, it might be, but also might not. The Jain claim will run:

> (J4) Some individual that I now introspectively experience has numerical identity to an individual that I remember having introspectively experienced.

The typical individual referred to by (J4) will, of course, be the person making the claim. Presumably, these are, or are close to, the minimal descriptions of an experience that would lend some support to Buddhist doctrine (in the case of [B4]) or Jain doctrine (in the case of [J4]).

One who correctly reported an experience via (B4) or (J4) would have to be able to *identify* individuals. Whether or not one needs a criterion to identify individuals, one will need some notion of what an individual is. Both whether one experiences any individuals at all, and if so how many, obviously will depend on what counts as an individual. It may well be that one "brings the relevant concept of an individual to" the experience in which one identifies them. By itself, this need cause no problem. That I already have the concept of a parrot does not raise the suspicion that my answer to the question "How many parrots are in the cage?" somehow is epistemically tainted. When there are relevantly competing ontologies, as is the case between Jainism and Buddhism – distinct ontologies that of course have different accounts of what an individual is – things can be more complicated.

Suppose that one has an afterimage. For the Jain, the afterimage (insofar as it is individual at all) is an individual state; strictly, it is a state or property of an individual, individuated by reference to whose state it is as well as by when it occurs. For the Buddhist, it is an individual in its own right, individuated by reference to when it occurs. But "whose" it is in part is individuated by reference to *it*, and not conversely. A person is a heap, and a heap at a time is individuated by reference to its constituents at that time, and (if it exists over time) it also is individuated by reference to its constituents at one time and its constituents at another.

Although an image, a pain, or any other mental phenomenon, being both an individual and a thing that endures, would falsify the claim that everything is impermanent, the obvious focus of the dispute concerns persons. The Jain monk claims to reidentify himself as the same individual as one previously experienced. The Buddhist monk claims at most to reidentify the same heap as previously experienced.

The philosopher and bishop George Berkeley once claimed that "there is no identity (other than qualitative) in any individuals besides persons" (Fraser, vol. 1, p. 72). Jains will disagree insofar as they think that physical objects or substances endure over time, but will agree that persons enjoy numerical identity over time; Sharon at noon is numerically the same enduring noncomposite individual as Sharon at midnight. Typical Buddhists will hold that persons altogether lack the identity that Berkeley ascribes to them. The question here concerns whether one or the other of these views concerning persons is substantiated by introspective experience.

The Jain metaphysic of personal identity is stated in various religious texts. For example, a Jain text tells us the following:

> The distinctive characteristic of a substance is being. Being is a simultaneous possession of coming into existence, going out of existence, and permanence. Permanence means the indestructibility of the essence of the substance. . . . Substance is possessed of attributes and modifications. . . . Attributes depend upon substratum and cannot be the substratum of another attribute. Modification is change of attribute. (*Tattvarthadhigama Sutra*, Chapter 5, Sections 29, 30, 31, 38, 41, 42; *Sourcebook*, p. 256)

A substance, we are told, has attributes – properties or qualities, if you please. No attribute can exist that is not the attribute of some substance. Second-order properties can be properties of first-order properties, but the latter are attributes of things or substances. One would guess that some attributes are essential to a substance and some are not. Thus it is no surprise to read elsewhere in the same text: "The self's essence is life, the capacity of being liberated, and the incapacity of being liberated. The distinctive characteristic of self is attention. . . . Those with minds are knowers" (Chapter 2, Sections 7, 8, 29; *Sourcebook*, p. 254). The idea, I take it, is that some selves or *jivas* are essentially alive and capable of achieving enlightenment and others are essentially alive and incapable of enlightenment – a sort of negative election without an elector. A self or person of course retains her essential properties, but over time continually gains some, and loses other, nonessential properties. As another text tersely says, "Selves are substances" (Chapter 2, Section 10).

Further, it is claimed that this concept of the person is derived from, and can be confirmed by reference to, intro-

Enlightenment and conceptual experience

spective experience. Thus one reads, "That which should be grasped by self-discrimination is 'I' from the real point of view" (*Samayasdra*, p. 325), and, "The soul has the nature of knowledge, and the realization of this nature is Nirvana; therefore one who is desirous of Nirvana must meditate upon self-knowledge" (*Atmanusasana*, p. 174). Knowledge of the nature of the self or person is achievable through self-awareness.

It is worth noting that for Jainism not even that most desirable modification – namely, enlightenment – changes the person's capacities for attention or removes its status as a knower: "After the soul is released, there remain perfect right-belief, perfect right-knowledge, perfect perception, and the state of having accomplished all" (*Tattvarthadhigama* Chapter 10, Section 4; *Sourcebook*, p. 260).

THERAVADA BUDDHISM

A Buddhist text tells us:

> Whether Buddhas arise, O priests, or whether Buddhas do not arise, it remains a fact and the fixed and necessary constitution of being that all its constituents are transitory. This fact a Buddha discovers and masters, and when he has discovered and mastered it, he announces, teaches, publishes, proclaims, discloses, minutely explains, and makes it clear, that all the constituents of being are transitory. . . . Whether Buddhas arise, O priests, or whether Buddhas do not arise, it remains a fact and the fixed and necessary constitution of being that all its elements are lacking in an ego (substantial, permanent self-nature). This fact a Buddha discovers and masters, and when he has discovered and mastered it, he announces, teaches, publishes, proclaims, discloses, minutely explains, and makes it clear, that all the elements of being are lacking in an ego. (*Anguttara-Nikaya*, Section iii, p. 134; *Sourcebook*, pp. 273, 274; the text is Theravadin)

A longer and more familiar passage reads as follows:

> Just as the word "chariot" is but a mode of expression for axle, wheels, chariot-body, pole, and other constituent mem-

288

bers, placed in a certain relation to each other, but when we come to examine the members one by one, we discover that in the absolute sense there is no chariot; and just as the word "house" is but a mode of expression for wood and other constituents of a house, surrounding space in a certain relation, but in the absolute sense there is no house; and just as the word "fist" is but a mode of expression for the fingers, the thumb, etc., in a certain relation; and the word "lute" for the body of the lute, strings, etc.; "army" for elephants, horses, etc.; "city" for fortifications, houses, gates, etc.; "tree" for trunk, branches, foliage, etc.; in a certain relation, but when we come to examine the parts one by one, we discover that in the absolute sense there is no tree; in exactly the same way the words "living entity" and "ego" are but a mode of expression for the presence of the five attachment groups, but when we come to examine the elements of being one by one, we discover that in the absolute sense there is no living entity there to form a basis for such figments as "I am" or "I"; in other words, that in the absolute sense there is only name and form. The insight of him who perceives this is called knowledge of the truth. (*Visuddhi-Magga*, Section 18; *Sourcebook*, pp. 284–85; the text is Theravadin)

The gist of the passages is put more succinctly by the terse claim "Consciousness is soulless" (*Sangutta-Nikaya*, Section 3, p. 66; *Sourcebook*, p. 280).

THE BASIC LINES OF ARGUMENT

The core of the Buddhist line is captured by these lines of reasoning:

(1) If I am a mental substance, then each introspective experience will include experience of myself as a mental substance.
(2) No introspective experience includes experience of myself as a mental substance.

Hence:

(3) I am not an enduring mental substance.

To this line of reasoning is added:

(4) I am at any given moment what I introspectively experience myself to be at that moment.
(5) I introspectively experience, at any given moment, only momentary states.

Hence:

(6) I am, at any given moment, only momentary states.

The core of the Jain line of reasoning reads:

(1) If each introspective experience includes experience of myself as a mental substance, then I am a mental substance.
(2) Each introspective experience does include experience of myself as a mental substance.

Hence:

(3) I am a mental substance.

To this line of reasoning is added:

(4) I am at any given moment what I experience myself to be at that moment.
(5) I introspectively experience, at any given moment, my having momentary states.

Hence:

(6) I am, at any given moment, something that has momentary states.

Obviously, the doctrine that a person *has* states and endures over time as a noncomposite agent is different from the view that a person *is* one or more conscious states at a given time and a succession of transitory states over time, each state being around only for a second. These lines of reasoning bring out some of the central ideas and claims of our competing perspectives. These perspectives agree that persons are objects of direct awareness, and that one's nature as a person lies open to introspective examination. How I appear to introspection is how I am. But they differ as to how I appear to introspection.

The Jain monk and the Buddhist monk obviously describe their introspective experiences differently. Each will claim that the other misdescribes. Each will defend that claim by appeal to texts that he (but not his opponents) regards as authoritative, and each offers arguments that are not appeals to introspective experience. Apparently the fact of the matter is this. One cannot nonarbitrarily decide between the Jain report of introspective experience and the Buddhist report of introspective experience by appeal to introspection. It was appeal to introspection that yielded the impasse, and further appeal to the same source will only give the same results. Suppose that the two views of personhood are not only exclusive but exhaustive. Then what follows is that one report expresses the correct account of what a person is, and one does not. Even then it does not follow that one can *tell* which report is correct by appeal to introspection. If one discovers that, say, Jainism is the correct view, it still does not follow that Jainism then is supported by introspective evidence. It does not follow that those who got it right did so by appeal to experiential evidence.

For the Jain, awareness of mental states is awareness of oneself as being in those mental states. The person is what is in those states – not the states by themselves (there being no such thing) but the very thing that is conscious in the ways in which it is aware of itself as being conscious. For the Buddhist, one is aware not of being in, but of being constituted by, one's states. Thus the Jain report form for introspective experiences is *Person S is aware of S's being in state A*, whereas the Buddhist's report form goes: *Person S is aware of S's being constituted by state A*. Even if these report forms are exclusive and exhaustive, it may well be that introspective experience will not tell us which report form matches, and which mutilates, the structure of introspective experience. Indeed, that seems to be the truth of the matter.

Further, even should a Jain philosopher accept the Buddhist description of introspective experience, it would not follow that he would have, in all consistency, to abandon his overall position. Suppose a Jain accepts the description:

(B*) All I am aware of is transitory mental states,

but also correctly embraces:

(J*) Every mental state is a state of some mental substance.

Together (B*) and (M*) will justify:

(J**) What I am aware of exists only if there is a mental substance.

Further, if he rightly also accepts:

(J') Any mental state that I am aware of is mine,

he may infer:

(J") I am a mental substance,

all compatibly with accepting (B*), a Buddhist-compatible description of introspective awareness.

MEDITATION

One might object that I have neglected the meditative traditions in which the Jain and Buddhist experiences (especially at their religiously most significant) occur. So I have, but for sufficient reason. The meditative traditions themselves are shaped by the doctrines in dispute, and what counts as a religiously genuine experience in part is decided by whether it is an experience in which the correct doctrine is "seen to be so." Thus if one appeals to a Jain meditative tradition and its experiences, one will have "verified" Jainism, and if one appeals to a Buddhist tradition (other than of the very minority personalist sort) and its approved experiences, one will have "verified" Buddhism. The appeal to meditation accomplishes nothing in terms of assessing the experiential evidence, since what is approved as a result of meditation is only what conforms to the relevant already approved doctrine. So we are left with conflicting introspective reports and the resultant impasse so far as appeal to introspection goes.

THE GENERAL ARGUMENT

One possesses *internal* epistemic certainty regarding P if and only if one believes that P, and it is a necessary truth that *If one believes that P, then P is true*, and P is logically contingent. One possesses *external* epistemic certainty regarding P if and only if one believes that P, and it is a necessary truth that *If one believes that P, then P is true*, and P is logically necessary. If one is not sure that P, one lacks psychological certainty that P. Of course one can be psychologically certain that P when P is false (and one lacks epistemic certainty regarding P). If one is epistemically certain regarding some proposition P, then one at least has the raw materials for being epistemically justified in believing that P. One need only become aware that one believes that P, and that necessarily if one does so, then P is true, and then make the proper inference. But one can possess epistemic justification and lack epistemic certainty. Psychological certainty can join epistemic justification without impropriety.

If our previous arguments regarding self-authentication have been correct, enlightenment experiences occur only if doctrines regarding which epistemic certainty necessarily is unavailable are known to be true. Yet, given intratraditional criteria, no experience counts as providing enlightenment in which doubt is present. Hence an experience in which epistemic justification joins psychological certainty regarding an enlightenment doctrine is the most, but also the least, one can hope for if there are genuine enlightenment experiences.

293

Remember the claims:

(B3) I now experience one or more individuals, none of which is numerically identical to any previously existing individuals.

(J3) I now experience one or more individuals, at least one of which is numerically identical to a previously existing individual.

These claims are essential, respectively, to the Buddhist and Jain experiential arguments in the sense that unless these claims can be experientially substantiated, the full Buddhist and Jain doctrines, expressed in stronger claims, cannot be experientially substantiated by appeal to introspection. Plainly (B3) and (J3) are the sorts of propositions that one might mistakenly believe. It is possible that one offer (B3) or (J3) as a report of one's experience, and be mistaken. Hence one cannot have epistemological certainty regarding them.

Further, if the *specific argument* is correct, claims such as (B3) and (J3) cannot be justified by appeal to the experiences that provide evidence for them *if* any experience at all plays that role. If that argument is correct, introspective (and meditational) experience does not provide evidence for either (B3) or (J3). Thus there is no experiential epistemic justification available for (B3) or (J3), or hence for the stronger Jain or Buddhist doctrinal claims that entail (B3) or (J3), since (B3) and (J3) – or claims much like them – are experientially minimal claims relative to what must be experientially established if experiential confirmation of Buddhist or Jain claims, based on introspective (or meditational) awareness, is to be a going enterprise, and the right sort of experiential evidence to consider is introspective.

It is of some interest that the Buddhist position differs from the views of David Hume. If we ask what the ontological status of each transitory state is, we get different answers. For Hume, each such state exists independently of all others; a single impression constitutes a logically and causally possible world. For the typical Buddhist tradition, each state depends for its existence on other states with which it "codependently arises." Similarly, the Jain position differs from Descartes's views. If we ask about the ontological status of a mental substance, we get different answers. For Descartes, each mental substance other than God depends for its existence on God, whereas for Jainism each mental substance enjoys independent existence. Here, too, I suggest, appeal to introspective evidence will be fruitless.

A FINAL CONSIDERATION OF
INTROSPECTIVE EVIDENCE

A simple and short way with the Jain claim that one is ontologically independent – that one depends on nothing distinct from oneself for one's existence – and that one can discern this from self-awareness is to reply that *being ontologically independent* is not a property that is discernible by self-awareness. Even if one has that property, one will not be able to tell that one has it simply by taking an extremely discerning introspective look at oneself. Correspondingly, when Pascal says that even a drop of water can destroy him, he is not giving us the benefit of an introspective report.

In contrast to *feeling tired, being dizzy,* and *feeling depressed and lonely,* and also in contrast to *being euphoric* and *feeling excited and alert,* a property such as *being ontologically independent* is not a possible object of inner awareness. The same, of course, goes for *being ontologically dependent.*

One range of properties that one can be introspectively aware of – *introspectible* properties – are those that one arguably cannot be mistaken about. Another range of introspectible properties consists of those that have this feature: One's believing that one has them is evidence that one has them. *Being in pain* falls within the former range; *not fearing to travel by air* falls within the latter range.

Introspectible properties are *aspectual;* they are aspects of the persons who introspect them. But not every aspect is introspectible. All of one's properties are aspects of oneself, since for any person S and property A, *S does not exist* entails *S lacks A.* But plainly *being an only child* and *having a pet gold-*

fish are not introspectible. There are a great many properties that involve both their bearers' having an aspect and there existing certain items that are objects relative to their bearers. My knowing that my dog is a golden retriever is an aspect of me, but it is an aspect that I can have only if a certain friendly creature exists and belongs to the indicated breed. For any person *S* and aspect *A*, if *S has A* entails *O, which is an object relative to A, exists,* then *A* is not an introspectible property of *S*. An aspect that I have only if I have properties whose nonintrospectibility arises in this manner is at best only partly introspectible; introspection alone cannot justify the claim that I have any such aspect. The aspects that persons allegedly have that are of religious interest typically, perhaps always, are object-entailing, and hence it is not introspectibly confirmable that persons have them. Claims about human nature are object-entailing, even if they are (quite atypically) construed as counterfactual.

Introspection is awareness of (non–object-entailing) aspects as sensory perception is awareness of objects. One's experiences frequently involve introspection and sensory experience – one tastes the coffee and finds it pleasing or hears the symphony and is soothed and relaxed. The religious experiences relevant to our concerns, however, are not sensory, nor do they contain sensory components. They are inner-directed and involve self-awareness (for the Jain, awareness of an enduring self; for the Buddhist, awareness of momentary states that compose a self). More explicitly, they concern the nature and structure of selfhood, or a representative example of same, as allegedly open to introspection. In fact, claims regarding the nature and structure of selfhood ascribe properties to selves that introspective experience does not, and cannot, confirm.

The gist of the problem of going from

(A1) *It seems to me that I am but a bundle of states*

to

(B) *I am but a bundle of states*

can be put in terms of the lack of possible falsification. The "seems" in (A1) is a "seems" of opinion, not a phenomenological "seems." The distinctive difference between one who asserts (A1) and one who affirms

(A2) It seems to me that I am an enduring being

is doctrinal, not phenomenological. Different things seem true to them. No doubt the overall cast of their experiences may be affected by their different beliefs. But the difference between them is not a matter of one being introspectively blind and the other being possessed of introspective sight – one is not an introspective hallucinator or the other an astute introspective observer. There is nothing that one could observe that would introspectively falsify (A1) or (A2). Hence there is nothing that would introspectively verify (A1) or (A2). But only if appeal to a sort of experience *could* falsify a claim does appeal to it provide possible confirmation for that claim.

If we replace (A1) and (A2) with

(A) I introspectively observe only states

then (as we have seen) the Jain will contend that this misdescribes what one introspectively observes – one observes not states but *one's own states* and observes them *as* one's own – and in any case (A)'s truth and adequacy are as compatible with the Jain analysis as with the Buddhist.

Short of thinking that Jains and Buddhists belong to different ontological species, the right explanation of the different introspective reports seems to be the difference in doctrine that we have noted; it is basic doctrinal discord that explains a cross-culturally represented difference in introspective reports. Perhaps arguments can refute one, or both, of the relevant doctrines. What has been argued here is that introspective experiences cannot confirm either doctrine, because introspective experience could not disconfirm either doctrine. But then it follows that introspective experiences do not meet the relevance conditions that a proper principle of experiential evidence will require any experience to meet that parades itself as evidence for either the Jain account or the Buddhist.

Whether or not, then, one could weave a Jain or a Buddhist account of personhood into a robustly monotheistic account of things, there is no experiential conflict – no conflict among experiential evidences – when we compare the evidence provided for the existence of God by strong numinous experiences and the lack of evidence provided for a Jain or a Buddhist account of what a person is by introspective experiences.

ADVAITA VEDANTA DISMISSAL OF EVIDENCE FROM STRONG NUMINOUS EXPERIENCE

Some varieties of Hinduism – Dvaita Vedanta as represented by Madhva and Vsistadvaita Vedanta as represented by Ramanuja, for example – are unreservedly monotheistic. Even when (as with Ramanuja) the universe is spoken of as God's body, the relationship between God and the universe is this: The universe is sustained in existence by God, who could exist even if it did not. The view is that between God and the universe there obtains an asymmetrical dependence relation; God everlastingly supports the world's existence but does not need the world around in order to sustain God's own being. The core religious problem is sin and the core human need is for forgiveness of sin and freedom from the power of sin, which a gracious God can provide. But Advaita Vedanta Hinduism, for all of its temples and hymns and rituals, in its doctrinal formulation regards God, as described thus far in this paragraph, as nonexistent and Brahman without qualities as comprising all there is. This is softened in terms of speaking of what is *true at the level of appearance* – that God exists – and what is *true at the level of reality* – that only qualityless Brahman exists. But the softening is pedagogical and psychological, not doctrinal or theological or philosophical. If the Advaita Vedanta perspective is true, then God does not exist. If strong numinous experience provides evidence to the contrary, it lies.

Essentially, the Advaita Vedanta grounds for the dismissal of the apparent evidential force of strong numinous experience involve two lines of criticism. One line begins by noting that strong numinous experience involves "the making of distinctions" and argues that since only Brahman without qualities exists, no distinction that anyone makes corresponds to anything that is distinct. There is only one thing, and it allegedly has no qualities, and so has no qualities that are distinct from other qualities. Thus any experience that involves there being distinctions – whose phenomenology is such as to involve distinctions and which is veridical only if there is more than one qualityless thing – is nonveridical; it is epistemically flawed in a manner that prevents it from being evidence about how things are. That, briefly, is how one dismissive line of reasoning goes. The other goes as follows. To become religiously enlightened is to have an enlightenment experience called *moksha*, which experientially confirms the Advaita Vedanta view of reality. Enlightenment experience trumps any other sort of experience so far as evidence is concerned (as well as in other ways). Since one cannot take both enlightenment experience and strong numinous experience as veridical, the latter must go. Here, then, the challenge to the notion of strong numinous experience as evidence for God's existence is direct. It is time to examine the case that we have briefly described.

THREE OBJECTIONS, SCHEMATICALLY STATED, TO ADVAITA VEDANTA

Advaita Vedanta seems to face insuperable objections. It maintains that only *nirguna*, or qualityless, Brahman exists; call this *the thesis of radical monism*. Three difficulties immediately beset this thesis. For one thing, it is logically impossible that there be anything that lacks all qualities; *X exists but for every property P, X lacks P* is simply a contradiction. Replacing "exists" by "subsists," or the like, of course will change nothing. So the thesis of radical monism is necessarily false. For another, the thesis is supposedly confirmed, allegedly firmly if not irrefutably, by *moksha*, or enlightenment, experience. Thus such an experience must be one in which someone learns something – in which some person *S* is such that *S learns the truth of the thesis of radical monism* is true. But of course in such an experience there are distinctions to be made – distinctions between *S* and *what S learns* and *S's learning it*, or between *S* and *what S intuits* and *S's intuiting it*, and the like. But it is also held both that the appearance of distinctions within experiences disqualifies other sorts of experiences from being veridical or providing reliable information, so in all consistency they should equally disqualify *moksha* experiences from being veridical or providing reliable information, and that the subject of even *moksha* experiences is not real but illusory, and so does not so much as exist, which would seem to be a serious barrier to obtaining knowledge. For a third thing, the thesis of radical monism runs dead against the testimony of all our experience. Many, perhaps most, of our experiences are *subject-consciousness-object* in form, where *O is an object of S's experience E* entails *If O exists at all, O's existence is not dependent on S's or E's*. Thus the experiences reported by *S reads his Koran* and *S sees a ghost* are both intentional (in structure, so to say), though the *Koran* is in *S's* hands and there are no ghosts, and whether *S* mistakes something else for a ghost or is purely hallucinating. Others of our experiences are what we might call *subject-consciousness-content*, or perhaps *subject-content*. Thus the experiences reported by *S feels dizzy* or *S is hungry and tired* are not such that the dizziness, or the hunger and weariness, exists independent of *S*. *S sees an afterimage*, on these criteria, is *subject-content*, as is *S is in pain*, for the afterimage and the pain are not such that, if they exist, they do so independent of the subject that experiences them. Both *subject-consciousness-object* and *subject-content* experiences confirm distinctions of a sort (and what sort is not?) incompatible with the thesis of radical monism – distinctions between subjects of experience, experiential states, and objects of experiences, or between subjects of experiences and experiential contents. So the thesis of radical monism flies directly in the face of the very occurrence of human experience, let alone of those particular claims about distinct terms, possessing qualities, for which various experiences provide splendid evidence. Thus Advaita Vedanta seems colossally false – false in a manner that makes such mere empirical falsehoods as *Peanuts mature into elephants* or *Alligators become teaspoons on Tuesdays* seem highly plausible by comparison. Advaita Vedantins, however mistaken they may be, are not unaware of the fact that such objections as those just briefly rehearsed have been made.

TWO INTERPRETATIONS OF ADVAITA VEDANTA

One issue that is crucial to understanding Advaita Vedanta is this: Is the Atman-Brahman distinction to be seen as metaphysical or as epistemological – as ontic or as epistemic? Suppose it is metaphysical or ontological. Then there is a distinction between Atman – that is, between *any* Atman, or "individual self" – and Brahman. In the context, one natural way of seeing this, then, is in terms of the Atman being dependent on Brahman; Brahman has and the Atman lacks independence, or *aseity*, as a traditional theologial would say. This can hardly be the way to understand the identity of Atman with Brahman; it requires their real and irreducible distinctness. Granted, there are traditions in which, if *A* depends for its existence on *B* (and not conversely), then *A* is *less real* than *B*. I think this way of putting the matter invites confusion and error, but in any case it is clear that such an *A* and *B* are not identical.

So presumably the Atman-Brahman distinction is epistemic. One *mistakenly* distinguishes an Atman from Brahman; one perceives Brahman as if it were an Atman. But in fact, "Atman" and "Brahman" have identity of reference, where "Atman = Brahman" is to be read *left to right*. Read *right to left*, it would say something of this sort: "Brahman" refers to the *set of distinct Atmans*; and *that* is not the Advaita Vedanta position. So perhaps Advaita Vedanta's thesis of radical monism can be stated as (i) "Atman" and "Brahman" have identity of reference (and the identity is to be read *right to left*); (ii) the referent of "Brahman" is misperceived when one refers to it as "Atman" in that it then seems to have properties it does not have. But seems *to whom*? Not to Brahman – Brahman is not the sort of entity to which error (a variety of defect) is ascribable, and Brahman allegedly has no properties at all and so is not in a position to perceive or misperceive anything – but, rather, to an Atman, that is, to some individual perceiver. But *S misperceives X as Y* entails *X exists* and *S exists*, though it does not entail *Y exists* or *X has Y*. That Ralph perceives his horse as a unicorn entails that Ralph and Ralph's horse are real, but not that unicorns are real or that Ralph's horse is a unicorn. Where Advaita Vedanta is construed as claiming that the Atman-Brahman distinction is only epistemological, that Ralph misperceives Brahman as an Atman entails that Ralph and Brahman exist, but not that an Atman does. But if Ralph misperceives Brahman as an Atman, then (since a misperceiver must be an Atman) Ralph must be an Atman, and not Brahman; thus the Brahman-Atman distinction is ontic, not epistemic. But that the Brahman-Atman distinction is ontic is incompatible with Advaita Vedanta; it is inconsistent with the thesis of radical monism.

Since *the Brahman-Atman distinction is epistemic* entails the *Brahman-Atman distinction is ontic*, that the Brahman–Atman distinction is epistemic is inconsistent with Advaita Vedanta. But then how *is* Advaita Vedanta to be put? Perhaps there is no way to put it. Perhaps there *is* no "thesis of radical monism" – no such claim that is true, no such claim that is false, no such claim whose acceptance is essential to enlightenment, no such claim whose acceptance is utter folly, no such perspective as Advaita Vedanta at all. So much for Advaita Vedanta. And so much for any challenge it might seem to present to strong numinous experience being evidence for God's existence.

These types of objections, of course, are familiar. There are a variety of ways of responding to them. In what follows, I consider some of these responses with Eliot Deutsch's *Ad-*

vaita Vedānta: A Philosophical Reconstruction providing a contemporary sourcebook.

I consider three types of response – an appeal to experience, a retreat from language, and an attempt at proof or argument.

ADVAITA VEDANTA'S APPEAL TO EXPERIENCE

One response concerns the notion of *sublation* or *subration;* the general idea is that one experience E_1 supports a proposition P, and another experience E_2 supports *not-P*, and E_2 epistemically outweights E_1. Thus if Ralph, having imbibed two quarts of rum, sees insects crawling wherever he looks in his room at the Delhi Hilton, whereas after a long night's rest and several cups of coffee he sees an immaculate room, presumably he but seemed to see the insects; the delirium tremens experience is *subrated* by the sober perception. Deutsch elaborates:

> *Subration* is the mental process whereby one disvalues some previously appraised object or content of consciousness because of its being contradicted by a new experience. A judgment about something is contradicted by a new experience when it is impossible – more as a psychological fact of one's being than as a purely logical state of one's mind – to affirm (to act upon or to orient one's attitudes upon) both the previous judgment and what is learned or acquired in the new experience. From the standpoint of the subject, *to subrate* means to undergo an experience – practical, intellectual, or spiritual – which radically changes one's judgment about something. An object or content of consciousness is *subrated* or is *subratable* when it is or can be so disvaluated, denied, or contradicted by another experience. (pp. 15–16)

We have, then, something of this sort:

(1) S's experience E_1 *subrates* S's experience E_2 if and only if (a) E_1's content or object is more valuable than the content or object of E_2, and (b) E_1's content or object supports proposition P and E_2's content or object sup-

> ports proposition *Q*, and *P* and *Q* cannot both be true
> (i.e., *P* and *Q* are either contradictories, or else con-
> traries).

The exact thrust of "content or object" is not made clear;
perhaps what is involved is acceptance of something like the
experiences-of-subject-consciousness-object-structure (*sco*) and *ex-
periences-with-subject-content-structure* (*sc*) distinction noted
earlier.

Some of Deutsch's remarks require discussion. The idea is
that ultimately *moksha* experience subrates all other sorts,
and the view is that *moksha* experience is the highest or most
valuable sort of experience to have. But, setting this aside for
the moment, subration is a relationship that is supposed to
hold between non*moksha* experiences. Thus if one mistakes a
tree for a bear at one hundred paces, and recognizes it as a
tree at five paces, then the second experience subrates the
first. But it is not clear that the content or object of the second, subrating, experience is more or less valuable (in a sense
of "being valuable" distinct from "being accurate") than that
of the first, subrated one. Suppose one misperceives a sea-
shell, taking it to be silver. Is the object of the content of the
experience in which the shell is recognized for what it is
more valuable than the first? Given that talk about the *value*
of experiences seems simply not to fit many, perhaps most,
of the cases of subrationing, I shall drop it in what follows.

I propose also to drop the remarks about psychological
impossibility. If Ralph waits until Randy holds Ruth's hand
to send an electric shock into Randy's body that brings Randy
to the verge of death, perhaps it will be psychologically impossible for Randy to hold Ruth's hand again, or even to see
Ruth without falling into a state of shock. It will not follow
that any of Randy's experiences have been subrated. Nor
need it be psychologically impossible for one who mistook
the shell for silver to mistake it for silver again in order for his
or her recognition that it is a shell to subrate the prior mis-
perception. So psychological impossibility of change of mind
is not a sufficient, or a necessary, condition of subrationing.

If the content-object distinction Deutsch reports is identical with the *sco-sc* distinction, as I suspect it is, it is worth reflecting on exactly what connections there may be between *sco* and *sc* experiences, and between claims based on *sco* experiences and claims based on *sc* experiences. Before doing so, we may note that the result of our dropping what we have dropped retains what seems epistemically central to the notion of subrating and gives us something like this:

> (2) *S*'s experience E_1 subrates *S*'s experience E_2 if and only if (a) E_1's content or object supports *P* and E_2's content or object supports *not-P*, (b) if E_2 is veridical, E_1 is not, and (c) E_2 is known to be veridical (where to be *veridical* is *to provide reliable information*).

Alternatively one could replace (c) with (c'); E_2 provides better evidence for *not-P* than E_1 provides for *P*. I think, and hope, that this captures the epistemological content of the notion of subration.

Sco experiences, we noted, are intentional – they seem to their subjects to be (and of course often are) experiences of objects that exist independent of subject and experience alike. Experiences of physical objects and other persons are of this sort; so are numinous experiences, or experiences of God, and at least most aesthetic experiences. The sorts of propositions, then, that such experiences support will concern the existence and properties of objects and persons – *The pen in my hand is black, My son is tall, The painting is magnificent,* and the like.

Sc experiences, we noted, are not intentional – they do not seem to their subjects to be (and of course are not) experiences of objects that exist independent of subject and experience alike. They are experiences whose content is provided by the psychological and other states of the subject – weariness, dizziness, pain, a ringing in the ears, and the like. *Being pained by, rejoicing over, blissfully contemplating* are intentional states – one is pained by, rejoices over, or blissfully contemplating something or other. But just as generalized anxiety (anxiety that has no real or imagined object but consists in simply "feeling anxious") is possible, so is general-ized bliss (not being happy *about* something but simply "feeling happy"). Feeling warm or hungry or comfortably full is an *sc*, rather than an *sco*, experience. Perhaps gener-alized anxiety or bliss is possible only given the presence of *sco* experiences – perhaps these generalized feelings are more affective tones that accrue to other experiences than experi-ences in their own right; nothing here will hang on whether this is so or not. The sorts of propositions, then, that *sc* experiences support will concern the conscious states of persons – *I am dizzy, There are butterflies in my stomach, I have a sense of well-being just now,* and the like.

Moksha, or enlightenment, experience, is supposed to *sub-rate sco* experiences:

> A relational experience that is founded on the distinction be-tween self and non-self – where the non-self is taken to be God or another person to whom one offers oneself in loving relation and in which the experience fulfills the emotional-intellectual-spiritual demands make upon it – cannot be sub-rated by another experience within the subject/object situation because, by its nature, it has already been valued as among the highest in the order of sense-mental experience; that is to say, it has been valued commensurate with the fulfillment that it yields. But this relational experience can be subrated by Reality, by an experience that transcends the dualistic distinctions upon which that relation is founded; for when pure identity shines forth as the content of conscious-ness, all distinctions and all experience constituted by these distinctions are necessarily cancelled. (Deutsch, p. 20)

But why suppose that enlightenment experience subrates other experiences? Not everyone who seems to have had both sorts values the former more highly; theistic mystics seem sometimes to have had experiences like those which an Advaitin regards as enlightenment experiences, and to have found them as only prologues to (what they at least held to be) higher experiences of a personal deity. To say that these could not have been enlightenment experiences because they did not lead to the required results seems but to rule out the possibility that the Advaitin is wrong by saying it very loudly. Further, suppose everyone who had such experiences did value them more highly than any other; why should this entail that such experiences were sources of reliable information, or confirmed the thesis of radical monism? That something is *valued* does not even entail that it *should be valued* or that it is *valuable,* let alone that it is *epistemically reliable.* Even if everyone who took heavy doses of soma (that *Brave New World* pleasure drug) valued their soma trips above all other experiences, this would not even make it likely, let alone guarantee, that the world is as it is seen within a soma trip.

But of course it will be claimed that this ignores the essentially cognitive content of *moksha* in which "pure identity shines forth as the content of consciousness." I agree that it is the *epistemic* or *evidential* force of *moksha* that is at issue, and that it is irrelevant to the present issue that people do, or do not, value *moksha* experiences; this was why we shifted earlier from one characterization of *subrationing* in (1) to the other in (2). Thus the suggestion, perhaps, is that *moksha* is an *sc* experience, which subrates all *sco* experiences. But once one considers the sort of claims that *sc* experiences can support, this suggestion loses whatever original plausibility it possessed, for "My Atman is Brahman" is not a mere report about what some have called "the immediate content of my consciousness." Rather, it is a metaphysical claim, not a mere psychological report. In contrast to such mundane propositions as *I feel elated*, it entails the ambitious *There is only qualityless Brahman. Sc* experiences license introspective autobiographical reports, and the thesis of radical monism is no such report. So *sc* experience cannot confirm it.

Let us investigate this a bit further. Deutsch tells us that the "higher knowledge"

> is not one form of knowledge among others but is so completely knowledge that it overrides and overcomes any pretension to "real" knowledge that may be put forward on behalf of any other type or kind of knowing. Consequently, parāvidyā, the higher knowledge, is self-certifying: no other

form of lower knowledge, such as inference or perception, is capable either of demonstrating or of refuting it. (p. 82)

The idea, I take it, is that one who has the "higher knowledge" knows that the thesis of radical monism is true in such a manner that either the proposition known, or the state one is in when one knows it, eliminates the possibility of one's being mistaken. How is this suggestion to be understood?

Some propositions cannot be false in that their denials are contradictory, but the thesis of radical monism does not have this feature. Some sentences have this quality: The proposition they express when someone asserts them is such that its truth is guaranteed by the fact that it was asserted; *I exist* and *I am conscious* and, perhaps, *I am in pain* are of this sort, their sincere assertion being sufficient for the truth of the proposition asserted. But these propositions are about the existence or momentary conscious state of the person with whom they are concerned, and the thesis of radical monism is not.

I suspect there has been some confusion in this regard. Suppose one puts the thesis of Advaita Vedanta as *I am identical with Brahman, not as I appear, but as I really am.* The propositions expressed by sentences whose sincere assertion is sufficient for their truth concern, in this language, how one appears to oneself, not how one allegedly really is. Suppose Ralph notices that the Advaitic thesis concerns Ralph or Ralph's nature or the like, and concludes that Ralph therefore cannot make a mistake regarding that thesis. Ralph will have made a mistaken inference. It is true of every one of the following propositions that it is "about Ralph" (in the sense that the subject term refers to him): *Ralph has had more orange afterimages than any person with red hair; Ralph is identical with the wisest person in town; Ralph has a good memory; Ralph has performed more evil actions than good ones;* and *Ralph is a kind person.* Yet in each case it is possible that Ralph believe the proposition and it be false, and that Ralph disbelieve the proposition and it be true, so that a proposition is "about Ralph" does not mean that Ralph cannot be mistaken regarding that proposition.

Why, then, cannot Ralph mistakenly believe that he is identical with Brahman? Not simply due to the striking character of *moksha* – other experiences are striking without thereby being veridical. The answer seems to be that the only reason Ralph cannot mistakenly believe this is that it is true; but this was something to be established by appeal to a self-certifying experience, not something that has to be assumed in order for the experience to be veridical, let alone self-certifying. The epistemological security provided by *sc* experiences extends only to reports of such experiences that stick to the momentary conscious states of the reporting subject, and the thesis of radical monism goes far beyond that scope.

Further, if an experience is *sc*, then its subject is distinct from its content; either, then, the thesis of radical monism is false since there is this distinction, or else there is no such distinction and the experience is not veridical and hence provides no evidence for the thesis of radical monism. One might put the matter this way: *Content* requires *distinctions,* at least between the subject of the experience that has the content, and the content itself; hence no *sc* experience can both be veridical and confirm Advaita (and, of course, nonveridical experiences do not confirm it).

Before we leave the topic of experiential confirmation, perhaps a word should be said about the claim that the thesis of radical monism is placed beyond all doubt in the case of the person who has had an enlightenment experience. That something is placed beyond *psychological* doubt is irrelevant to its having been established; that one could not doubt that one's head was made of glass would not establish, or even be relevant to establishing, that it was.

The security of such claims as *I exist* or *I am conscious,* relative to their sincerely being proffered, has a perennial and understandable attraction; if one can ground particular metaphysical or religious doctrines, or *any* significant claims, on experience in the tight-fitting way in which such claims as these apparently can be grounded, that would be very cheering indeed to those who held, or wanted to hold, those particular doctrines. Notoriously, however, the sorts of propositions capable of such tight experiential fit (so to say) are propositions tensed only to the time at which they are made (*I exist now*), not entailing past or future claims (e.g., *I shall be conscious a moment hence*), not concerning matters beyond what can be introspectively discerned (e.g., *I am in pain*), and so not encompassing even whether to be a person is to be an enduring subject, let alone one's identity, or lack thereof, with Brahman. One might put it sloganwise as follows: The price of utter epistemological security is unmitigated ontological triviality.

I cannot find, then, in the appeal to experience an adequate reply to the objections considered earlier.

THE RETREAT FROM LANGUAGE

Another response to these objections lies in a quite different direction. The familiar theme appealed to is that human language is too limited or frail to bear the heavy burden of communicating deep truth; adequate for banking and buying bread, it breaks asunder at the feet of Brahman. Thus there is a retreat from language to something else; I have never understood what the "something else" is supposed to be:

> A person's essence is unapproachable through his name; and in the Spirit, in the Absolute where pure silence reigns, all names are rejected. The application of a label to someone too often implies that in the deepest ontological sense that someone is a "something." Labels are mere conventions and sounds; and to disown all labels in a penetrating inward intuition means not only to recognize the "nothing" that one is but also to become the silence, the "everything" that alone is. (Deutsch, pp. 47–48)

Concepts are abused as mere *names*, and one is led (without argument) from the suggestion that just as nothing in Ralph's daughter intrinsically requires his naming her Sarah rather than Sally, so there is nothing intrinsic in her that requires her being called human rather than feline or bovine. But of course she *is* (nonconventionally) female and human *rather than* being feline or bovine, though how one chooses to say that is conventional. Elephants are mammalian not by convention but by nature, although it is not by nature but by convention that we mark their mammalhood by means of the word "mammal." Choosing to mark it instead by means of the word "ivy" would not turn elephants into plants. Words, expressing concepts as they do, are not mere labels; distinguish between what *Elephants are mammals* says on the one hand, and the fact that we say it by using the sounds and marks we do on the other, and this becomes evident.

Behind such cavalier treatment of language, one suspects, lies a theory of concepts. Nor is the suspicion unfounded:

> The *via negativa* of Advaita Vedānta also safeguards the unqualified oneness of that state of being called Brahman and silences all argument that would seek either to demonstrate or to refute it. Human language has its source in phenomenal experience; hence, it is limited in its application to states of being that are beyond that experience; logic is grounded in the mind as it relates to the phenomenal order; hence, it is unable to affirm, without at the same time denying, what extends beyond that order. "All determination is negation"; to apply a predicate to something is to impose a limitation upon it; for, logically, something is being excluded from the subject. The Real is without internal difference and, in essence, is unrelated to the content of any other form of experience. The Real is thus unthinkable: thought can be brought to it only through negations of what is thinkable. (Deutsch, p. 11)

The theory of concepts thus expressed is not particularly clear, nor is any reason given for accepting it. In the absence of a clear account of what is intended (e.g., of exactly how "language has its source in phenomenal experience" is to be understood), one is limited to offering a rather general, as opposed to a specific and detailed, assessment; still, the prognosis is not cheering.

Consider these features of the exposition. First, we are told that "the Real is without internal difference and, in essence, is unrelated to the content of any other form of experience"; presumably, this is intended to tell us something about "the Real." But on the theory presented this cannot be so, for on that theory one simply cannot say anything about what transcends, or is not part of, the "phenomenal order"; hence "The Real is without internal difference," far from expressing a reason for rejecting one or more views incompatible with Advaita Vedanta, expresses exactly nothing. What might be called "the ineffability canceler" cancels the Advaitin's claims to whatever degree it is supposed to cancel the non-Advaitin's.

Second, we are told that "all determination is negation." If something exists, it does not have the distinction of not existing. If someone knows something, one has not the distinction of inexhaustible ignorance. But why should *existing* and *not being completely ignorant* be limitations? And, if they are, surely we are wise to embrace some limitations with genuine fervor.

Third, if one asserts something whose proper forms is *X is, and is not, A,* then of course one utters a necessary falsehood; but this applies *whatever X is* – a brick, a bone, or Brahman; even to *deny* this is to apply concepts to Brahman, and to suppose that one's denial is true, and not false.

Fourth, Deutsch cannot so much as state the Advaitin view without contradiction; no doubt, on Advaita's behalf, he will say that this is due to the limits of language or logic or some such; why not instead suppose it is due to exactly what it seems to be due to, namely, that the view cannot be expressed without contradiction because it is contradictory, and so necessarily false?

Fifth, *part* of what seems to give the ineffability perspective whatever force it has is an assumption, or family of assumptions, expressible in some such way as this: If we abstract our concepts from sensory and introspective experience, it can only apply to the objects and contents of such experiences. But of course (as Kant saw in his opening sentences in the introduction to his first *Critique*) this reasoning is fallacious; the *source* of our concepts does not tell us what their *range of application* is. One might as well argue that because sight has its source in an organ in a dark womb, the open adult eye cannot see in the light.

Sixth, the claim, I take it, is that *no* concept applies to "the Real" or Brahman, not merely that only some do or that only complex ones do, or the like. A being is ineffable only if *no* concepts apply to it – no concept *at all* applies to it *at all*. But then how does *there not being any Brahman* differ from *Brahman's being ineffable?*

In sum: Appeal to ineffability, or retreat from language, seems not so much a reply to refutation as an admission that one had nothing to say in the first place. A false view might at least be interesting; the retreat from language rules out even this.

THE APPEAL TO ARGUMENT

Endeavors to prove Advaita Vedanta, so far as I am aware, are not nearly so characteristic of this tradition as are the other themes addressed here, and I will be very brief in discussing the topic. In fact, I will be concerned with only one argument, which Deutsch characterizes as follows:

> In further criticism of *asatkāryavāda* (the theory that effects do not pre-exist in their causes), Śamkara argues that it would lead to an infinite regress (*anavasthā*), for the granting of independence to two distinct realities – the cause and the effect – requires the positing of a third entity which is the relation of invariable concomitance that holds between them. And then this third entity (which must be distinct from the two terms that it relates) requires a fourth relating entity that would relate the third entity with each of the first two terms, and so on to a fifth, sixth, . . . (p. 36)

The British philosopher F. H. Bradley, presumably independently, offered this sort of argument for his view (he talked about "the Absolute" rather than about "Brahman"), which at least bore some strong resemblances to Śamkara's. Both Bradley's strategy and Śamkara's is to offer a reductio argument – roughly, to begin with a proposition that is logically contradictory to the thesis of radical monism and then to derive a contradiction from it alone, or else from it plus other propositions essential to the opponent's perspective. Although the argument, as Deutsch's expression of it makes clear, has to do with cause and effect taken as distinct, the argument presumably is viewed as generalizable to any claim that includes at least two distinct entities among its truth conditions – that is, among the things there must be if the proposition is to be true.

The argument can be represented as follows: Suppose that A and B are distinct items (i.e., either can exist without the other existing); then A and B bear some relation R to each other; the relation R they bear to each other is a *third* entity, so that A and B are joined by a third item R on our list of things heaven and earth contain; but then R and A are related (say, by R_1) and R and B are related (say, by R_2) and so there are *five* items $(A, B, R, R_1,$ and $R_2)$ if there are *two* items. By seeing that in principle there can be an endless repetition of this strategy, one can see that it is the case that *If as many as two things exist, then an infinite number of things exist.* This last claim is said to "involve an infinite regress" and is thus thought somehow to be defective.

One thing this argument requires is that there be a *vicious*, or *objectionable*, infinite regress involved. This is not clear; indeed it is not *obvious* what makes an infinite regress vicious rather than not, but it is in particular not obvious that the argument discerns any vicious regress. One can argue that if *one* is a number, then *one plus one* is a number, as is *one plus one plus one*, and so on absolutely forever. But this raises no problems. Suppose *If there are as many as two things, then there are an infinite number of things* is true; what is *incoherent* or even *objectionable* about that?

Further, it *looks* as if this argument assumes something along the lines of *If x exists, then x is a substance* (a *substance* being something that has properties, is not itself a property or set of properties, and endures through time); but this seems false. *Perhaps* it is true that *If x exists, then x is a substance, a quality of a substance, or a relation of a substance;* perhaps a still more catholic list of types of existents is requisite.

But the argument seems to require the assumption noted, which is a very dubious assumption.

Suppose we grant the assumption. Perhaps then the idea is that if A and B are distinct, they cannot bear any relation to each other, since there is always another relation *between,* say, A and any relation R^n, namely, R^{ntl}, and so on ad infinitum. But then there always *is* an R^{ntl} to relate A and R^n. So how does the conclusion that A and R^n are not related follow?

The core of the Advaita objection *may* be, or include, this: For Advaita Vedanta, Brahman is *infinite* in the sense of *including everything;* if there are an infinite number of distinct things, then there is no room left for Brahman. I do not want to press this. For one thing, if there be *one* thing with properties, then the thesis of radical monism is false. For another, while it is not clear that *saguna* Brahman (Brahman *with qualities*) could not coexist with an infinite number of distinct contingent items, it is clear that *nirguna* Brahman (Brahman *without qualities*) could not, nonetheless there being an infinite number of such items is not *more* incompatible with the thesis of radical monism than there being one. But *perhaps* the idea is that *less revision* of Advaita would be required in the latter case. I am not sure that this *is* thought, or that, if thought, then thought truly.

It is very plausible that the only chance the thesis of radical monism has of being true is that the objections noted earlier all rest on some absolutely incoherent assumptions. So the *reductio* strategy seems appropriate for defenders of that thesis. But I know of no reason whatever to think the strategy successful.

THE RETENTION OF ADVAITA VEDANTA, EVEN IF THE REFUTATIONS ARE SUCCESSFUL

I think it is fair to say that the answers we have considered to the objections raised are unsatisfactory. I think it is also fair to say that an Advaita Vedantin, at least one of the perspective Eliot Deutsch describes, would not therefore automatically abandon that perspective – not even if it were agreed by all sides that the refutations are genuine and unanswerable refutations. This raises two questions: Why would anyone continue to hold a perspective that was agreed on by everyone, himself or herself included, to be refuted? Can this attitude be defended?

I set aside one sort of answer to the first question. One might answer: from fear, from need, from peer pressure, from a sense of loss of meaning to life if the perspective is abandoned, from stupidity, from insanity, from loss of a sense of one's own identity, and so on; for any belief, that belief may come to be held with psychological tenacity for any of quite a lot of causes. But what I mean is this: What *grounds* or *reasons* – what *evidence* – might one present for continuing to be an Advaita Vedantin, even though one admitted the view had been refuted? How might one defend doing this (and by "defend" I mean "rationally defend")? I take it that the answer comes in terms of appeals to intuition (in contrast to reason), to incommensurability, or to the "practical" purpose of philosophy and theology, but in one way or another to some fashion or other of negating, not the *fact*, but the *significance*, of the refutations.

The appeal to intuition versus reason comes in such terms as, first, a quotation from Śamkara:

[If Sŕuti, i.e., Scripture] shows that reasoning also is to be allowed its place [this] must not deceitfully be taken as enjoining bare independent ratiocination, but must be understood to represent reasoning as a subordinate auxiliary of intuitional knowledge. (quoted in Deutsch, p. 94; *Brahmasūtrabhāsya*, II, I, II)

Then Deutsch's remark:

In its epistemology, Advaita Vedānta is like a phenomenological art. Its main concern is to describe the primary moments of spiritual experience and to lead the mind to it. Reason is of value in enabling one to function in the world; and it is of greatest value when it enables one to transcend oneself and acquire thereby immediate understanding. (p. 94)

My concern here is not with the view that intuition "subrates" reason but with the different suggestion that reason is simply incompetent as a means of knowing what there really is. It is easy to confuse, and so to conflate, two quite different theses. One concerns *reasoning*, or inference, as a *source* of knowledge. The other concerns *cognizing*, or understanding, as a *condition* of knowledge. Suppose Ralph cannot understand what a proposition means, no matter what sentence we use to express it; then while he may come to believe (perhaps from our testimony) something like "Proposition *P*, namely, what my friend expresses by sentence *S*, is true – but I do not have the vaguest idea what *P* is" – it seems simply false that Ralph knows that *P*. Without the cognizing or understanding that Ralph lacks regarding *P*, "intuition" or "direct experience" is as impossible as is reasoning without at least an understanding of the logical skeleton or form of what one is reasoning about. Intuition presupposes reason, if reason includes cognizing; relevant to a tradition different from Śamkara's, so does revelation.

Reasoning, or inference, requires premises. Not everything one knows can be known by inference, on pain of vicious circularity or vicious infinite regress; that is, if one requires that *Ralph knows P only if Ralph validly infers P from something else Ralph knows*, then either the chain of inference includes *P* or it does not. If so, Ralph reasons in a fashion representable by *P, so Q, so R, so S, so . . . P* so that Ralph knows *P* noninferentially or else not at all. If not, then in order to know that *P*, Ralph must infer *P* from *P1* and *P1* from *P2*, and so on in a never-ending process that yields always another inference from a premise as yet not known to be true. So, once again, if *P* is known, it is known noninferentially. Of course, that inference cannot be the only source of knowledge is nothing against it.

Any source of knowledge, then, requires *reason* in the sense of *cognizing* or *understanding*. Without one's possessing reason, in this sense, relevant to a proposition *P*, one cannot even entertain or consider it, let alone know it to be true. One could not distinguish between the thesis of radical monism and such nonsense as *Plitters pluf plantically*. The attempt, then, to contrast reason (as *cognizing*, rather than *inferring*) and intuition endeavors to introduce a distinction without a difference. Intuition, or "direct" experience, *includes* reason, or cognizing, as an essential component. But then one cannot appeal to intuition *over* or *against* reason.

One attempt to solve the problem – to escape the refutations without descent into ineffability – is to claim that the monistic thesis is incommensurable with the claims that provide evidence against it. Deutsch countenances this "solution":

> These two kinds of knowledge must be incommensurable; for, according to Advaita, the higher knowledge is sui generis: it is reached not through a progressive movement through the lower orders of knowledge, as if it were the final term of a series, but all at once, as it were, intuitively, immediately. *Parāvidyā*, by the nature of its content, possesses a unique quality of ultimacy that annuls any supposed ultimacy that might be attached to any other form or mode of knowledge (e.g., reason or the senses). Just as Brahman is not a reality among other realities but is so completely Reality that all other orders of being, when taken as independent or separate from Brahman, are condemned to *māyā*, so *parāvidyā*, the higher knowledge, is self-certifying: no other form of lower knowledge, such as inference or perception, is capable either of demonstrating or of refuting it. (p. 82)

What this means, I take it, is this: Propositions *A* and *B* are incommensurable if and only if *no* logical relationship holds between them. *A* entails *B* if and only if *A, but not B* is a contradiction. *A* and *B* are *logical contraries,* if any, only if *Both A and B are true* is a contradiction but *Both A and B are false* is not. *A* and *B* are *logically independent* if neither entails the other. Thus *Seven men are in the boat* entails *At least five men are in the boat; There are exactly eight men in the boat* and *There are exactly nine men in the boat* are logical contraries; *Some elephants are albino* and *All books have green covers* are logically independent. But even logically independent claims can be commensurable, for *Everything albino is white* and *If something is white, then all books have green covers*, plus *Some elephants are white*, entail *All books have green covers*. But if a set of three propositions together entails a fourth, none of those three propositions is incommensurable with one another, or with the fourth.

One difficulty, then, with the incommensurability doctrine is that it is very hard to see that there *are* any propositions that are incommensurate with one other. Logical independence does not generate incommensurability; I suggest that nothing does.

But suppose I am wrong about this, and the thesis of radical monism is incommensurable with those claims that many hold are both true and inconsistent with radical monism – say, *My pen is black*. Why should *My pen is black*'s being true be problematic for *Only qualityless Brahman exists?* For the obvious reason that *being black* is a quality, and if my pen has it, then my pen exists and has a quality, and so is not Brahman; hence it is false that only qualityless Brahman exists. If *My pen is black* is *not* logically inconsistent with *Only qualityless Brahman exists*, what does this latter claim mean? Insofar as one can attach any sense to the thesis of radical monism, it seems plainly inconsistent with there really being black pens or gray elephants or anything whatever that we have any reason at all to think exists. At this point, apparently, incommensurability degenerates into ineffability, which we have already discussed.

Perhaps it should be added that it is not clear that Śamkara's Advaita, at any rate, intended to embrace the incommensurability theme. He writes, at 111, 5, 1 of his commentary on the *Brhad-āranyaka Upanishad*, that "knowledge and ignorance cannot coexist in the same individual, for they are contradictory, like light and darkness." Even if we refuse to read "contradictory" as "logically contradictory" and take it in some weaker way, there seems to me no reason why "knowledge" and "ignorance" cannot coexist in the same person *if they are incommensurate*. But I will not press this issue of interpretation.

A standard move at this point is to recite the doctrine that all doctrines (save this one?) are but pointers to ultimate truth or steps on the ladder to ultimate reality, to be cast away on reaching the goal. So, whatever problems or however many refutations these doctrines face, all is still well. I will not press, but only raise, the question of whether a doctrine facing grave epistemic difficulties might not suggest that it was pointing in the wrong way or was a broken step on a distressingly shaky ladder leading nowhere.

Two other issues are more important. One is that the doctrines are not *mere* "pointers" or "ladder steps." What reason one has to accept the perspective on whose behalf reasons and arguments and experiential reports and doctrinal claims (religious or philosophical) are offered is just those reasons, arguments, reports, and claims. If these reasons and arguments are so weak as to provide no real support for the views on whose behalf they are offered, if those experiential reports are utterly challengeable as *accurate* reports of the phenomena they present, and if those doctrines seem open to crushing refutation, then there simply is no reason to suppose that there is anything significant to which they point or lead. The grounds, if any, for supposing anything *is* being "pointed to" or resides at the ladder's end are provided by the reasons, arguments, reports, and doctrines. Their very role as "pointers to the Real" rests utterly on their being epistemically sound – sound as evidence – in the first place. Epistemic failure removes the plausibility of the view that they are in fact "pointers" at all. Arrows drawn on a map that is itself shown to be utterly inaccurate are not reasonably given geographical significance. That is the first issue.

The second issue is this. The doctrines, if not also the reasons and arguments and reports, at least partially constitute the perspective in question. If the perspective is correct, then the doctrines are true. Remove the doctrines, and replace them with no others, and you simply have no perspective. The result is not a profound silence; it is merely a matter of having nothing to say. If there are profound silences, they are the pregnant pauses between profound claims. The Greek philosopher who allegedly "expressed his philosophy" by waving his arms, if he *only* waved his arms, had no philosophy to state; in this respect, Athens does not differ from Benares. We saw this, I suggest, in our discussions of the retreat from language.

When reasons and arguments fail, when experiential reports are dubious, when doctrines appear to be refuted, the temptation to appeal to incommensurability, to ineffability, to self-authentication, to doctrines as mere pointers or ladder steps, apparently is irresistible. A perspective is inherently cognitive; appeals to incommensurability or ineffability, whatever their intent, make a perspective noncognitive, that is, erase the perspective. The result is not philosophy, or religion, but nothing at all. Appeals to self-authentication (of the sort noted earlier) do not render a tradition noncognitive; they merely trivialize the claims allegedly so authenticated that can be so only by becoming trivial. But to trivialize a tradition, of course, does it no favors. The view of reasons, arguments, reports, and doctrines as pointers or ladder steps *presupposes* that the overall perspective they support or constitute is *correct; it does not sidestep this issue,* but supposes it to have been decided in the perspective's favor.

What follows from this? Not that Vedanta is false; for Vedanta has its non-Advaitic varieties. Not that the "religion of the people" is false; for they do not much consider the thesis of radical monism. Not even that Advaita Vedanta is false; for that, one would need to deal directly with Advaita Vedanta as Śamkara (and other traditional figures) presents it. What follows, I think, is that one attempt to reconstruct it yields no adequate version of Advaita. And perhaps that is not simply a feature of this particular, not atypical or unrepresentative, endeavor.

Religious experiences vary in structure and content, and no attempt has been made here to cover them all. What has been attempted is a discussion of some of the more important and interesting varieties that might form the basis of a challenge to the view that strong numinous experience provides evidence in favor of *God exists.* Such challenges as we have considered seem entirely unsuccessful.

14

Conceptual experience and religious belief

ARE "GOD EXISTS" AND "THERE IS EVIL"
LOGICALLY COMPATIBLE?

Religious experience is not the only source of evidence relevant to religious belief. It is only to be expected that conceptual matters – whether the concept of God (or Brahman or
Nirvana or *achieving* nirvana or the like) is logically consistent, whether two or more doctrines cohere, and whether
other sorts of claims are consistent with religious claims –
also enter into the assessment of religious traditions. There is
plenty to consider along these lines. I limit myself here to
some central issues concerning evil, the concept of God, divine autonomy and divine moral agency, and divine omniscience and human freedom. The overall purpose is not so
much to settle these issues as to provide illustrative argument for the claims that they are not beyond human ken and
that it is possible rationally to assess alternative positions on
these matters. It is also to argue that there is more than one
monotheistic perspective on these matters, so that disprov-
ing one such perspective is one thing and refuting monotheism another.

EVIL

That there is evil in the world is something that none of the
monotheistic traditions can deny without becoming inconsistent. Sin is moral evil construed as an offense against a

322

holy God. Our basic religious problem, for monotheistic traditions, is that we are sinners who make ourselves the center
of our lives. We need God's forgiveness and help in recon-
structing our lives so that we worship God and live as if
others are what they actually are, namely, as important as
we are. Upon our repentance and confession before God,
forgiveness and help are available. No tradition that so construes our basic religious problem and its solution can go on
to deny the existence of sin. Hence no such tradition is in a
position to deny the existence of evil. This makes particularly
pressing the common objection that it is logically impossible
that *God exists* and *There is evil* are both true.

This common objection misses its mark. Consider the
claims (G) *God exists* and (E) *There is evil*. Then consider these
claims: (A1) Any free agent that God created in fact would
sin and it is better that a free agent who sins be created than
that she not be created at all; (A2) A world of high moral
value will contain such virtues as compassion, fortitude, self-
giving love, and the like that are achieved, not just hard-
wired in, and any world in which these virtues are achieved
will contain such evils as suffering, pain, and the like; (A3)
God has a morally sufficient reason for allowing evil to exist,
although we do not know what that reason is. Then note
three things about these claims. First, it is not at all obvious
that any of these claims is self-contradictory. Second, if any
of them is self-contradictory, one actually could discover this
(as opposed to merely assuming it) only by doing considerable philosophy, especially moral philosophy. Third, there
are various versions of virtue ethics and autonomous agent
ethics (and combinations of same) that provide a context for
(A1) and (A2), and a fortiori for (A3). Proofs that any of the
(A)-claims is contradictory are hard to find. I suspect that
this is so simply because they are not self-contradictory.

Next, consider any of these sets of claims:

Set One

(G) God exists.
(A1) Any free agent that God created in fact would sin,

and it is better that a free agent who sins be created rather than not having been created at all.

(E) There is evil.

Set Two

(G) God exists.

(A2) A world of high moral value will contain such virtues as compassion, fortitude, self-giving love, and the like, that are achieved, not merely hard-wired in, and any world in which these virtues are achieved will contain such evils as suffering, pain, and the like.

(E) There is evil.

Set Three

(G) God exists.

(A3) God has a morally sufficient reason for permitting evil, though we do not know what this reason is.

(E) There is evil.

Of course other suggestions might be added by considering other (A)-claims. One could add a utilitarian analogue of (A1) and (A2). One could consider a probabilistic world in which evils might not occur, but do occur, which God nonetheless could create since that world's existing would be better than its not existing.

If *any* of our three sets, or any other created by replacing an (A)-claim with some other candidate, is logically consistent, then (G) and (E) are logically consistent. Since the point is the logical consistency or otherwise of (G) and (E), we need not be concerned with whether (A1) or any of its successors is *true*. All that is relevant is whether (A1), or some successor, is *noncontradictory*.

The explicit argument, often and successfully used, is this: If a set of three statements is logically consistent, then any two statements from that set are consistent. Set One (or Two or Three) is consistent. Hence, (G) and (E), two statements taken from that set, are consistent. The very least that this sort of argument establishes is that showing that (G) and (E) constitute an inconsistent pair is much, much harder than many have thought. In fact, claims like (A1) and (A2) and (A3) are not inconsistent, and hence neither are (G) and (E). If one takes (E) to be inconsistent, one cannot consistently think that there is any evil; if one supposes (G) to be inconsistent, that needs independent argument beyond appeal to the problem of evil.

One might object that (A1) and (A2) refer to autonomous agents and achieved virtue, and thus presuppose that moral philosophies in which persons enjoy incompatibilist freedom are logically consistent. The short answer is that they do make this assumption, and the assumption is true. A different answer notes that (A3) makes no such assumption.

One might reply that if the assumption is false, then (A3) also is false, for only if (A1) and (A2), or at least the assumption on which they rest (that incompatibilist freedom is logically possibly true) are true could God have morally sufficient reason for allowing evil. This reply is mistaken. Suppose:

(A4) For any world God creates, it is logically possible that God create a better world.

(A5) There are worlds in which compatibilist freedom is possessed by agents who act wrongly, and are better created than not.

(A6) Even if, for any world God creates, it is logically possible that God create a better world, if God creates, God will create some world that is better created than not.

If (A4–A6) are true, God could have a morally sufficient reason for creating a world in which there was evil but no incompatibilist freedom. If (A6) is true, then the objection that God could create a better world than the one God did create is without force. It *always* could be made, no matter what God did, even if God created a world with all good and no evil. If (A6), so to speak, tells us what God's obligations are on the assumption that there is no best possible world, then creating a world of the sort (A5) describes is morally permis-

sible. If (A4), (A5), and (A6) are true, then (A3) is true even
if (A1) and (A2) are false.

Again, one could argue that (A6) is not strong enough to
describe what a good God would do. A world merely better
to create than not nonetheless could contain things a good
God ought not to allow. So (the argument goes) one ought to
raise the standard for divine behavior higher than the one
that (A6) offers. For example, a world in which God tortured
an innocent person to death every one hundred years contains every one hundred years an event that God ought not
to perform but overall such a world might be better created
than not. Whether it was or not would depend on what else
it contained. Perhaps this suggestion is correct, and (A6)
should be strengthened. But it does not follow that it should
be strengthened in any manner that makes (A4) or (A5)
false.

In considering how to strengthen (A6), various things
should be kept in mind. First, *It would be wrong that God do X*
does not entail *God should not allow anyone to do X*; that God
should not lie does not entail that God should not allow lies
to be told. Second, *God allowed X* does not entail *God did X*.
That God allows John to lie to James does not entail that God
lied to James. Third, even among mortals, what one should
do depends on what one can do. I ought not to perform
operations, and if a friend needs surgery, my duty is to en-
courage that friend to seek a competent surgeon, not to
sharpen my knife and go to work. What concrete duties one
has is a function of what powers and capacities one has, or
has a duty to acquire. This applies both to what one has a
duty to try to do and what one has a duty to try to prevent.
If I can prevent an infant from dying, then unless I know
something that speaks otherwise (for example, that the infant surely will die a week hence from an incurable medical
problem it now has, and will suffer terribly until then) my
overriding duty is to save its life. If God exists and is morally
perfect, God does not have that overriding duty, for a morally perfect God acts rightly and God does not always save
infants' lives. Death places anyone beyond our power to aid

or hinder; not so with God, who (at least on traditional conceptions) continues to sustain a person in existence through death and beyond. God's plans and purposes, relative to a human person, can thus range longer and deeper than our own, God's powers being greater than ours. Hence it does not follow that because we ought not to allow something, God ought not to allow it, or that because it is permissible or right for God to allow something, it is permissible or right for us to do so. When these considerations (and others like them) are taken into account, it is not clear that the standard that (A6) expresses should be raised so high that it is always impermissible that God allow evil. This is so even if the standard that (A6) expresses indeed is too low – so that (A6) should be replaced by:

(A6*) If for any world God creates, it is logically possible that God create a better one, then if God creates, God will create some world such that it is better created than not and such that it contains nothing that God ought not to create or allow.

Certainly various things occur that anyone would be hard pressed to explain as really being good. But typical monotheistic doctrine does not entail that whatever exists is good. It recognizes that some things are profoundly evil, and its religious kernel (its account of our basic religious problem and its solution) is constructed in that light. *God allows X to happen* does not entail *It is good that X happen* but only *God did not do wrong in allowing X to happen.* God's powers to overcome evil being greater than any human being's powers to do so, *It would be wrong of any human being to allow X when she could prevent it* does not entail *It would be wrong of God to allow X.* Thus, if we accept typical monotheistic doctrine, *God allowed X to happen* is perfectly compatible with *X was wicked* or *It was very bad that X happened.* That it was very bad that X happened does not entail that it was bad to allow X to have happened. It does not follow that there is nothing a good God could not allow to happen. There will be limits on what a good God can do, and (different) limits on what a good

God can allow to occur. I conclude, then, that there is little reason to suppose that *God exists* and *There is evil* are logically inconsistent propositions.

There is no good reason to think that we should be able to explain the evils there are in the light of the claim that God exists. There is no reason to suppose that *God exists and is omnipotent, omniscient, and morally perfect* was concocted as a hypothesis for explaining the fact that there are the particular evils we observe or the *sorts* of evil we observe, or that its success as such an explanatory hypothesis is high. If we take the second of these facts in the light of the first, there is much less rationale than otherwise to suppose that our inability to explain the existence of evil is evidence against the existence of God. Perhaps the evils that occur are as tragic as we take them to be only if persons have the high status of being made in God's image. But even if it is a necessary truth that whatever things there are, are sustained in existence by God, it does not follow that one can usefully explain the particular moral features of whatever exists by reference to God. Even if there being logically contingent and dependent beings is best explained by reference to creation by an independent divine being, it does not follow that we should be able to explain all of the particular things that occur by reference to divine creation. The failure of the New York Yankees to dominate the American League during the 1980s is not easily explained by reference to God's existence, but there is no reason to think it should be.

A REMAINING UNEASE

There remains an unease about evil and monotheism, even if one grants that *God exists and there is evil* is not self-contradictory, and that *God exists* is not supposed to be a hypothesis to explain the fact of evil. That unease does not come merely from confusion or prejudice, though it is not easy to state it clearly in unobjectionable ways. That the world is not as we might expect if a good God exists is not much to the point; why suppose that we are in a position to have highly plausible relevant expectations?

Perhaps we can put the unease in terms of something monotheism can explain. Given a typical monotheistic perspective, it is understandable that persons have great value. God is a person, possessed of self-consciousness, knowledge, power, and love. God is also the locus – the source and model – of value, as good a being as beings get. God has maximal worth. Being like God in value-relevant ways, persons also are of great, if derivative, worth. Our confidence that real tragedies occur to people is sound if monotheism is true; the truth of monotheism entails that people are of a value to make talk of tragedy appropriate. Then such talk reflects reality, not just our feelings and prejudices.

Neither infant mortality nor the state of the elderly in nursing homes suggest that nature highly prizes persons, and behind nature, monotheism tells us, is God, who does prize them. How are we to explain infant mortality on monotheism's assumptions? Do persons who die at birth automatically go to Hell? to Heaven? Neither seems fair, though the latter is nicer. If God prizes our growth to mature, moral adulthood, why are people who do so allowed to lose their memories and ability to identify even family and friends? Why are people who were moral saints allowed to survive and become shrews who curse everyone in sight? Such questions could be multiplied for a long time.

Curiously, perhaps, the problem here is not that we die. Roughly and inadequately, the monotheistic account of death tells us that death is both a punishment for sin and a way of transferring us from a less to a more elegant cosmic context – one without the other effects of sin and without further death. There, a coherent account is available.

The remaining unease, insofar as it is rational, arises largely, I suggest, from explanatory indeterminacy. What is lacking is a *coherent* as well as *consistent* account of a variety of disturbing facts. Consistency is a matter of absence of contradiction. Coherence is a matter of mutual explanatory relevance. Thus *17 and 19 are 36, Milwaukee is not in Arizona,* and *George Jones and Tom T. Hall both sing songs in which whiskey is mentioned* are collectively consistent, and even true. But one would be hard pressed to name some explanation-requiring phenomenon for which they together provided the best explanation. A set of propositions comprising only those three lacks coherence. What is lacking, then, is an explanation, consistent and coherent in itself and with the tenets of monotheism, that explains such things as there being infant mortality and sad cases in nursing homes (taking these as representative of other cases). This is compatible with the existence of evil not being inconsistent with the truth of *God exists* and with the truth of monotheism explaining why these things are tragic.

What would remove the explanatory indeterminacy? First, a view that illuminatingly discussed such things as mind-body dualism, mind-body materialism, conditions of personal identity, the nature of persons, and the like. Second, a view that added to the first an account of its relevance to the relevant portions of contemporary science. Third, added to this, an extrapolation or speculation regarding such traditional topics as the origin of the soul or mind, its possible survival, and the like. Fourth, an ethical theory consonant with the value of persons. Finally, taking all these into account, we would need suggestions as to morally acceptable possible narratives that included such phenomena as infant mortality and sad cases in nursing homes. Thus a lot would be needed to remove the indeterminacy. Even then, one would have (I suspect) diverse possible accounts, not one account that alone was consistent and coherent, considering everything relevant that we knew – and perhaps not only one not falsified by what we know. It is entirely proper to note, and worry about, this explanatory indeterminacy. Were it removed, even as described earlier, there would be other explanatory indeterminacies. The presence of such indeterminacies is not evidence against a view. The indeterminacy discussed here is no more an indeterminacy in monotheism than it is an indeterminacy in the metaphysics of persons generally.

Plainly, a lot more can be said about the problem of evil. The intention here has been to argue that there is no easy and successful move to be made from *There is evil* to *There is no God*. The existence of evil is not logically incompatible with the existence of God. There is an explanatory indeterminacy regarding monotheism and evil. This is frustrating and unwelcome, and no reminder, however accurate, of this showing us our limitations excuses our trying to reduce the explanatory indeterminacy or lessens the frustration and unwelcomeness that accompany it. But however much more monotheism is than a conceptual system, it is not less than that and any such system of any interest is likely to have its share of explanatory indeterminacy. The fact that it has that is not evidence against it. We turn next to the consistency of the concept of God.

OMNIPOTENCE

The concept of God traditionally involves the claim that God is omnipotent. A proposition is that which has truth-value – what is true or false. Declarative sentences, typically used – used, that is, to make an assertion – express propositions. Different sentences (in the same language or in different languages) can express the same proposition. Typically, philosophers think of omnipotence along the lines of being able to make any noncontradictory proposition true. But it is not clear that the notion of *making* a necessary truth true expresses anything that even an all-powerful being could do.

It is typical among philosophers to state the notion of divine omnipotence by reference to God and propositions. One way of doing this is by saying *God is omnipotent* if and only if *God can actually make true any proposition that it is logically possible that God make true*. Presumably one could analogously say what it would be for me to be omnipotent and recognize that I am not omnipotent. Thus while it is logically possible that I open the door by shouting "Door, be open," in fact I cannot open the door in that fashion. So I am not omnipotent.

This definition of divine omnipotence leads one to reflect on what the phrase "any proposition that it is logically possible that God make true" amounts to. Here are some suggestions:

(1) Making proposition P true does not fall within the scope of divine omnipotence if P is a contradiction. Thus "John is and is not six feet tall" does not fall within that scope. (Also, perhaps, if P is a logically necessary truth, there is no such thing as *making P true* and so no such thing that God might do.)

(2) Making proposition P true does not fall within the scope of divine omnipotence if "God makes P true" is a contradiction. Thus "God makes it true that there is an uncreated world" does not fall within that scope.

Consider the claim that "Richard Q. Jones wrote the autobiography of Richard Q. Jones." This can be true. Where Samuel M. Smart is a different person from John Q. Jones it cannot be true that "Samuel M. Smart wrote the autobiography of Richard Q. Jones" (setting aside things like ghost writing on the one hand, and Smart having hypnotized Jones and telling him to write on the other). God cannot write Jones's autobiography. God cannot know what it is to be Jones, for God is not Jones (this is different from God knowing what it is *like* to be Jones, which presumably is possible). Call propositions that can only be true of X because X is X rather than someone else *X-specific propositions*.

(3) Making proposition P true does not fall within the scope of divine omnipotence if P is a non-God-specific proposition.

(4) Making proposition P true does not fall within the scope of divine omnipotence if "having property A" is included in God's essence and "having property A" entails "not making P true."

Every religious tradition has a rational kernel – a particular analysis of the basic religious problem that human beings face, the cosmic environment within which they face it, and the solution to that problem in that environment. Monotheistic rational kernels ascribe to God the power to solve the basic religious problem (perhaps only if asked to do so). Thus for some particular monotheistic kernel, let us say that the properties that God must have if God can solve the problem as that kernel construes it are kernel properties. Then we can say that:

> (5) Making proposition *P* true does come within the scope of divine omnipotence if *God has the kernel properties* entails *God can make P true*.

If (1–5) are true, then we get results like these. The proposition *God creates a round square* is not possibly true. Whereas perhaps *There is an uncreated world* is possibly true or non-contradictory, *God makes an uncreated world* is *not* possibly true or *is* contradictory. *God writes John Smith's autobiography* and *God lives Mary Jones's life* are not possibly true. God could create a book qualitatively identical to John's but could not write it as a life God had lived. If *being omnipotent* is a metaphysically essential property of God, then *God exists and is not omnipotent* is not possibly true. If property *A* is a kernel property, and *God does X* entails *God lacks A*, then *God does X* is not possibly true if the kernel properties are essential properties. Roughly, metaphysically essential properties are properties such as *being omnipotent, being omniscient, being existentially independent,* and (perhaps) *being morally perfect*. Kernel properties vary from *being providential over human history,* and *providing redemption from sin* to tradition-specific properties such as *having called Abraham to be the founder of the Hebrew people, becoming incarnate in Jesus Christ,* and *giving a revelation to Mohammed*. One can, without prejudice to them, call the former properties *generic* kernel properties and the latter *specific* kernel properties. Specific kernel properties typically are not taken to be essential properties of God. Neither are some generic kernel properties. Typically, *creating the world* is not taken to be an essential property of God, who typically is viewed as being well able to exist without having created. Still, *being the Creator, if there is a world* and *being providential, if there is human history* might be, or follow from, essential properties. When we come, then, to the fifth consideration relevant to divine omnipotence, we must phrase it carefully.

Given that *being morally perfect* is an essential divine property, the properties *creating a world not wrong to create if creating at all* and *creating a world not lacking providential oversight* also are essential divine properties. Then *God created the world and it would have been better had the world not existed* and *God created the world and does not providentially oversee it* are not possibly true.

For orthodox or classical Christianity, it is impossible that God act unjustly and it would be unjust for God to forgive sins for which no objective atonement was ever to be made. Hence part of what *God is omnipotent* amounts to in orthodox Christian terms does not include its being possibly true that *God forgives sins and no objective atonement for sins ever occurs,* and hence divine omnipotence does not include making that proposition true.

Objections to the consistency of the notion of omnipotence rarely make the effort to understand what the term means within any specific religious tradition. I have tried to illustrate here what are some not implausible considerations concerning how the notion of divine omnipotence is to be understood. It should be realized that there is some operating room available to the thinker who wishes to render the claim that God is omnipotent clear and distinct. It may well be that more than one analysis would serve all the theological purposes to which the concept is put. If there are deep philosophical difficulties with some, but not with other, analyses of *God is omnipotent,* that constitutes no theological problem. Only if every analysis that would do theologically has been shown to be philosophically unworthy has a strong negative critique been mounted. Many of the attempts to mount such a critique fail if one accepts the sort of construal of *God is omnipotent* suggested earlier.

KERNEL PROPERTIES AGAIN

Some have held that God lacks certain important properties –
that God cannot know the meaning of terms like "fear" and
"pain" and "guilt" since (i) one cannot know the meaning of
these terms without having had certain experiences, and (ii)
one cannot have (or imagine having or successfully pretend
to have) these properties without actually having certain beliefs that would be false if God had them, and (iii) God
cannot have certain important properties unless God knows
the meaning of these terms. Although (i) seems plausible,
(ii) is dubious. Suppose that it is logically necessary that one
who has the concepts of fear and pain must have certain
experiences. It will not be sufficient for the argument in question that one must have certain experiences if one is to learn
the concepts *pain* and *fear*; if God is omniscient (and presumably *God is omnipotent* entails *God is omniscient*), then God
always has the concepts *pain* and *fear*, and *learning* concepts
is not in question. If this is so, then God must be able to
imagine what it is like to be in pain or afraid. But there is no
reason to think that (say) God can imagine what it is like to
be afraid only if God (falsely) believes that God is in danger.
So if (as seems possible) God can have the concept *being
afraid* by imagining what it is like to be afraid, then God can
have the concept.

OMNISCIENCE, OMNIPOTENCE, AND
DIVINE SIMPLICITY

To say that God is omniscient is to say that if it is logically
possible that God know the truth-value of a proposition,
then God does know its truth-value. It is logically possible
that I know the truth-value for the proposition that the score
of the first game the Boston Celtics ever played was 85–70
and that the weight of the smallest adult armadillo in Texas
is two pounds. Since I do not know their truth-value, I am
not omniscient. If a proposition is self-contradictory, then
God cannot know that it is true, but God can know that its
truth value is "false." God cannot know what it is to be a

dependent being or what it is to begin to exist – that is, God cannot know "firsthand" what it is to be dependent or to have begun to exist. But God can know the truth-value of *God depends for existence on something else* and *God began to exist* as God can know the truth-value of *The universe depends for its existence on something else* and *The universe began to exist*. Cross-culturally, there is an interesting variety of opinions among monotheists as to the truth-value of *The universe began to exist*. The claims *The universe never began to exist* and *The universe depends for its existence on something else* are compatible propositions, provided *Time did not begin (there was no first moment) and the universe everlastingly has depended for its existence on God* is possibly true. The view of *creation* as *beginningless asymmetrical dependence* seems to have been held by some Hindu monotheists, and Aquinas thought it philosophically coherent but incompatible with the results of proper biblical interpretation. If he was wrong on the latter point, perhaps this view of creation is open to Judaism and Christianity.

PHILOSOPHICAL THEOLOGY AND ENTAILMENT

It seems logically impossible that a being be omnipotent but not omniscient, and logically possible that a being be omniscient but know how to do things that she lacks the power to do and hence lack omnipotence. (I know *how* to "stuff" a basketball through the net; I just cannot jump high enough to do it.) But there is an argument to the effect that it is not logically possible that God be omniscient without being omnipotent. The argument is this: *God is omniscient* is a necessary truth. (More carefully, *If God exists, then God is omniscient* is a necessary truth.) *If God exists, then God is omnipotent* is also a necessary truth. Then it is logically impossible that God (exist and) not be omniscient. So it is logically impossible that God exist and not be omnipotent or that God exist and not be omniscient. So it is not possible that God be omniscient and not omnipotent, even though it is possible that a being not essentially omniscient possess omniscience and lack omnipotence.

This argument can be put as follows. The propositions (G1) *If God exists, then God is omnipotent* and (G2) *If God exists, then God is omniscient* are necessary truths. One proposition entails another if it is logically impossible that the former be true and the latter false. It is impossible that any necessary truth be false. So it is impossible that (G1) be true and (G2) be false, and impossible that (G2) be true and (G1) be false. So (G1) entails (G2) and (G2) entails (G1).

Suppose that (G) *God exists* is a necessary truth. Then note that (G) and (G1) entail (G1A) *God is omnipotent* and (G) and (G2) entail (G2A) *God is omniscient*. Since what necessary truths entail is also a necessary truth, (G1A) and (G2A) are necessary truths. So each member of the group (G), (G1), (G1A), (G2), and (G2A) entails every other member.

If one accepts the principle of meaning:

(M) Proposition P is identical in meaning to proposition Q if and only if, for every proposition R, P entails R if and only if Q entails R,

then each member of our quartet is identical in meaning to every other. Further, consider the criterion of property identity that says:

(I) Property P is identical to property Q if and only if the proposition X *has* P entails X *has* Q and the proposition X *has* Q entails X *has* P.

On this account of propositions, *God is omnipotent* and *God is omniscient* are the same proposition, and *God's being omnipotent* and *God's being omniscient* are the same property. This chimes in nicely with the doctrine of divine simplicity, which says that God has only one property with which God is identical.

The supporter of simplicity doctrine may be a tad less enthusiastic about the proposition *God is omnipotent* and the proposition *God is not identical to Socrates* being the same proposition, though (each being a necessary truth and thus each entailing the other) they are the same proposition on the criterion just noted. The same holds for *God is omnipotent* and

$17 + 24 = 41$ or *No round square exists* or *If John draws a circle, then John draws a figure*. It simply cannot be that all of these propositions are one proposition. For that matter, even though *God is omnipotent* and *God is unextended* entail each other, *God's being omnipotent* and *God's being unextended* are distinct properties if the notion of distinct properties has any content.

If one holds that *God exists* is logically contingent, then while *If God exists, then God is omnipotent* is a necessary truth, *God is omnipotent* is contingent since it entails *God exists*. *God is omniscient* is also (for the same reason) contingent, and while presumably it is entailed by *God is omnipotent*, it does not entail that claim. There then will be no reason to suppose that *God's being omnipotent* and *God's being omniscient* are identical properties. Neither will there be any reason to think that *God is omnipotent* and *One plus one equals two* are the same proposition, since each entails every proposition that the other entails, including each other. For if *God exists* is logically contingent, then none of this will be true.

If one holds that *God exists* is a necessary truth, then the inelegancies already noted arise. One can attempt to escape them by offering a different criterion of propositional identity than the one noted earlier, or a different criterion of property identity. It is hard to see how proposition *A* can entail absolutely every proposition that proposition *B* entails and *B* entail absolutely every proposition that *A* entails (including, of course, *A* and *B* themselves) and yet be different propositions. How could that be?

Perhaps there is an answer to this question. Consider three propositions:

(A) God is omnipotent.
(B) God cannot turn a white swan black.
(C) If *X* is a Euclidean triangle, then *X* is not three-sided.

If *God exists* is a necessary truth, then (A) is a necessary truth and (B) is a contradiction or necessary falsehood; for then the truth is *Necessarily, God can turn a white swan black*. Further, (C) is necessarily false no matter what the status of (A) is.

Now consider this suggestion: (A) is *contradicted by* (B), but (A) is not *contradicted by* (C).

Consider the claims:

(D) God is omniscient.
(E) God does not know that 2 + 2 = 4.
(F) If there are circles, then they have no circumferences.

It seems clear that (D) is *contradicted by* (E) and (D) is *not contradicted* by (F). Then consider this definition:

> If *P* is a necessary truth, then *P* *nonvacuously entails Q* if and only if *P* entails *Q* and *not-Q* contradicts *P*.

Then (A) will nonvacuously entail (B) but not (C) and (D) will nonvacuously entail (E) but not (F). Further, we can say that:

> Property *A* is identical with property *B* if and only if *X has A* nonvacuously entails *X has B* and *X has B* nonvacuously entails *X has A*.

On these criteria, *God is omnipotent* is not the same proposition as *God is omniscient* (the latter proposition does not nonvacuously entail the former) and so *God's being omnipotent* is not the same property as *God's being omniscient*. This will be so, even if *God exists* is necessarily true.

We can gain a further grasp of the notion of nonvacuous entailment among necessary truths if we consider some rules for such entailment.

We begin with two definitions. In (1), *A* and *B* range over all propositions.

> (1) *Entailment:* *A* entails *B* if and only if it is logically impossible that *A* be true and *B* be false.

Thus, since it is impossible that a necessary truth be false, any necessary truth is entailed by any proposition, including of course any other necessary truth. Part of this broad scope of entailment can be pared back by the standard definition of nonvacuous entailment. In (1C), *A* and *B* range over all propositions:

(1C) *A* nonvacuously entails *B* if and only if *A* entails *B* and *A* is not necessarily false and *B* is not necessarily true.

But obviously this will not rule out one necessary truth's nonvacuously entailing another. That, we are suggesting, can be done via (1N), in which *A* and *B* range only over necessary propositions:

(1N) *A* nonvacuously entails *B* if and only if *A* entails *B* and not-*B* contradicts *A*.

As perhaps is obvious, (1C) covers nonvacuous entailment between contingent propositions (propositions neither necessarily true nor contradictory) and (1N) covers nonvacuous entailment among necessary propositions.

The idea behind (1N) can be put in another way. *God is omniscient* entails *God knows that 7 and 9 are 16*. The second proposition states part of the truth conditions of the first. If *God exists* is necessary, then *God is omniscient* entails *No triangle lacks angles* and *Whatever has color is extended*, but these propositions do not state part of the truth conditions of *God is omniscient*. We can put this notion to work in defining nonvacuous entailment among necessary propositions:

(1N1) *A* nonvacuously entails *B* if and only if *A* entails *B* and *B* states (all or part) of the truth conditions of *A*.

Now for some rules. Concerning ordinary entailment among necessary propositions, these rules hold:

(R1) If *A* entails *B*, then *B* entails *A*.
(R2) If *A* entails *B*, and *B* entails *C*, then *A* entails *C*.

What (R1) says is that entailment is symmetrical. (R2) tells us that entailment is transitive. For *nonvacuous* entailment among the necessary, we have instead:

(RN1) *A* can nonvacuously entail *B* without *B* nonvacuously entailing *A*.

(RN2) If *A* nonvacuously entails *B*, and *B* nonvacuously entails *C*, then *A* nonvacuously entails *C*.

Thus transitivity is retained, since if B states at least part of A's truth conditions, and C states at least part of B's, then C states at least part of A's truth conditions. That much is guaranteed by plain entailment, and thus is not eliminated by nonvacuous entailment. But that A entails B does not guarantee that A states part of B's truth conditions, so it does not guarantee that B nonvacuously entails A. Indeed, that B states at least part of A's truth conditions does not entail that A states at least part of B's truth conditions, so that A nonvacuously entails B does not entail that B nonvacuously entails A. Symmetry is not retained.

Concerning entailment among necessary propositions, it is true that

(R3) If A and a necessary truth C entail B, then A alone entails B.

It is not true that if A and a necessary truth C nonvacuously entail B, then A nonvacuously entails B. For C alone might nonvacuously entail B and A alone might not. That is, not-B might contradict C, but not contradict A; B might state at least part of C's truth conditions, but not state at least part of A's truth conditions.

A further rule governing entailment among the necessary is:

(R4) if A entails B, then A entails B *entails A.*

The analogous rule of nonvacuous entailment, of course, would not do; for A can nonvacuously entail B without B's nonvacuously entailing A. True statements to the effect that one proposition entails another are *necessarily* true and false statements to the effect that one proposition entails another are necessarily false. Thus if it is false that B *nonvacuously entails A*, A cannot entail that proposition. The truth of A *nonvacuously entails B* does not rule out its being false that B *nonvacuously entails A*. So (R4) lacks a parallel in nonvacuous entailment. By way of contrast, the rule:

(R5) If A entails B, then A entails B *or C*

can be paralleled by the rule:

(RN3) If A nonvacuously entails B, then A nonvacuously entails B *or* C.

Of course the rule that

(R6) If A entails B and B entails A, then A if and only if B.

is paralleled by the rule:

(RN4) If A nonvacuously entails B and B nonvacuously entails A, then A if and only if B.

Nonvacuous entailment should be truth-preserving; one should never have a case of a truth nonvacuously entailing a falsehood. Every case of nonvacuous entailment is a case of entailment, though not every case of entailment is a case of nonvacuous entailment. Since entailment is truth-preserving, and nonvacuous entailment comprises a subclass of entailment, nonvacuous entailment is truth-preserving.

If the notion of nonvacuous entailment is in order, then one can replace the entailment criteria for propositional identity and property identity by the nonvacuous entailment criteria for propositional identity and property identity. Then *God is omnipotent* and *God is omniscient* are distinct propositions, and *God's being omnipotent* is a property distinct from *God's being omniscient*. Thus these presumably desirable philosophical results are yielded either by taking *God exists* to be a contingent proposition while accepting *either* set of criteria for propositional and property identity or by taking *God exists* to be a necessary truth and adopting the nonvacuous entailment criteria. Of course either way simplicity is sacrificed. Some theists will regard that as unfortunate, but others will regard it as desirable.

NECESSITY, TEMPORALITY, AND DEPENDENCE

If *God exists* is logically contingent, then presumably God is everlasting, not eternal; this will be so if the notion of an eternal entity that does exist, but might not have existed, is contradictory. Then God has such temporal properties as *having temporally preceded Abraham* and *existing at the time at which Socrates took hemlock*. If *X is eternal and Y is eternal and X depends for its existence on Y* is consistent, then so long as *Y sustains X* is contingent, *X exists* also can be contingent. Presumably, those Christian theologians who talk of eternal generation of the Son by the Father regard asymmetrical dependence relations between eternal beings as a genuine possibility. It is a genuine possibility provided it is not also held that the sustainer and the being sustained have logically necessary existence. If a being enjoys logically necessary existence then its nonexistence is logically impossible. *Existence,* but not *logically necessary existence,* can be sustained by something distinct from its owner (or by its owner relative to itself). If *X* has logically necessary existence, then *X* exists whether *Y* eternally acts in relation to *X* or not; *X's existence is logically necessary, and its logical necessity (or its existence) is sustained by Y* is contradictory.

Suppose one holds that *God exists* is necessarily true. Can one then hold that God is not eternal? One can do so by also holding that necessary truths are everlastingly rather than eternally true; a necessary truth cannot be false and is true (not timelessly but) at all times.

There are, then, various alternatives regarding necessity, time, and God. Monotheism comes in varieties. The truth of one variety of course does not entail the truth of another, and the falsehood of one variety need not entail the falsehood of another variety. The net result of this for the task of appraising monotheism is that the results of assessing one of its varieties, if negative, may have very little impact on the assessment of other varieties. A proof of one variety would entail, of course, that any other variety of theism (or anything else) incompatible with the proved variety was false. A disproof of one variety would be a proof that anything that entailed the disproved version was false, but none of the other versions of monotheism need have any such entailment.

Philosophical theology is a wide, deep field. No one volume, let alone one chapter, can canvass all of it. Here I will raise only two further questions. Can God be a moral agent? Is divine foreknowledge of free choices possible?

DIVINE FREEDOM

Suppose that God is everlasting, existing at every moment. Suppose, further, that God is omniscient, and that it is logically possible that God knows all the choices any free agent (God included) will make. Given these assumptions, any free choice God makes, God makes at some time or other. Further, any free choice God makes is one that God always knows God will make – God knows both *that* God will make it and *how* God will make it, so to speak. But if God at (say) 100,000 B.C. knows that God will choose to call Abraham at (say) 3000 B.C., God at 100,000 B.C. already has chosen to call Abraham at 3000 B.C. For any earlier time, for that matter, God has known that God would choose to call Abraham at 3000 B.C. So God always has chosen to call Abraham at 3000 B.C.

We might put the point this way. Consider the claims:

(A) At 3000 B.C. (and not at any other time), God decides to call Abraham at 3000 B.C.
(A1) God decides to call Abraham at 3000 B.C.
(A2) God calls Abraham at 3000 B.C.
(A3) At any time before 3000 B.C. that you like, God knew that God would call Abraham at 3000 B.C.
(A4) At any time you like before 3000 B.C., God already has chosen to call Abraham at 3000 B.C.

Then we reason: If (A2) is true, then (A3) is true. If (A3) is true, then (A4) is true. So if (A2) is true, then (A4) is true. If (A4) is true, then (A1) is true at any time before 3000 B.C. If (A1) is true at any time before 3000 B.C., then (A) is false. Deciding to call Abraham is not something God does at 3000 B.C. It is something that God always has decided to do, since God always knew that God was going to do it. So if God makes choices at all, they are choices that it is never true that

God has not yet made. If we distinguish between divine actions that are choices and divine actions that are not, then divine actions need not always occur (God need not call Abraham until 3000 B.C.) but divine choices always already have been made (God cannot wait until 3000 B.C. to decide whether to call Abraham or not, for God has always known that God would call Abraham).

AN OBJECTION

This sketch of an account of divine freedom faces an objection that is captured by a two-step argument. The first part goes like this:

(C) For God always to know how God's choices are made is for God always to have made those choices.

(C1) For God always to have made God's choices is not different from God's making no choices at all.

Hence:

(C2) For God always to know how God's choices are made is not different from God's making no choices at all.

Behind (C1) are these claims:

(C*1) If God is everlasting, then if God makes a choice, there is a time at which God makes it.

(C*2) If God makes a choice at a time as opposed to having made it earlier, then prior to that time God does not know what choice God will make.

The other part of the argument has this shape:

(C3) If God does not know the way God will choose, God does not know those truths about the world that are true as a result of how God will choose.

(C4) If God does not know those truths about the world that are true as a result of how God will choose, then God's "omniscience" is anemic.

Hence:

(C5) God's "omniscience" is anemic.

One core claim of the (C–C3) argument is that no choice is made unless someone *comes to* make it, and an omniscient everlasting being never *comes to know* she will make a choice and so never comes to make a choice. The other core claim is that for an omniscient everlasting being always to know that she will make a certain decision is tantamount to her already having made it. If either core claim is false, the argument fails.

There is a distinction between God's everlastingly knowing that God will cause the Red Sea to part and God's everlastingly causing the Red Sea to part. God so knowing is one thing. God's causing it to part is another. If God is omniscient and everlasting, the former considerably predates the latter. But nothing in the argument challenges the distinction between God's knowing that God will do A at t and God's actually doing A at t.

Since *God knows that P* entails P, it cannot be the case that God knows that God will choose to part the Red Sea, and God not so choose, nor that God choose to do so and not do it. God can choose to do something long before God does it. *God knows that God will choose A at time t* entails *God will choose A at t*, and conversely. But if God exists and P is true, *God knows P if and only if P* is true for any value of P, and it does not follow that *God knows that P* is identical to P itself. So mutual entailment considerations do not help to establish that God's knowing how God will choose is the same as God's choosing. The best reason for claiming that God's knowing that God will choose to do A is tantamount to God's choosing to do A is this scenario: At time t, God comes to decide what God will do. But at t God, who is everlastingly omniscient, already knows what God will do. So God's "decision" is a sham – if God already knows how the choice shall be made, there is no choice to be made.

The suggestion that God is eternal, not everlasting, and if only we remembered this our supposed problem would vanish, seems to me false. It seems to me logically impossible that *God made choice C* and *There is no time at which God made C* both be true. Further, the proponents of the claim *God is eternal* tend to use temporal metaphors. For example, they suggest that God is eternal and so simultaneous to every time. But what is simultaneous to every time is everlasting, not eternal. So far as I can see, these metaphors are ineliminable from the account; without them, there would be no account. But then God is said to be eternal (and so timeless) from within a theory whose intelligibility rests squarely on God's being temporal, albeit everlasting. Finally, if *God eternally knows how God chooses* is true, then (to use one of the temporal metaphors that seem to me to give the eternalist's view its content) there is no eternal moment when God does not know what God's choice is and so no eternal moment when God has not chosen. How is this an *escape* from whatever problem the argument just offered may pose?

One who accepts the account of divine choice just sketched must grant that God never comes to choose anything, just as God never learns anything. An everlastingly omniscient being always knows whatever it is logically possible that she know. Similarly, the choices of an everlasting omniscient being are everlastingly made. What this amounts to is this: God chooses to do *A* at *t* if and only if God knows that God will do *A* at *t* and it is logically possible that God not do *A* at *t*. Of course *It is logically possible that God know that God will do A at t and yet God will not do A at t* is a contradiction. That is one reason for distinguishing it from the noncontradictory *God knows that God will do A at t and yet it is not logically necessary that God do A at t* or the equivalent *God knows that God will do A at t and yet it is logically possible that God not do A at t*. Similarly, *Necessarily, if God knows P, then P is true* is true, but *If God knows P, then P is necessarily true* is false.

On this analysis, God's knowing that God will choose to part the Red Sea for the Israelites and God's choosing to part the Red Sea for the Israelites are the same, although of course God's knowing that God will part the sea or God's choosing to do so is different from God's actually parting the sea. (For one thing, the knowledge choice considerably predates the event known and chosen.)

347

To put the analysis of, say, *God freely chooses to call Abraham* formally, consider:

(GF) God freely chooses to call Abraham if and only if (i) God does call Abraham, (ii) God everlastingly knew that God would call Abraham, (iii) it is logically possible that God did not call Abraham (= *God called Abraham* is logically contingent) and (iv) not calling Abraham was within God's power.

What (ii) rules out is God's *coming* to choose to call Abraham, not God's *choosing* to do so.

To (GF) we can add:

(GF1) *God calls Abraham* if and only if *God always knows that God calls Abraham*

and:

(GF2) *God chooses to call Abraham* if and only if *God always knows that God calls Abraham*.

From these it follows that

(GF3) *God calls Abraham* if and only if *God always knows that God calls Abraham*.

It is false, then, that choices that always have been made really were never made. To say that God always knows what choices God will make is to say that God always already has chosen, and in turn that is to say that the divine intentions always are in place and there never is deliberation about them. It does not follow that God could make no choices, nor does it follow that God's choices are not free. It only follows that God's choices, if freely made, are everlastingly freely made. It also follows that God's knowing what God will do is not distinct from God's choosing to do what God will do; if God's choices are free, so is some of God's knowledge.

A DIFFERENT SKETCH

One might argue differently, beginning with the ideas that God is a moral agent only if God has moral autonomy or freedom of choice, that God is a moral agent, and that an agent who foreknows her choices is not free regarding them. (God cannot be morally perfect without being a moral agent.) Can God have freedom of choice if God is omniscient and everlasting? One might reason as follows. Suppose that God is omnipotent. Knowing that moral perfection is essential to being divine, God will so act as to be morally perfect and thus so as to be a moral agent. Hence, the reasoning continues, God will choose not to know the choices that God will make. This is a second-order choice – a choice not to know about how certain choices will be made – and of course an everlasting and omniscient God always will know that God has made this second-order choice. But with respect to any specific divine choice – the choice as to whether or not to do some specific X – that choice is not made until it is time to act in a way that depends on how X is made. Then God's choice will be simultaneous with God's decision as to what to do – knowledge of God's choice about X will be simultaneous with God's choice about X. The freedom of an omniscient, everlasting God then itself will be freely chosen (everlastingly, of course) by God, and will rest on a voluntary everlasting limitation on divine omniscience, a limitation justified by the rationale of possessing moral perfection. *Necessarily, God is a moral agent* is true. Then *Necessarily, God is an autonomous being* is true. Since the truth is that *It is logically impossible that God have freedom of choice and know in advance how God shall choose*, it follows that *It is logically impossible that God know in advance how God shall choose*. Hence, this is a type of knowledge not included in omniscience.

PROBLEMS WITH THE DIFFERENT SKETCH

There are at least apparent problems with the results of this line of reasoning. According to it, until 3000 B.C. comes along, God does not know that *God calls Abraham* is true; for God calls Abraham only if God chooses to do so, and God does not know until then that God will so choose. Suppose that, in fact, there will be a Hebrew people only if Abraham

favorably responds to God's call and of course Abraham responds favorably to God's call only if there is such a call.
Then God does not know, prior to 3000 B.C., that there will
be a Hebrew people. To make this clear, consider this more
formal statement of our argument. Begin with

   (H) There will be a Hebrew people only if Abraham re-
      sponds favorably to God's call.
   (H1) Abraham does respond favorably to God's call.
   (H2) The conditions necessary to there being a Hebrew
      people, other than Abraham's response, will obtain.

On the view under consideration, prior to 3000 B.C., God
cannot know *all* of (H), (H1), and (H2). If God did, the
inference to *God called Abraham* will not be beyond divine
capacity. Neither will the further inference to *God chooses to
call Abraham*. In the present context, the simplest move is to
deny that God knows (H1). But then since God knows (H)
and (H2), but not (H1), God does not know.

   (H3) There is a Hebrew people.

If God knew (H3), God could infer (H1) from (H), (H2),
and (H3). God's not knowing that there will be a Hebrew
people until, say, 3000 B.C. cuts omniscience a little short,
especially if one considers other results ascribed in the Judeo-
Christian-Islamic tradition to God. For monotheistic traditions of this sort, where God's actions are said to affect the
world in significant ways, there will be a variety of arguments analogous to the one that we have been considering –
arguments related to David's being king, the prophets' being
sent, the birth of Jesus in Bethlehem, (for Islam) the giving of
the Koran to Mohammed, and the like.
   Consider the act of creating the universe. If God's act of
creating the universe is the result of a free choice, then (on
the line of reasoning being investigated here) God did not
always know that God would create. A few million years
before creation, God would be of an open mind as to whether
someday a world would exist; that is, God did not know
whether there would be a world someday or not. At this

point, God does not look like a strong candidate for omniscience.

On the account being investigated, then, *God is a moral agent* and *God is omniscient in a sense that includes knowledge of God's future choices* are logically incompatible. Insofar as a monotheistic tradition maintains that God is omniscient and a moral agent, then God must not be able to know in advance how God will act, and so omniscience cannot be unlimited. One might define "omniscience" and argue as follows:

(O1) God is omniscient if and only if, for any proposition *P*, if it is logically possible that God knows that *P*, then God knows that *P*.

(O2) Necessarily, God is a moral agent.

(O3) For any proposition *P*, if *God knows that P* and *God is a moral agent* are logically incompatible, then it is logically impossible that God knows that *P*.

(O4) *God is a moral agent* and *God knows God's future choices* are logically incompatible.

Hence:

(O5) It is logically impossible that God knows God's future choices.

If it is logically impossible for God to know something, God's not knowing that thing does not count against God's omniscience. Further, even if (O1–O5) are true, God does know, at any time *T* and always thereafter, whatever is true at *T*. If *God is a moral agent* and *God knows in advance whatever will happen* are incompatible, presumably the astute theist develops her theology so as to preserve the former and reject the latter. A strong notion of providence is retrievable provided at each time God knows what is true at that time as well as at all earlier times, and the view in question allows for that.

Of course, despite the alternative just discussed, it is not at all clear that *God is a moral agent* and *God knows in advance what will happen* are incompatible. As was noted, one can hold that God's knowledge of God's actions and God's choices of actions are identical. God's knowledge being everlasting (or else eternal), God's choices are everlasting (or else eternal). But this is not incompatible with God's choices being free, nor hence with God being an omniscient moral agent who knows what God's actions will be. That alternative remains open.

OTHER ALTERNATIVES

There are ways out of the problems about God's knowledge of God's own free choices that are worse than the problem. One denies that God is a moral agent, saying instead that divine goodness is of a nonmoral sort. This line removes the core of the content of the doctrine of our creation in God's image as an autonomous moral agent, the basis of much of monotheistic morality. It also removes half of the crucial pairing of otherness and oughtness in the notion of divine holiness. Another is compatibilism, the view that determinism and freedom of choice can coexist in the same world. If determinism is true, then a combination of propositions that comprises laws of nature and propositions true before I was born entails that I shall choose and act as I do, however that may be. Of course, even then it is not likely that I or anyone else will be able to identify those propositions, but as good determinists point out (no one gets everything wrong) ignorance of causes is not freedom of choice or action. I have no control whatever over what the laws of nature are. I have no influence on what was so before I was born. Such things lie utterly beyond my power. I have no freedom regarding what lies utterly beyond my power. So, if determinism is true, I have no freedom regarding my choices and actions. So compatibilism offers no comfort not based on illusion.

HUMAN FREEDOM

Some philosophers deny that God can know, in advance of Sally's freely choosing to decline Robert's invitation to adultery, that she would so choose. One claim relevant to this view is that a proposition of the form *Sally freely chooses to do A at time t* has no truth-value before time *t*, so that there is nothing to be known before time *t*. (One could apply this to God's knowledge of God's future choices.) But I can see no reason to think this true. If the future is not yet, the past is no more. That we now experience the effects of some things past does not mean that these things now exist to make reports of their occurrence true. Past-tense propositions are true or false. The same holds for future-tense propositions, as I argue later.

The view that God is eternal sometimes is said to solve the problem that otherwise arises when one holds that God has knowledge of human free choices that does not wait for the choices to be made. If God is eternal and omniscient, then God's omniscience is eternal. *God knows how Sharon will choose at time t* is not true at time *t* or any other time. Hence God's knowledge does not predate any human free choices. Hence its predating human free choices cannot be appealed to as a basis for denying or doubting human freedom.

Although I argue later that the alleged incompatibility between divine foreknowledge and human freedom is only apparent, there plainly also is an apparent incompatibility between eternal divine knowledge of human free choices and human freedom. The prima facie incompatibility between foreknowledge and freedom is that the past is "fixed" or "frozen" and God's knowledge is past relative to any choice; hence (the idea is) the choice cannot be free. But there is as much reason to think of eternity as fixed or frozen as there is to think of the past in these terms. In both cases, something frozen or fixed entails the truth about what choices anyone freely makes. If in the one instance there is incompatibility, why not also in the other?

Perhaps there is an answer to this question. *God eternally knows that X freely does A at time t* entails *X freely does A at t.* So if future-tense propositions have no truth-value until the time to which they are tensed (the time referred to by "at *t*"), propositions of the form *X freely does A at t* have no truth-value until *t* (and so *God eternally knows that X will freely do A at t* has no truth-value until *t*). Then, if *God eternally knows that X freely does A at time t* entails *X freely does A at t,* then God's knowledge changes in that it increases when time *t* arrives, which no defender of divine eternity will allow. Hence the indicated entailment does not hold.

The problem with this line of reasoning is that the entailment plainly does hold – for *any* proposition *P, God eternally knows P* entails *P.* This sets up a dilemma. If future-tense propositions have truth-value, then a "frozen" eternal knowledge provides the same sort of block to freedom, if block there be, as does a "frozen" past divine knowledge. If future-tense propositions have no truth-value, then neither the eternal frozenness nor the past frozenness even appears to block human freedom from gracing the world, and appeal to eternal rather than everlasting knowledge is pointless as a defense of freedom. Finally, since in fact future-tense propositions have truth-value, the second horn of the dilemma is (to mix metaphors) a broken reed. So the alleged incompatibility between divine knowledge, past or eternal, and human freedom remains.

THE SUGGESTION THAT GOD LACKS KNOWLEDGE OF FUTURE HUMAN FREE CHOICES

Some have thought that even though future-tense propositions have truth-value, God cannot know the truth or falsity of propositions concerning future human free choices. Suppose that in 1994 Stan is considering stealing Tom's heart medicine, thereby keeping Tom from taking it in a timely manner and thus killing him. Suppose, too, that Tom will die in 1994 only if Stan steals Tom's medicine, and otherwise Tom will live a long time and find a cure for cancer in 1999. It is true, we are supposing, that

(T) Tom will die in 1994 only if Stan freely steals Tom's medicine.

(T1) If Tom does not die in 1994, then Tom will discover a cure for cancer in 1999.

354

If God knows (T) and (T1) and also knows

(T2) Tom will discover a cure for cancer in 1999,

Then God can infer:

(S) Stan will not (freely or otherwise) steal Tom's medicine.

So, on the view in question, God cannot know all of (T), (T1), and (T2). Suppose God knows

(T3) Tom will die in 1994.

Then if God knows (T), God can infer from (T) and (T3) that:

(S1) Stan will freely steal Tom's medicine.

So God cannot know both (T) and (T3), since God, on the current view, cannot know (S1). But (T1–T3) are not claims about anyone's free actions. Hence, if God cannot know what free actions anyone will perform, and people actually do act freely, then God's knowledge of our world will be far more restricted than a mere lack of knowledge of future free choices. God will not know anything that entails how anyone will freely act.

This can be very restrictive. Suppose that William Windom will be elected governor of Rhode Island in 1996 by the freely cast votes of 51 percent of the electorate. ("Freely cast" here is a *metaphysical*, not a political, term.) God, on the view under consideration, cannot know that the votes, freely cast, will have this result. Suppose, however, that were the votes cast other than freely, Windom would lose; suppose that the truth is

(V1) If the voters vote unfreely, they do so because bribed.
(V2) If the voters are bribed, they will vote against Windom.
(V3) If the voters vote against Windom, Windom will lose.

Now (V1–V3) entail

(V4) If the voters vote unfreely, Windom will lose.

Suppose God knows that (V4) is true. It is also true that

(V5) Windom will not lose.
(V6) The voters will not vote unfreely.

But God cannot know both (V5) and (V6), since God cannot know

(V7) The voters freely elect Windom.

So, on the view in question, God cannot know both (V5) and (V6).

The way to put the restriction on divine knowledge that a denial that God can know in advance what choices people shall freely make is this: Any one-or-more-membered collection of propositions that entails a proposition of the form *Person X does A freely at time t* is not a collection of propositions all of which God can know to be true at any time before *t*. This is a significant restriction on omniscience *besides* that involved merely by subtracting, so to speak, all propositions describing the future free actions of persons.

There is an argument against the view that at time *t* a proposition of the form *Sally freely chooses to do A at time t + 1* has no truth-value. Here it is. Suppose

(W) Will will become Mary's father in 1998 unless Harry freely kills Will in 1997.
(W1) Will will become Mary's father in 1998.

Now (W) and (W1) entail

(W2) Henry will not freely kill Will in 1997.

One can deny that in 1997 (W1) has any truth-value, but since it does not deal with any choice, the ground for this denial will have to be, not that no proposition asserting future free choice can have truth-value, but that no future-tense proposition whatever can have truth-value (or at least none of the non-future-choice-asserting sort as [W1]). (This really will truncate omniscience, although if it is logically impossible that future-tense propositions have truth-value, the notion of omniscience must be so trimmed.)

Suppose, then, that (W) is true in 1997. On the doctrine that no proposition about future free choices can be true, (W) was not true before 1997. Then (W) and (W1) did not in 1996 together entail anything, although in 1997 they entail (W2). Yet it seems perfectly plain that (W) and (W1) do now entail (W2), no matter what year it currently is. If (W1) is not true or false, then (now) it is meaningless. For what is true or false if it is meaningful – namely, assertions as opposed to questions and commands – is meaningless if it lacks both truth and falsehood. Only in 1997 does (W) become meaningful and thereby become a part (with [W1]) of a valid argument that entails (W2). On this account, the notion "X will be true" (if X ranges over propositions) or "Y will express a truth" (where Y ranges over sentences) should be unintelligible, since no meaningful value of X or Y is available. But sentences of the form "It will be true by 5:00 P.M. that I am in Chicago," spoken at noon of the same day as that on which the intended 5:00 P.M. occurs, can express a true proposition, and they do not become meaningful only at 5:00 P.M.

FUTURE-TENSE STATEMENTS HAVE TRUTH-VALUE

Imagine that a journalist is hired in 1994 to record the progress and product of a 1996 election from the viewpoint of the campaign of a candidate named Alicia Griffin. At the outset, the journalist will know that

(1) Either Griffin will win the election or Griffin will not win the election.

Of course there are various ways of not winning; if Alicia drops out of the election, is convicted of committing a major crime, dies, or receives fewer votes than some other candidate, presumably she will not win. But all of that does not detract from (1). No journalist who does not even know that (1) is true will be hired. Since one is hired, it is true that

(2) In 1994, the journalist knows (1).

If (2) is true, then so is:

(3) In 1994, (1) is true.

Now (1) is a disjunct. It is true only if one or the other of its composing propositions is true. Thus if (3) is true, so is

(4) In 1994, it is true that Griffin will win in 1996, or it is true that Griffin will not win in 1996.

From (4) it follows that

(5) Some future-tense proposition is now true.

The scenario just sketched is straightforward and unproblematic. Plenty of real-world scenarios correspond to it. Hence (5) is quite in order.

One might object to the scenario by suggesting that the journalist can know, and so only does know, something like this:

(1') It will be true that Griffin wins in 1996, or else it will be true that Griffin does not win in 1996, although neither claim is true now.

If we ask when one of these things will be true, the answer is: in 1996. So what (1') tells us is tantamount to

(1") In 1996, it will be true that Griffin wins in 1996 or it will be true that Griffin does not win in 1996.

But (1") explicitly, and (1') more shyly, is a claim that is true now about a later time. Hence neither can form the basis of a consistent argument that no future-tense propositions can be true.

A PROPOSED SOLUTION

Suppose, then, as seems true, that future-tense statements, in general and regarding the free choices of agents, are either true or else false before the time at which the events or choices or actions that they are concerned with occur. Is there any way of saving both divine omniscience and human moral agency?

Let us first make what capital we can out of the source of our problem. What makes the claim, spoken at breakfast, that "for lunch today, I shall have fruit and refuse pizza" a true claim is not anything that occurs until lunchtime. If I then have fruit and refuse pizza, what I said at breakfast is (and was and will be) true. If I accept pizza, then whether I also have fruit or not, what I said is (and was and will be) false. Suppose that I have promised my family to follow faithfully a diet my doctor has prescribed that unconscionably fails to mention pizza. Further, I freely refuse pizza in the light of my promise and stick to the fruit I am allowed. Then if God is everlasting, God knows when I am at breakfast that what I say then is true. It is true because of a free choice that I make, and if I add to myself at breakfast, "and I shall freely so choose," after my remark about fruit and pizza, God knows that this is true because God knows what free choice I shall make. The claims

(F) I shall freely choose to stay on my diet this coming noon.

(F1) God knows the truth-value of (F)

entail

(F2) God knows what I shall do regarding freely choosing to keep my diet this coming noon.

If (F1) is true, then so is (F2). Divine foreknowledge entails that I choose freely, and so is not incompatible with my doing so. It is hard to see why anyone would think otherwise so long as one keeps certain things in mind.

First, what makes a sentence of the form *X occurs at time t* true is something that happens at time t, not something that happens before t. Even if Y's occurrence at $t - 1$ *causes* X's occurrence at t, Y's occurrence makes *X occurs at t* true only by virtue of Y's causing X to occur at t.

Second, God's foreknowledge is not causative; God's knowing that free choice X will occur at time t is not the same as God's causing free choice X to occur at t. It is logically impossible for God to cause free choice X to occur at t; it is not logically impossible for God to know everlastingly that an agent will freely make X at t.

Third, the modal status of a proposition does not change. Consider the proposition *Larry Bird signed with the Celtics right out of college in 1981*. That proposition was logically contingent in 1981. It was logically contingent when Plato wrote *The Republic*, when Hannibal crossed the Alps, and when Lincoln freed the slaves. It will be contingent in A.D. 3001 and is so now. In the senses that matter, we cannot change the past. One thing we cannot change about the past is this: Whatever modal status (necessarily true, contingent, contradictory) a proposition enjoyed yesterday, it has now. Any proposition of the form *Person X freely does A at time t* is logically contingent. So it *always* is logically contingent – at t, before t, and after t. Finally, it is logically possible for free choices to be made by agents. If such choices are made, and God exists, God knows how they have been, are, and will be made (possibly with the exception of God's own free choices). Hence it is possible for there to be divine foreknowledge and human freedom of choice.

CONCLUSION

The discussion of divine foreknowledge and human freedom has been conducted on the assumption that there is a prima facie incompatibility between them. Save insofar as this merely means that some people have thought this, it is false: There is no such incompatibility, and there is no good reason to think that there is one. What problem there is can be stated without reference to knowledge or God; it concerns the fact that *Mary will freely do A at t*, if true at all, is true before time t. What there is by way of paradox can be put in terms of two claims: (i) It is true before the time that Mary will freely do what she freely does; (ii) Mary is free when she does what she freely does. What must be true if there is a

problem is: (iii) If it is true before she does it that Mary does
A at *t*, then Mary cannot be free in doing *A* at *t*.

Of course (iii) is false. It is crucial here to distinguish between what we might call *direction of truth determination* and
direction of entailment. Consider the propositions

(M1) On Tuesday Mary freely accepts a contract to write a
book on Chaucer.
(M2) On the preceding Monday, it was true that on Tuesday Mary will freely accept a contract to write a book
on Chaucer.

It is true that (M2) entails (M1); it is also true, for that matter,
that (M1) entails (M2). But what makes (M1) true is something Mary does on Tuesday, namely, her freely accepting
the Chaucer contract. Truth determination goes from Mary's
free action to (M1), and via the truth of (M1) to the truth of
(M2). While the direction of entailment is mutual, the direction of truth determination is one-way, and it is one-way in
a manner that prevents the alleged problem from arising.

This chapter contains discussions of a few issues in philosophical theology. Its intent is to argue for two claims: (i)
There are ways of assessing alternative views in philosophical theology (and hence of assessing theological views, for
views in philosophical theology tend to be theological views
stated with some philosophical precision), and (ii) there are
various alternatives that a monotheist can hold, so that the
refutation of some versions of monotheism is not a refutation
of monotheism. Monotheism, in one respect anyway, is like
materialism: Refuting one of its versions has hardly any effect on the question of its truth. These days, everyone knows
that about materialism; not everyone knows that about
monotheism, although the delightful renewal of interest in
philosophical theology may change that.

Bibliography

Baillie, John. *Our Knowledge of God* (London: Oxford University Press, 1939).

Beardsworth, Timothy. *A Sense of Presence* (Oxford: Religious Experience Research Unit, 1977).

Berger, Peter. *The Sacred Canopy* (New York: Doubleday, 1969).

Bowker, John. *Licensed Insanities* (London: Darton, Longman, & Todd, 1987).

The Religious Imagination and the Sense of God (Oxford: Clarendon Press, 1978).

The Sense of God (Oxford: Oxford University Press, 1973).

Broad, C. D. *Religion, Philosophy, and Psychical Research* (London: Routledge & Kegan Paul, 1953).

Christian, William A., Sr. *Doctrines of Religious Communities* (New Haven: Yale University Press, 1987).

Conway, David. "Mavrodes, Martin, and the Verification of Religious Experience." *International Journal for the Philosophy of Religion* 2, no. 3 (Fall 1971).

David, Caroline Franks. *The Evidential Force of Religious Experience* (Oxford: Clarendon Press, 1989).

Deutsch, Eliot. *Advaita Vedānta: A Philosophical Reconstruction* (Honolulu: University of Hawaii Press, 1969).

Donovan, Peter. *Interpreting Religious Experience* (London: Sheldon Press, 1979).

England, F. E. *The Validity of Religious Experience* (London: Ivor Nicholson & Watson, 1937).

Forman, Robert K. C. (ed.). *The Problem of Pure Consciousness* (Oxford: Oxford University Press, 1990).

Fraser, Alexander Campbell. *The Works of George Berkeley.* 4 vols. (Oxford: Clarendon, 1901).

Bibliography

Garrigou-Lagrange, R., O.P. *The Three Stages of the Interior Life,* vols. 1 and 2, trans. Sister M. Timothea Doyle, O.P. (London: Herder, 1951, 1948).

Goodier, Alban, S.J. *An Introduction to the Study of Ascetical and Mystical Theology* (Milwaukee, Wis.: Bruce, n.d.).

Gutting, Gary. *Religious Belief and Religious Skepticism* (Notre Dame, Ind.: University of Notre Dame Press, 1983).

Happold, F. C. *Mysticism: A Study and an Anthology* (Harmondsworth: Penguin, 1970).

Hardy, Alistair. *The Spiritual Nature of Man* (Oxford: Clarendon Press, 1979).

James, William. *The Varieties of Religious Experience* (Glasgow: Collins Fount Paperbacks, 1977).

Katz, Steven (ed.). *Mysticism and Philosophical Analysis* (Oxford: Oxford University Press, 1978).

(ed.). *Mysticism and Religious Traditions* (Oxford: Oxford University Press, 1983).

Larson, Gerald J., and Eliot Deutsch (eds.). *Interpreting across Boundaries* (Princeton: Princeton University Press, 1988).

Leach, Edmund. *Lévi-Strauss* (London: Fontana, 1970).

Leuba, James H. (ed. C. K. Ogden). *The Psychology of Religious Mysticism* (London: Kegan, Paul, Trench, Trubner, 1925).

Lewis, H. D. *Our Experience of God* (London: Allen & Unwin, 1959).

Lott, Eric. *Vedantic Approaches to God* (London: Macmillan, 1980).

Martin, C. B. *Religious Belief* (Ithaca, N.Y.: Cornell University Press, 1959).

Mavrodes, George. *Belief in God: The Epistemology of Religious Experience* (New York: Random House, 1970).

Oakes, Robert. "Religious Experience and Rational Certainty." *Religious Studies* 12 (1976): 311–18.

Otto, Rudolf. *The Idea of the Holy* (Oxford: Oxford University Press, 1936).

Mysticism East and West, trans. Bertha C. Bracey and Richenda C. Payne (London: Macmillan, 1932).

Religious Essays (Oxford: Oxford University Press, 1931).

Parrinder, Geoffrey. *Avatar and Incarnation* (London: Faber & Faber, 1970).

Radhakrishnan, Sarvepelli, and Charles A. Moore. *A Sourcebook in Indian Philosophy* (Princeton, N.J.: Princeton University Press, 1959).

Reichauer, August Karl. *The Nature and Truth of the Great Religions* (Rutland, Vt.: Charles E. Tuttle, 1966).

Rowe, William. "Religious Experience and the Principle of Credulity." *International Journal for the Philosophy of Religion* 13 (1982): 85–92.

Skorupski, John. *Symbol and Theory* (Cambridge: Cambridge University Press, 1976).

Smart, Ninian. *Beyond Ideology* (New York: Harper & Row, 1981).
  Concept and Empathy, ed. Donald Wiebe (New York: New York University Press, 1986).
  A Dialogue of Religions (London: SCM Press, 1960).
  Doctrine and Argument in Indian Philosophy (London: Allen & Unwin, 1964).
  "Interpretation and Mystical Experience." *Religious Studies* 1 (1965): 75–87.
  Reasons and Faiths (London: Routledge & Kegan Paul, 1958).
  Religion and the Western Mind (Albany: State University of New York Press, 1989).
  The Science of Religion and the Sociology of Knowledge (Princeton: Princeton University Press, 1973).
  Secular Education and the Logic of Religion (New York: Humanities Press, 1969).
  The Yogi and the Devotee (London: Allen & Unwin, 1968).

Swinburne, Richard. *The Coherence of Theism* (Oxford: Clarendon Press, 1977).
  The Existence of God (Oxford: Clarendon Press, 1979).
  Worldviews (New York: Charles Scribner's Sons, 1983).

Taylor, A. E. *Does God Exist?* (London: Collins/Fontana, 1945, 1961).

Von Hugel, Baron. *Essays and Addresses*, 1st and 2nd ser. (London: J. M. Dent & Sons, 1921, 1926).
  The Mystical Element in Religion, vols. 1 and 2 (London: J. M. Dent & Sons, 1908).
  The Reality of God and Religion and Agnosticism (London: J. M. Dent & Sons, 1931).

Wainwright, William J. *Mysticism* (Madison: University of Wisconsin Press, 1981).

Webb, Clement C. J. *Religion and Theism* (New York: Charles Scribner's Sons, 1934).

Yandell, Keith. *Christianity and Philosophy* (Grand Rapids, Mich.: Eerdmans, 1984).

Bibliography

Hume's "Inexplicable Mystery" (Philadelphia: Temple University Press, 1990).

Zaehner, R. C. *The Comparison of Religions* (London: Faber & Faber, 1958).

Mysticism Sacred and Profane (Oxford: Clarendon Press, 1957).

Zen, Drugs, and Mysticism (New York: Pantheon, 1972).

Index

Index

Critique of Pure Reason, 194, 195, 312

de facto evidence, 44
Descartes, René, 179, 295
description: and evidence, 43; phenomenological, 16–17
Deutsch, Eliot, 302–3, 310, 311, 313, 315, 316, 318
direct relevance conditions, 40
disconfirmation. *See* lateral disconfirmation; polar disconfirmation
discreditation: of propositional belief, 146–7, 158; of psychological beliefs, 135, 142–3, 158; of religious belief, 149–50
discreditor, 123
divine choices, 344–5
divine crisis condition, 231
divine foreknowledge, 354
divine freedom, 344
divine moral agency, 348–9
doctrines as pointers, 315–16
doxastic practice, 205, 206
dretskes, 254, 255
dualism, idealistic, 127, 132; physicalistic, 125, 132
Dvaita Vedanta, 298

effability, restricted, 83
effective evidence, 44
Elias, Thomas D., 205
enlightenment experience, 280–1, 299; and memory, 284, 285
entailment, 336–7
entailment rules, 340–1
epistemic certainty, 169
epistemic constellation, 137, 138
epistemic duty vs. moral duty, 130
eternal, 342, 343, 346, 347, 353, 354
ethics of belief, 129–30, 142
everlasting, 342, 343, 344
evidence: de facto, 44; description and, 43; total relevant, 234

evidence cancellation alternative, 240
evidential association, 137
evil, 322–3
existential veridicality, 46, 47
experience, 42–3; conditions of, 201; imprisoned by concepts, 197–8; kinds of, 23–4, 236, 237; perceptual, 42, 43; pure, 184–5, 192; *sc* and *sco*, 300, 304; self-authenticating, 170–1; structure of, 19. *See also* numinous experience; religious experience; sensory experience
experiential confirmation scope, 243, 244
experiential disconfirmation, 243, 244
experiential object claim, 37
explanatory indeterminacy, 329–30
explanatory simplicity, 125
external epistemic certainty, 293

faith, 1–2
falsificationism, 114; complex, 156
fitting of concept, 65, 98
foreknowledge, divine, 354
full confirmation, 168
future-tense propositions and truth-value, 356–7

generic epistemic explanation, 128

high-claim assertions, 218–19
Hinduism, 298
historical claims, 155, 156
human freedom and divine foreknowledge, 354
Hume, David, 3, 144, 254

idealism, 127–8, 132
idealistic (nonphysicalistic) dualism, 127, 132
incommensurability, 319, 320
indirect relevance conditions, 40

Index

omnipotence, 74, 331–2
omniscience, 74, 335
one-type-of-religious-experience-per-tradition view, 183, 193–4
one-type-of-religious-experience view, 183–4
origin of concepts, 102–3
Otto, Rudolph, 16, 261, 262
overturnability, 179

paralysis questions, 8
Parton, Dolly, 205, 206
perceptual experience, 42, 43
perfection, 92
persons, 282–3
phenomenological description, 16–17
phenomenology, 164
physical chains, 258; causal, 260; experiential, 259
physical event, 258
physicalistic dualism, 125, 132
physiological explanations, 256–7
plain theism, 109
polar disconfirmation, 245, 249, 251
positive epistemic explanation, 128
positive (affirmative) religious beliefs, 151
possibility of assessing religious belief, 1–2
principle: of existential accessibility, 242; of experiential evidence, 37, 52–3, 235, 239–40, 249, 262, 266–7, 274; of explanatory simplicity, 126
problem of evil, 322–3
proper analogy, 70, 76
properly basic belief, 137–8
properly coordinated epistemic constellation, 138
properties: and descriptions, 85–6; introspectible, 295–6
property, 71, 78–9, 84
property identity, 91, 92, 95–6, 337

property instance, 71
property scope, 84
proportional predication, 100–1
propositional belief, 120
propositional identity, 92–3, 337
propositions, 331
psychological belief, 120
psychological claims, 280–1
pure experience, 184–5, 192

radical monism, 298, 309
Ramanuja, 298
rational kernel, 333
reason, 317–18
reasons and causes, 119
rebutting condition, 228–9
reciprocal checking sets, 222
reducing condition, 228–9
relativism, 196–7
relevance conditions, 38–40
religion, 1–2, 15, 151
Religion, Philosophy, and Psychical Research, 215
Religious Belief, 216
religious doctrines and truth-value, 2–3
religious doxastic practice, 206–7
religious experience, 7–8, 15; introspective, 280, 291–2
restricted effability, 83
Rowe, William, 121, 227–8

Śamkara, 313, 319
sc experiences, 300, 304
sco experiences, 300, 304
scope of one-type view, 203
second-order choice, 349
self-authenticating experience, 170–1
self-authentication, 165–6; and reasonable belief, 180; and religious beliefs, 181–2
sensory checking argument, 217
sensory doxastic practice, 206–7